The Sound System of French

Jean Casagrande

Georgetown University Press, Washington, D.C. 20057

à
A.L.C.

Chapter 13 is (apart from the excision of notes and minor revisions) essentially the same as an article submitted by the author to the editors of *Kritikon Litterarum* (Darmstadt: Thesen Verlag) and published in Vol. 3:4 (1974), pp. 346-355.

Copyright © 1984 by Georgetown University

All rights reserved.

Printed in the United States of America

Library of Congress Cataloging in Publication Data

Casagrande, Jean.
  The sound system of French.

  Includes bibliographies.
  1. French language—Phonology. 2. French language—Phonetics. I. Title.
PC2131.C34 1983   441'.5   83-20594
ISBN 0-87840-085-0

Contents

Acknowledgments

Preface

Part One. Phonetics and phonetic differences:
Foundation and building blocks of a sound system   1

1 By way of introduction   1

1.1 Sound and spelling   1
1.2 Grammar   2
1.3 Underlying representation and phonetic representation   3
1.4 Verbal intercourse   4
1.5 The speech chain   4
1.6 Questions   5

2 The nature of sound   6

2.1 Waves   6
2.2 Vibrations   6
2.3 Frequency and pitch   7
2.4 Amplitude and intensity   8
2.5 Sound propagation   9
2.6 Harmonics   9
2.7 Compound sounds   10
2.8 Resonators   11
2.9 Questions   12

3 The organs of speech   13

3.1 A superimposed system   13
3.2 The bellows   13
3.3 Speech production   14
3.4 The larynx   14
3.5 The vocal tract   15

       3.5.1 The pharynx   15
       3.5.2 The nose   15
       3.5.3 The mouth   16
  3.6 Questions   18

4 Articulatory properties of French sounds   18

4.1 Articulation   18
4.2 Manner of articulation   18
4.3 Point of articulation   19
4.4 Vowels (syllabic sounds)   19
    4.4.1 Oral vowels   19
    4.4.2 Nasal vowels   20
    4.4.3 Summing up the vowels   21
4.5 Consonants (nonsyllabic sounds)   21
    4.5.1 Bilabials   21
    4.5.2 Labiodentals   22
    4.5.3 Dentals   22
    4.5.4 Alveolar fricatives   23
    4.5.5 Alveopalatals   23
    4.5.6 Palatal nasal   23
    4.5.7 Velar stops   23
    4.5.8 Consonantal system   23
    4.5.9 Liquids   23
    4.5.10 Glides   24
4.6 Summary   25
4.7 Questions   26

5 The atomization of segments   27

5.0   Introduction   27
5.1   Major class features   28
    5.1.1 Consonantal   28
    5.1.2 Sonorant   28
    5.1.3 Syllabic   29
5.2   The neutral position   29
5.3   Features defined in terms of resonators   30
    5.3.1 Anterior   30
    5.3.2 Coronal   30
    5.3.3 Low   30
    5.3.4 High   32
    5.3.5 Front   32
    5.3.6 Back   32
    5.3.7 Round   32
5.4   Features determined by the manner of articulation   32
    5.4.1 Continuant   33

	5.4.2 Strident	33
	5.4.3 Tense	33
5.5	Features defined by secondary articulation	33
	5.5.1 Nasal	33
	5.5.2 Lateral	33
5.6	A glottal feature	33
	5.6.1 Voice	33
5.7	Diacritic features	34
	5.7.1 Aspirated	34
	5.7.2 Length	34
	5.7.3 Stress	34
5.8	The distinctive features of French	34
5.9	The components of segments	34
5.10	Why features?	36
5.11	Questions	36

Part Two. Phonology: Influences, reactions, and consequences in the society of sounds — 38

6 The rise and fall of segments — 38

6.0 Introduction — 38
6.1 Vowel insertion — 39
6.2 Vowel deletion — 40
    6.2.1 Apocope — 41
    6.2.2 Elision — 41
    6.2.3 Syncope — 42
6.3 Consonant deletion — 42
    6.3.1 Final consonant deletion — 42
    6.3.2 Cluster simplification — 44
    6.3.3 Failure to link — 44
6.4 Consonant insertion — 45
    6.4.1 Liaison mal à propos — 45
    6.4.2 Homorganic consonant insertion — 45
6.5 Diphthongization — 46
6.6 Reduction — 47
6.7 Questions — 48

7 Birds of a feather — 50

7.0 Introduction — 50
7.1 Assimilation — 50
    7.1.1 Voicing assimilation — 50
    7.1.2 /R/-Devoicing — 52
    7.1.3 Some remarks — 53
7.2 Palatalization — 54

vi / Contents

7.3 Nasalization	55
7.4 Contraction	55
7.5 Glide formation	56
7.6 Historical evidence	56
7.6.1 Voicing assimilation and nasalization	56
7.6.2 Palatalization	57
7.6.3 Total assimilation	58
7.7 Questions	58

Part Three. French phonological rules: The forces that shape the main traits of the French sound system   60

8 It's what's up front   60

8.1 Fronting	60
8.1.1 Tonic/pretonic vowel alternations: /a ~ ɛ/, /ɔ ~ œ/	60
8.1.2 Defining Fronting	61
8.1.3 Another round vowel alternation: /œ ~ u/	62
8.1.4 An alternation with schwa: /ɛ ~ ə/	62
8.2 Basic classes of French morphology	62
8.2.1 Two kinds of alternations	62
8.2.2 Native and learned forms	63
8.2.3 Derivational and inflectional classes	64
8.3 Some rules	64
8.3.1 Pretonic Vowel Raising	64
8.3.2 Pretonic Vowel Reduction	64
8.4 Fronted vowels in pretonic position	65
8.5 Divisions in French vocabulary	65
8.6 The rules with morphological conditioning	67
8.7 Questions	67

9 The more it changes   68

9.0 Introduction	68
9.1 Pretonic/tonic vowel alternations	69
9.2 Alternations with schwa	69
9.3 A more complex alternation	70
9.4 Some rules	71
9.4.1 High Vowel Lowering	71
9.4.2 Pretonic Vowel Raising	71
9.4.3 /wa/-Adjustment	72
9.5 Diphthongized vowels in pretonic position	72
9.6 More on vocabulary divisions	73
9.7 Ordering the rules	75
9.7.1 Diphthongization and Fronting	75
9.7.2 High Vowel Lowering and /wa/-Adjustment	75
9.8 Questions	76

10 High vowels . . . front!   77

10.0 Introduction   77
10.1 The vowels of learned vocabulary   78
10.2 Fronting   78
    10.2.1 /u/ and /y/ in native and learned forms   78
    10.2.2 Nonalternating /y/ and /u/   80
10.3 Generalizing rules   81
    10.3.1 Fronting   81
    10.3.2 High Vowel Lowering generalized   81
    10.3.3 Generalizing Pretonic Vowel Adjustment   82
    10.3.4 Back Vowel Raising   83
10.4 Two fronting rules   84
10.5 Ordering the rules   84
10.6 Conclusion   85
10.7 Questions   86

11 Other oral vowels   87

11.0 Introduction   87
11.1 The syllable   87
11.2 Nonalternating vowels   87
    11.2.1 /a/, /u/, /ɔ/, /y/, and /i/   87
    11.2.2 Vowels in unrelated words   88
    11.2.3 Alternations with syllabic conditioning   89
    11.2.4 Vowel harmony   89
11.3 The vowels /o/ and /ø/   90
    11.3.1 Low vowels alternating with nonlow vowels:
    /œ ~ ø/, /ɔ ~ o/   90
    11.3.2 /o/-adjustment rules   91
        11.3.2.1 /o/ from /ɔs/   92
        11.3.2.2 Coalescence: /al/ becomes /o/   92
        11.3.2.3 Coalescence: /ɛl/ becomes /o/   93
11.4 Review of the vowels   94
11.5 Questions   95

12 To glide or diphthongize   96

12.0 Introduction   96
12.1 Glides and vowels   96
12.2 Gliding   97
    12.2.1 Prevocalic glides   97
    12.2.2 Ordering Gliding   98
    12.2.3 A constraint on Gliding   99
    12.2.4 Yod-Insertion   99
12.3 The postvocalic glide   100
12.4 Glide or diphthong   102

12.4.1 An apparent counterexample — 102
 12.4.2 The diphthong as a partial explanation — 103
 12.4.3 To glide or to diphthongize — 103
 12.4.4 Diphthongizing back vowels — 104
12.5 Conclusion — 104
12.6 Questions — 104

13 Three nasals from two — 106

13.0 Introduction — 106
13.1 Distribution — 106
13.2 The cluster argument — 107
13.3 The homorganic argument — 108
13.4 The source of the palatal nasal — 108
13.5 Distribution reviewed — 109
 13.5.1 Word-final palatal nasal — 109
 13.5.2 After a liquid — 109
 13.5.3 Intervocalically — 109
 13.5.4 Word-initially — 110
 13.5.5 Before a nasal — 110
 13.5.6 After a consonant — 110
 13.5.7 In the context of nasalization — 110
13.6 Why /ɲ/ behaves like a cluster — 111
13.7 The rule — 111
13.8 The orthographic trap — 111
13.9 Conclusion — 112
13.10 Questions — 112

14 Velum down, nasal out — 113

14.0 Introduction — 113
14.1 Alternations — 113
 14.1.1 Alternations with /ɛ̃/ — 114
 14.1.2 Alternations with /ã/ — 116
 14.1.3 Alternations with /œ̃/ — 116
 14.1.4 Alternations with /ɔ̃/ — 117
 14.1.5 Alternations in a prefix — 117
14.2 The rules — 118
 14.2.1 Nasalization and borrowing — 118
 14.2.2 Two rules, not one — 119
 14.2.3 Nasalized Vowel Lowering — 120
 14.2.4 *en*-Adjustment — 120
14.3 Ordering — 120
14.4 The conditioning nasal — 120
14.5 Questions — 121

15 Schwa, the chameleon — 122

15.0 Introduction — 122
15.1 Reduction — 123
    15.1.1 Posttonic Vowel Reduction — 123
    15.1.2 Reduction of pretonic /a/ — 123
    15.1.3 /ɛ/ reduced to schwa — 124
    15.1.4 Alternations of schwa with diphthongs — 124
    15.1.5 Low Vowel Reduction — 124
15.2 Syllabicity — 125
    15.2.1 The phonetic stuff of schwa — 125
    15.2.2 Syllabic liquids — 127
    15.2.3 In postvocalic position — 130
    15.2.4 After a glide — 131
    15.2.5 Tonic schwa — 131
15.3 Demotion — 132
    15.3.1 Prevocalic demotion — 133
    15.3.2 Phrase-initial demotion — 134
    15.3.3 Contiguous syllable segments — 135
    15.3.4 In word-final position — 138
15.4 Questions — 141

Part Four. Some practical observations, eclectic remarks, and drill-oriented applications — 143

16 Sound production — 144

16.1 The buckshot effect — 144
16.2 Glottal aperture — 145
    16.2.1 Aspiration — 145
    16.2.2 Closure — 146
16.3 Articulatory habits — 146
16.4 Posture and breathing — 147
16.5 Keep up interest — 147
16.6 Assessment — 148

17 Segment production — 149

17.1 Preeminence of the vowel — 149
17.2 Even-stressed rhythm — 149
17.3 Vowel distinctness — 151
17.4 Consonants — 153
    17.4.1 Unaspirated initial stops — 153
    17.4.2 Word-final stops — 154
    17.4.3 Word-medial stops — 154
    17.4.4 Point of articulation — 155

x / Contents

17.5 Liquids — 155
    17.5.1 Uvular consonant vs. retroflex vocoid — 155
    17.5.2 Nonvelarized /l/ and its environment — 156

18 Transcription — 157

18.0 Introduction — 157
18.1 Memorizing French sounds — 157
18.2 Consonantal contrasts — 158
    18.2.1 Voiced vs. voiceless stops — 158
    18.2.2 Voiced vs. voiceless fricatives — 159
    18.2.3 Voiced vs. voiceless segments — 160
    18.2.4 Nasal vs. oral segments — 160
        18.2.4.1 Nasal consonantal segments — 160
        18.2.4.2 Nasal oral segments — 161
    18.2.5 Vowels vs. glides — 161
18.3 Vowels in contrast — 162
    18.3.1 Front vowels: /i/, /e/, /ɛ/ — 162
    18.3.2 Front rounded vowels: /y/, /ø/, /œ/ — 163
    18.3.3 Back vowels: /u/, /o/, /ɔ/ — 163
18.4 Transcription — 164
18.5 The importance of transcription — 165

19 Liaison and elision — 165

19.1 Enchainment and liaison — 165
    19.1.1 Their nature — 165
    19.1.2 Practical steps — 165
    19.1.3 Voicing and devoicing in liaison — 166
    19.1.4 Practice — 167
19.2 Elision — 167
19.3 Syntactic conditioning — 168
    19.3.1 *Liaison obligatoire* — 168
    19.3.2 *Liaison interdite* — 170

20 The front rounded vowels — 172

20.0 Introduction — 172
20.1 Phonologically derived front segments — 172
    20.1.1 Low front rounded /œ/ — 172
    20.1.2 Mid front rounded /ø/ — 174
    20.1.3 Front rounded /y/ — 176
20.2 Generalized fronting — 179

21 Nonhigh oral vowels — 180

21.0 Introduction — 180

21.1 Front unrounded nonhigh vowels: /e/, /ɛ/	181
21.1.1 Verb forms exhibiting the /ɛ/ ~ /e/ contrast	181
21.1.2 /ɛ/ alternating with /ɛj/ and /eje/	182
21.1.3 /ɛ/ in closed syllables	183
21.1.4 Comparison with English	185
21.2 Rounded nonhigh oral vowels: /ø/, /œ/, /o/, /ɔ/	185
21.2.1 Mid vowels before /z/	185
21.2.2 Nonhigh rounded vowels in other checked syllables	187
21.3 Low central tense vowel: /a/	188

22 Glides and diphthongs — 189

22.1 Glides	189
22.1.1 Phonetic production	189
22.1.2 Constraints on Gliding	194
22.2 Stem-final /j/	195
22.3 Diphthongs	196
22.4 Glides and spelling	197
22.4.1 The front unrounded glide /j/	197
22.4.1.1 /V/-*il*	197
22.4.1.2 -*ill*-	198
22.4.1.3 -*i*/V/	198
22.4.1.4 /j/ as the letter *y*	198
22.4.1.4.1 *y* pronounced as /i/	198
22.4.1.4.2 *y* pronounced as /i/ or /j/	198
22.4.1.4.3 *y* pronounced as /j/ only	198
22.4.1.4.3.1 Word-initial *y*	198
22.4.1.4.3.2 Intervocalic *y*	198
22.4.1.4.3.3 Word-final *y*	199
22.4.1.5 /j/ as the letter *ï*	199
22.4.2 The front rounded glide /ɥ/	199
22.4.2.1 Silent *u*	199
22.4.2.2 *u* as either /w/ or /ɥ/ in *qu* and *gu* sequences	199
22.4.2.3 *u* as a vowel or a glide	200
22.4.2.4 *u* before /j/	200
22.4.3 The back glide /w/	201
22.4.3.1 /w/ spelled *u*	201
22.4.3.2 /w/ spelled *ou*	201
22.4.3.3 /wa/ spelled *oe*	201
22.4.3.4 /wa/ and /wɛ̃/ spelled *oi* and *oin*	201
22.4.3.5 *ou* before /j/	201
22.4.3.6 *w* pronounced as /w/ or /v/	201
22.5 Glides in poetry	201
22.5.1 Generally bisyllabic sequences in French poetry	202
22.5.1.1 *ia*	202

22.5.1.2	*ie*	202
22.5.1.3	*ian*	202
22.5.1.4	*iai* (a variant of *ie*)	202
22.5.1.5	*ion*	202
22.5.1.6	*io*	202
22.5.1.7	*iau*	202
22.5.1.8	*ieu*	202
22.5.1.9	*oe*	202
22.5.1.10	*ue*	202
22.5.2 Monosyllabic sequences in poetry		202
22.5.2.1 *ie*		202
22.5.2.2 *oi*		202
22.5.2.3 *oe*		202
22.5.2.4 *ui*		203
22.5.2.5 *ion*		203
22.5.2.6 *oin*		203
22.5.2.7 *ouin*		203

23 Nasals and nasalized vowels — 203

23.1 Phonetic production	203
23.1.1 Drilling /VN/	203
23.1.2 /Ṽ/ not /ṼN/	206
23.1.3 Drills for the nasalized vowels (/Ṽ/)	207
23.1.3.1 /œ̃/	207
23.1.3.2 /ɛ̃/	208
23.1.3.2.1 /ɛ̃/ ~ /in/ alternation	208
23.1.3.2.2 /ɛ̃/ ~ /ɛn/ alternation	208
23.1.3.2.3 /ɛ̃/ ~ /ɛɲ/ alternation	208
23.1.3.2.4 /an/ ~ /ɛn/ ~ /ɛ̃/ alternation	208
23.1.3.3 /ã/: The sequence /an/ as alternant of /ã/	209
23.1.3.4 /õ/	209
23.1.4 Liaison after nasalized vowels	211
23.1.4.1 *Liaison obligatoire*	211
23.1.4.1.1 Fixed expressions with a prenominal modifier	211
23.1.4.1.2 Satellites	211
23.1.4.2 *Liaisons facultatives*	212
23.1.4.3 *Liaisons interdites*	212
23.1.4.3.1 Drills	213
23.1.4.3.2 Odds and ends	213
23.2 Sound to letter relationship	213
23.2.1 The spellings of /ã/	214
23.2.1.1 *an*	214
23.2.1.2 *am*	214

23.2.1.3 *en* 214
23.2.1.4 *em* 214
23.2.1.5 *aen, aon, ean* 214
23.2.2 The spellings of /œ̃/ 214
   23.2.2.1 *un* 214
   23.2.2.2 *um* 214
   23.2.2.3 *eun* 214
23.2.3 The spellings of /õ/ 214
   23.2.3.1 *on* 214
   23.2.3.2 *om* 214
   23.2.3.3 *un, um* 214
23.2.4 The spellings of /ɛ̃/ 214
   23.2.4.1 *in* 214
   23.2.4.2 *im* 215
   23.2.4.3 *ain* 215
   23.2.4.4 *aim* 215
   23.2.4.5 *en* 215
   23.2.4.6 *ein* 215
   23.2.4.7 *eim* 215
   23.2.4.8 *yn* and *ym* 215
   23.2.4.9 *ing* 215
23.2.5 The spellings of /ɲ/ 215
   23.2.5.1 /ɲ/ 215
   23.2.5.2 /gn/ 215
   23.2.5.3 Either /ɲ/ or /gn/ 215
23.2.6 The spellings of /n/ 215
   23.2.6.1 *pn* for /pn/ 215
   23.2.6.2 *mn* for /mn/ 215
   23.2.6.3 Pronounced as /n/ when Nasalization does not apply 215
23.2.7 The spelling of /m/ 215
   23.2.7.1 See Section 23.2.6.2 215
   23.2.7.2 Pronounced as /m/ when Nasalization does not apply 216

24 Schwa as 'mute *e*'   216

24.0 Introduction 216
  24.0.1 The diacritic (ˌ) for syllabic 216
  24.0.2 Syllabicization 216
  24.0.3 A generative solution for traditional 'mute *e*' 217
  24.0.4 Organization of the chapter 217
24.1 Schwa in alternations 217
  24.1.1 In verbs 217
  24.1.2 As an epenthetic segment 219

  24.1.3 Word-medially   221
24.2 Before the so-called aspirated *h*   221
24.3 Demotions   222
  24.3.1 Word-final Demotion   222
  24.3.2 Postvocalic Demotion   224
  24.3.3 Phrase-initial Demotion   226
  24.3.4 Specific Demotion   227
  24.3.5 Demotion of adjacent syllabicized segments   227
24.4 Demotion in poetry   228

Appendix 1: An IPA chart of English   230
Appendix 2: The RULES   231
Appendix 3: RULE Ordering chart   235

References   **236**

Acknowledgments

I am indebted to many people, only a few of whom I will be able to name. I wish to thank first the National Endowment for the Humanities, whose award of a nine-month fellowship enabled me to increase my understanding of language. I am particularly indebted to Sanford Schane, whose pioneering work in French generative phonology constitutes the framework of the description proper. Here and there I have endeavored to go beyond his work within the tradition of abstract representation which he established for French phonology. Because the purpose of this book is to inform scholars and students not trained in linguistics, I have kept away from extensive quoting, from footnoting, and from frequent references. The reader not thoroughly familiar with Schane's work will not know the extent of my model's contribution. Let weaknesses be ascribed to me and strengths to him. As for the work of other French linguists whose example I have attempted to emulate, references to their contributions can be found in the bibliography.

With the perspective of time I have come to appreciate even more some of the advice and example of my former instructors: Robert Champigny, Albert Valdman, Joe Campbell, Andreas Koutsoudas, Gerald Sanders, Richard O'Gorman, and Francis Gravit. I am also thankful to Albert Valdman, Pierre Cintas, Web Donaldson, and Bill Henning, with whom I participated in an experimental program and whose excitement about the topic awakened my love for language study. I am particularly indebted in yet a third regard to Albert Valdman, namely for his encouragement and example over the years. His ideas on phonology permeate my thinking to this day, not just in the descriptive but even more in the pedagogical views I hold regarding the teaching of French pronunciation.

A number of friends have been kind enough to give me helpful comments. I wish to thank Bohdan Saciuk, Bob Hammond, and Jean-Hugues Boisset, who have used parts of this book in their own courses. I thank Shannon Anderson, Andy Crooks, Don Greco, Margot Mahler, Tom Ratican, Hyta Mederer, Gail Sheperd, Pat Sivinski, Jean Singleton, Chris Edson, Abdu Benhallam, and Megan Gideon, for their challenging questions in and out of class. I am also grateful to Andy and Jean for their contributions to questions at the end of some chapters. I would like to thank Tina Bassi, who drew the illustrations. I would also acknowledge the encouragement and the resourceful help, academic and professional, of J. Wayne Conner, a friend and colleague. My gratitude to these people, however, should in no way suggest that they agree with what is proposed herein. I alone take the responsibility for the contents of this volume.

I also owe a great debt of gratitude to my family: to my children, for being, to my parents, Michel and Adrienne Casagrande, for their support and their linguistic insights as speakers of French, and especially to my life's companion, Juanita Casagrande, whose French and English intuition, numerous suggestions, and unequalled patience I wish to publicly acknowledge once again.

JC
Gainesville, 1983

Preface

In more than ten years of teaching French conversation, pronunciation, corrective phonetics, and other topics relating to spoken French, I have found time and again that students thirst for information about the hows and whys of French sounds and their systematic arrangement. Responding to this intellectual need, however, has proven extremely difficult because available materials are too technical for students in a humanistic discipline. This book is intended to fill the gap by providing the necessary background and the desired content to meet the intellectual challenge expected in a senior level course on the study of French sounds. It should also be of help to any humanist wishing to become familiar with some of the tenets of French generative phonology. Written in an order of increasing difficulty, *The Sound System of French* will prepare its reader for further readings in French phonology and, more importantly, it covers the main points in the study of French sounds.

The intellectual challenge is not, of course, the only goal of this work. *The Sound System of French* attempts to balance description and practice. After an introductory portion (Chapters 1-7), it is evenly divided between a descriptive and a practical portion (Chapters 8-15 and 16-24, respectively). Depending on the time available, the previous background of students, the level of the course for which the book may be used, each part can be covered extensively or lightly. The assignments in the descriptive and practical chapters are designed to run conjointly. Suggested schedules for semester and quarter terms are given on the following page.

The Sound System of French is composed of four parts. Part One is an introduction to phonetics and distinctive features. It includes one chapter on the physiological and another on the acoustic properties of sounds. Chapter 5 constitutes an appendix to the first part, detailing the feature organization of all French sounds. Part Two is an introduction to phonological processes. Together, these two parts constitute the introductory portion of this book. Part Three, the descriptive portion, covers such processes as fronting, diphthongization, various raising and lowering rules, gliding, pala-

Table. Suggested schedule for presenting chapters describing the sound system of French and chapters containing practical applications.

A semester schedule:			A quarter schedule:		
Week	Description	Application	Week	Description	Application
1	Ch. 1,2	...	1	Ch. 1, 2, 3	Ch. 16
2	3	Ch. 16	2	4	17
3	4	17	3	5	18
4	5	18	4	6, 7	19
5	6	19	5	8, 9	20
6	7	19	6	10	20
7	8	20	7	11	21
8	9	20	8	12	22
9	10	20	9	13, 14	23
10	11	21	10	15	24
11	12	22			
12	13	23			
13	14	23			
14	15	24			

talizations of different sorts, nasalization, harmony, syllabic demotion, and syllabic deletion. Part Four, the practical portion, focuses on problems which confront the teacher of French. It points out learning problems and offers solutions. It is not, strictly speaking, a drillbook for improving French pronunciation but students can nevertheless improve their speaking habits while learning tips on how to teach French pronunciation to others. Since teachers agree that one of the best ways to learn a given topic is to prepare to teach it, I feel that the approach is sound.

Each of the 15 chapters is followed by a set of questions. In the case of the early chapters these questions are merely a review of the information presented. As readers progress through the book, however, they will gain in their ability to interpret the material presented. Consequently, they will not be satisfied with questions that merely review the contents of chapters and will find with satisfaction that some of the objections or queries they may have formulated as they read the text are taken up in the questions.

Humanists, who are notoriously averse to formalism, will be happy to know that all formal notions, tables, graphs, and symbols have been kept to an absolute minimum. Rules are stated in plain though sometimes inelegant English rather than with features, pluses, alpha signs, arrows, and other symbolic devices. Phonetic, phonological, and underlying representations are not formally distinguished. All transcriptions are in slanted lines. Redundancy statements have been eliminated. The phonetic symbols used are those of the International Phonetic Association, in accordance with a long established practice in French language studies.

There are three appendices. Appendix 1 is an IPA chart of English segments; Appendix 2, an ordering network showing the order in which the rules apply; and Appendix 3, an alphabetically ordered list of the rules.

A linguist reading these introductory remarks will want to know why an abstract phonology approach is chosen in the descriptive part of the book over more concrete descriptions. No theoretic import should be attached to this choice. It is simply felt that on the practical level a more abstract approach to phonology mirrors history better and provides the reader with a clearer perspective of word families. I have found that students who went through earlier versions of the book were able to appreciate courses on the history of French or other Romance languages far more than those with no knowledge of the sound system of a Romance language. Those instructors more prone to work in a concrete vein will be able and no doubt quite willing to champion that approach. Personally, I feel that an introduction should lean toward the abstract tradition before any argumentation aimed at theory construction is presented. For that reason this book goes beyond published abstract analyses of French, notably Schane's. In particular, historical information is allowed here and there to influence the analysis.

To some degree one might say, then, that for the sake of presenting a broader picture of word families I have written rules likely to characterize the grammar of an ideal speaker whose faculté de langue is far more developed than that of the average person. As a rather observant undergraduate put it: 'You can find language rules living through the speech of the people, or you can find them in the language itself. Your book has given me a perspective of the latter.'

Part One.
Phonetics and phonetic differences: Foundation and building blocks of a sound system.

Although the purpose of this book is to describe the sound system of French, it is not inappropriate to place these sounds in a context which might make them more easily understood. For this reason the first three chapters of this part contain some facts about how speech sounds are produced from the physical point of view (Chapter 2), and from the anatomical point of view (Chapter 3). The place of phonetic information within the grammar of French is the subject of Chapter 1 along with a few assorted misconceptions which should be put aside at the outset.

Chapters 4 and 5 deal specifically with French sounds. The articulations required for the production of all French sounds is covered in Chapter 4. Chapter 5 introduces the linguistic terminology necessary for identifying these sounds and families of sounds within the French sound system.

In short, Part One corresponds to a brief survey of facts, principles, and terms needed to understand the rest of the book.

Chapter 1
By way of introduction

1.1 Sound and spelling. The orthographies of languages with long literary traditions are seldom true reflections of their sound systems. This was brought out strikingly by George Bernard Shaw's spelling of *fish* as *ghoti* on the basis of the spelling of *enough*, *women*, and *nation*. Moreover, stringing letters together can yield surprising results. The word *do*, for example, can be changed to rhyme with *sew* by adding an *e* or *ugh*, yielding *doe* and *dough*, respectively. Here are three words sharing the same vowel sound but spelled differently. Adding *e* or *ugh* to other words, even very similar words, does not have the same effect. *To*, for example, gives *toe*, which rhymes with *doe*, but also *tough*, which does not rhyme with *dough*. *Tough* has a final consonant. It rhymes with *stuff*. Furthermore, its vowel sound is different from that of *dough*. Another example of the difference between sound and spelling is shown by the unpredictable results that adding a letter can cause. Consider the word *no*. Adding a *w* changes its vowel from the simple sound *o* to the more complex *ow*. But adding the letter *k* to *now* yields *know* and causes the word to sound like *no*. There is an explanation for these oddities. Orthography is initially a reflection of the sounds of a language. But sounds change with time while orthography lags behind.

In this book (unless specifically stated otherwise) references are made to the sound of French utterances, not to their spelling. Hence, when I refer to the first sound of *philosophie*, I mean *f*; to the last sound of *neuves*, I mean *v*; and to the last sound of *doigt*, I mean *a*. There is no *p* or *h* sound in *philosophie*; final consonants are generally pronounced when a vowel follows, and the final *e* of *neuve* is not pronounced; finally, the *g* of *doigt* has never been pronounced in French even though its Latin equivalent, *digitem*, had a *g*. This *g* disappeared very early. It is of utmost importance to distinguish between orthographic and the phonetic sign, of which only the latter is of concern here.

1.2 Grammar. The word *grammar* can be many things to many people. To some it is a set of higher principles which they would defend with their lives. This meaning of grammar is clearly illustrated by the greying English teacher who asserts that a cigarette tastes *as* it should, not *like* it should. If grammar is used to refer to a published book, then it can be a teaching tool, as used to teach foreign languages, or it can be a reference text. It can also be a piece of empirical research on a language making theoretical claims about language. But a grammar need not be a book. All of us have a grammar which is the set of principles governing our use of this most complex and little understood part of us: our language.

The main goal of linguistic study is to find the principles (rules) which associate the sounds of all utterances possible in a language with the respective meanings of all these utterances. A set of rules which accomplishes this feat for a language is its 'grammar'. All normal human beings internalize a set of rules of (at least) one language, i. e. they acquire a grammar. This process of language acquisition is not a conscious one. No speaker can state all the principles at work in any one utterance. Each of us knows what the result of those rules is, namely, the utterance in question. Linguists want to make explicit what is known subconsciously by speakers. Hence even in this context, the term *grammar* is ambiguous: it can be an abstract set of principles which the speaker uses and it can mean a set of principles about language which a linguist formulates. In this book the term 'grammar' is used in one or the other sense interchangeably.

The model of grammar assumed here is one with a semantico-syntactic set of rules which precedes a set of rules applying to sounds. A sentence is generated in approximately the following way: a thought is given a structure, called its conceptual structure, upon which the semantico-syntactic rules apply. The end result of the application of these rules is another structure, the surface structure. Some of the rules which relate the conceptual to the surface structure create words. These words and the structures within which they occur constitute the input to the rules of the sound system: the phonological rules.

1.3 Underlying representation and phonetic representation. Phonology distinguishes between two levels of structure: underlying representation (UR) and phonetic representation. In a sense, a large portion of this book explains why such a distinction is made, but for purpose of illustration, consider the adjective *clair* and the noun *clarté*. *Clarté* is composed of a stem *clar-* resembling *clair*, and a suffix whose property is to make an adjective into a noun, as in *propre/propreté, beau/beauté, bon/bonté*. Cases like *propre/propreté* only require adding *-té* (a rule of suffixation) to make the adjective into a noun, but *clair* is different, requiring something other than suffixation because of **claireté* (preceded by an asterisk to show that it is not French). Similarly, *sain/santé* appear to contradict the rule of suffixation. Nevertheless, that rule is intuitively correct.

It could be assumed that there is a factor clouding one's perception and that the rule of noun formation by suffixation is indeed correct. Given the fact that in French, a word is stressed (accentuated) on its last vowel sound, one can see that in *clair* the stress falls on *ai*, while in *clarté* it falls on *é*. Note, then, that one difference between the first vowel sound of *clair* (i.e. *ai*) and the first vowel sound of *clarté* (i.e. *a*) is that the first is stressed while the second is not. On the basis of this observation it is possible to postulate a rule which states that an unstressed *a* becomes *ai* when it is stressed. This rule can therefore yield *clair* from *clar*. If *clar-* is followed by *-té*, then the rule does not apply because the *a* of *clar-* is not stressed; hence *clarté*. If *clar-* is not followed by *-té*, then the rule does apply because it is stressed. The result is *clair*. This rule has one important implication. It applies to an abstract form of *clair*, namely, *clar*. Thus by allowing rules to apply as just illustrated, the intuitively correct rule of noun formation can be retained. Thus *clair/clarté, sain/santé*, and a number of apparent counterexamples to noun formation are shown to be regular.

All phonological rules participate in a process similar to this. They relate abstract forms to phonetic representations. Rules apply in order. Before any rule of the phonology has applied to a form produced by the syntax, this form is abstract. It is called the underlying representation. Applying all pertinent phonological rules to that form changes it to its phonetic representation.

4 / 1 By way of introduction

In Part Three a number of cases similar to the foregoing are examined. All are solved in the same fashion. It is also shown that the underlying representation of a phonological sequence is related to its phonetic representation by more than one rule. The rules which relate these two levels of structure apply in a particular order, whose detail will be of greater concern to the readers as they advance through this book.

1.4 Verbal intercourse. Verbal communication takes place in the following way. A speaker conceives a thought (meaning). He uses the grammar of his language to formulate it linguistically, generating phonetic material which corresponds to the thought in question. The speech apparatus produces the appropriate phonetic message, which is perceived by the ear of the listener and transmitted as nerve impulses to his brain, where the grammar of the listener's language converts it into meaning.

A number of short circuits can prevent the message from reaching the listener's brain unchanged: laryngitis, excessive background noise, deafness, and similar physical or physiological disturbances. There may also be a break in this process if the speaker is tired or sleepy (in which case the message is incorrectly altered), if the listener is inattentive for similar or other reasons (in which case he will decode the message only in part, if at all), or if both the speaker and the listener are eager to communicate but cannot because they have different grammars, i. e. they speak different languages.

These factors do not come into play in this book, which focuses on an ideal speaker/hearer of French, or more specifically, on the ideal grammar of a speaker of French. It is easy to see that incomplete competence in the sound system of a language may cause problems in communication. French speakers learning English often have difficulty producing the *h* sounds of such words as *hair, handy, happen, hash, hear, heat, heel, high*. English speakers are likely to interpret these as *air, Andy, a pen, ash, ear, eat, eel*, and *eye*, respectively.

To speak English, a French speaker must learn to produce the *h*. Furthermore, he must learn to produce it in all and only those words where a phonetic (not orthographic) *h* occurs. Hence, he must learn that *honesty, hour, herbs, honor*, and *heir* are in a sense *h*-less words. Gaps in the communication system occur unless the grammar of the language used is fully shared by the interlocutors. Depending on the nature of the gap created by a speaker's inability to produce a language correctly and the ability of the listener to reconstruct the message with the help of context or by means of his knowledge of the speaker's language, a message uttered by that speaker may or may not be decoded properly by the listener.

1.5 The speech chain. When transcribing speech sounds with phonetic symbols, it is assumed that speech is made up of discrete elements, of segments which do not overlap. If, however, recorded graphs of speech are examined, one can see that the so-called segments are, at times, not at all distinct from one another. Machines which record speech and transform it into a visible record show clearly that from an acoustic point of view, the noise-like message which humans send or receive and identify as speech is quite different from written records. Individual sounds, which are represented in orthography and in phonetic transcription by sound symbols, can be grossly enlarged, quite reduced, or even appear as empty space in recorded graphs. The acoustic image, therefore, is drastically different from the conceptual image.

On the other hand, there is a great deal of evidence that, although the acoustic image is so different from our conceptual image, humans rely exclusively on the latter in their use of language. No examples are given here because it would be like putting the cart before the horse. Let it simply be said that there is a gap between the way humans conceptualize speech and the way machines record it.

1.6 Questions.

1. To outdo George Bernard Shaw, make up a word that looks just like an English word but is composed of silent letters from other words. You can then claim that it is not pronounceable.

2. List two reference grammars and two pedagogical grammars. If need be, use the card catalog in your library.

3. Find three different suffixes that change words into masculine nouns.

4. Find three different suffixes that change words into feminine nouns.

5. Give pairs of nouns which differ in sound when they are changed from masculine to feminine.

6. Give pairs of adjectives that differ in the same ways as in Question 5.

7. Determine where a short in communication has taken place in the following verbal exchanges:

 (a): —Bonjour, Ça va?
   —Prego? Non capisco.
 (b): —Elève De Lapalisse. Quels sont les mois de l'année?
   —Ce sont les douze périodes consecutives qui composent un an.
 (c): —Pardon Monsieur. Avez vous du feu?
   —Oui. Dans ma cheminée.
 (d): Avant de l'embrasser, le Prince Charmant aurait demandé permission à la Belle Au Bois Dormant.
   Réponse: ZZZZZZZZ

Chapter 2
The nature of sound

2.1 Waves. People talk about waves: radio waves, sound waves, light waves, tidal waves. Identifying the crest of a surface wave in water as 'a wave', they refer to the position of a swimmer as being 'between two waves'. As is the case of most words in language, the term *wave* is used nontechnically by the average speaker, for whom words like *FM*, *AM*, *short waves*, etc. are likely to refer to places on a radio dial, not to the actual properties of the waves in question. Since the study of the sound properties of a language involves the notion of sound wave, the physics of sound is examined briefly.

The term 'wave' is, of course, taken from the everyday meaning of the word *wave*. Sound waves are but one example of physical phenomena that involve vibration. Vibration is a technical term for repeated motion. All waves are produced by the vibration of matter or energy. Radio and light waves are electromagnetic in nature. They consist of the vibrations of electrical particles and magnetic fields. Surface waves in water consist of the vibration of water particles. Sound waves in the air consist of the vibration of air particles. Since vibrations seem to play such an important role in the formation and nature of wave motion, it is useful to examine them first.

Also treated in this chapter are the nature of the cycle (simple and complex), the concepts of frequency, pitch, amplitude, intensity, resonance, and harmonics.

2.2 Vibrations. A vibration can be periodic or nonperiodic, simple or complex. The movement of a pendulum is a good example of periodic and simple vibration. If one were to place a pen at the tip of the pendulum, and slide a piece of paper at an even speed perpendicularly to the line of motion of the pendulum, in such a way as to cause the pen to write evenly on the paper, the resulting shape would be a curved line (*K*), as illustrated in Figure 2.1.

Figure 2.1

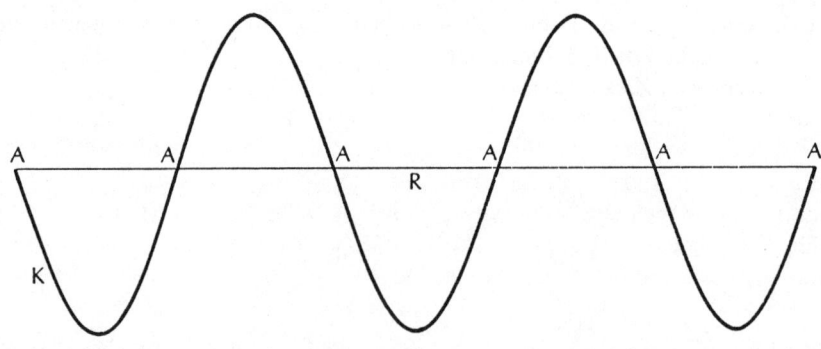

2.3 Frequency and pitch

If the pendulum is at rest and the paper is pulled in the same way as before, the resulting shape is the straight line R, in Figure 2.1. Line R represents the point of rest of the pendulum. It is a line and not a dot because the operation described requires that one pull the paper. If the paper were not pulled, the resulting shape would be a dot. The sliding corresponds to time, which remains constant.

The points of K which intersect with R, namely, the points of rest of K, are labeled A. The motion described by a curved line K from one A to the next A is a vibration. A period (or cycle) is composed of two successive vibrations. As the pendulum moves, it crosses the point of rest A and moves away from R to a point B farthest away from R, then returns toward R, crosses it at the next A, moves away from R to a point C farthest away from R, and starts the same motion again. A period or cycle is represented as $ABACA$. $ACABA$ is also a period. $ABAC$ and $BACABA$, however, are not periods.

2.3 Frequency and pitch. If the distance $ABACA$ is covered in 1/20 of one second, the frequency is said to be 20 cycles per second; in 1/440 of one second, 440 cycles per second; 1/20,000 of one second, 20,000 cycles per second. The human hearing range is between 20 c/s and 20,000 c/s. Middle A on the piano keyboard vibrates at 440 c/s. Sound frequency is interpreted by humans as pitch.

A particular frequency corresponds to each vibrating body. The heavier the body, the lower its frequency of vibration. The larger cords in a piano, for example, correspond to the lower frequencies; the thinner cords to the higher frequencies. Other qualities determine the frequency of vibrations: tension of cords, for example, as any string instrumentalist well knows. The volume and shape of a cavity, as well as the size of its opening, also determine frequency. The relationship of the volume of a cavity to the size of its opening is somewhat intricate. Let us consider it in terms of examples. The piccolo is an instrument with fixed cavity volume. Cover all holes and blow, and you get the lowest pitch (frequency). As holes are uncovered, the frequency increases. Hence, given a fixed cavity, the greater the opening(s), the higher the pitch. The slide trombone is a fixed opening instrument with variable volume. When the slide is pushed out, it makes the cavity longer and frequencies are lower. When the slide is in, it makes the cavity smaller, and the frequencies are higher. Hence, given a fixed opening, the smaller the cavity, the higher the frequency (or pitch).

A given frequency corresponds to a particular tone. People perceive sound frequencies in such a way that the doubling of a given frequency is interpreted as its equivalent at the next higher octave in music. Half the frequency of a sound is interpreted as the equivalent of that sound at the next lower octave. Thus the interval between middle A (440 c/s) and the next lower A (220 c/s), which is an interval of 220 c/s, is interpreted in the same way as that between middle A and the next higher A (880 c/s), which is an interval of 440 c/s. People do not perceive a given frequency in the same way at different points of the scale: the difference between 100 and 200 c/s is interpreted as an octave, while the same difference of 100 c/s between 1700 and 1800 is perceived as a semitone.

The way that a vibrating body is set in motion does not affect its frequency. A violin string plucked or rubbed by a bow will vibrate at the same frequency. If no change is brought to a vibrating body, its frequency remains constant, but it loses in intensity.

2.4 Amplitude and intensity. The amplitude of a vibration is measured in terms of the greatest displacement of the vibrating body from its position at rest. Suppose that we pluck a guitar string. The resulting vibration of that string has the frequency of the given string. Depending on the force exerted on the string in question, it will be slightly or greatly displaced. Its vibrations act upon the medium around it, air particles, which vibrate at the same frequency. Because of the relative inertia of air, the intensity of the vibration is diminished ('damped', in the technical jargon) by time and distance. A tuning fork, a plucked string, or any vibrating body loses intensity. An exploding bomb or mine can be deafening at close distance and a vague rumble from afar.

The amplitude of a vibration, then, is the distance d (see Figure 2.2) between points A and B or A and C, where B and C are the points of K farthest away from R and A is a point of R at the intersection of a perpendicular line drawn from B or C.

Figure 2.2

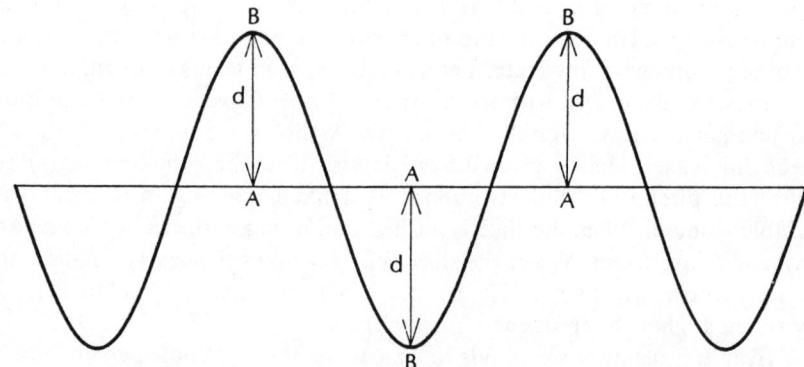

Amplitude is constant only if the intensity of a vibration is maintained constant. If not, a vibration loses in amplitude at a given rate. If this loss of amplitude is rapid, the vibration is heavily damped; if the loss is slow, the vibration is lightly damped (see Figure 2.3).

Figure 2.3

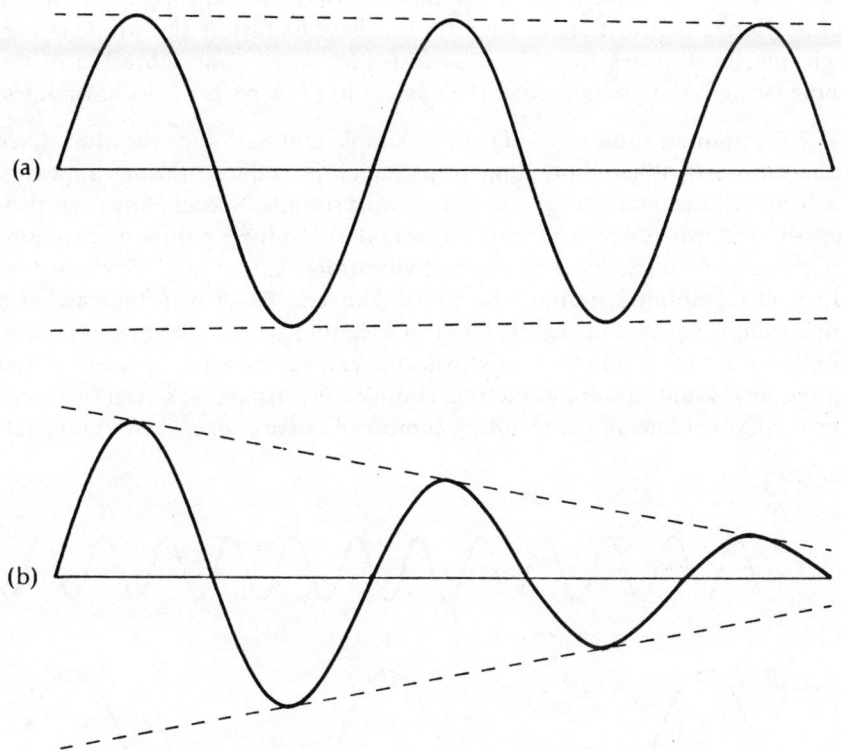

Of these two waves, the one labeled (a) is less heavily damped than (b). Note that, although intensity decreases in both, their frequencies remain constant.

2.5 Sound propagation. Sound travels in air at 1100 feet per second, or 770 miles per hour. The greater the density of the medium, the faster sound travels and the greater the amplitude needed. As a body vibrates it disturbs the particles of the medium in which it is located, displacing these particles at the frequency and with the amplitude of its vibrations. These disturbed particles in turn disturb other particles in the same way, and so on. The fewer the particles in a medium, the weaker the amplitude needed to make them vibrate. The number of particles is in direct proportion to the amount of friction created by the moving particles. Hence, the more particles, the greater the tendency to damp the sound. In a vacuum, however, these principles cannot apply: vibrations are not propagated because there are no particles to be disturbed and to pass motion to other particles.

2.6 Harmonics. The sounds that we humans generally hear around us are not simple sounds. This is so because vibrating bodies create not only a fundamental sound but also the harmonics of that sound.

10 / 2 The nature of sound

When a string vibrates, for example, each part of that string vibrates simultaneously with a frequency that corresponds to its relationship to the whole string. Hence half of that string vibrates twice as fast as the whole string, each quarter vibrates four times as fast, and so on. The vibration of the whole string is the fundamental; the vibrations of its parts are its harmonics.

2.7 Compound sounds. So far, only simple and periodic vibrations have been examined. When plotted on graph paper, periodic vibrations appear in the form of sinusoidal curves: they are simple sounds. Speech, however, produces sound waves which are not sinusoidal: it produces compound sounds.

Compound sounds have compound vibrations. Compound vibrations result from combining simple vibrations. This can be seen in the case of a single pebble thrown in still water. The resulting waves are concentric and simple. In a heavy rain or hail storm one can see no such concentric and simple waves, but rather interacting, complex disturbances. Given two sinusoidal curves A and B, the resulting combined curve is like C, in Figure 2.4.

Figure 2.4

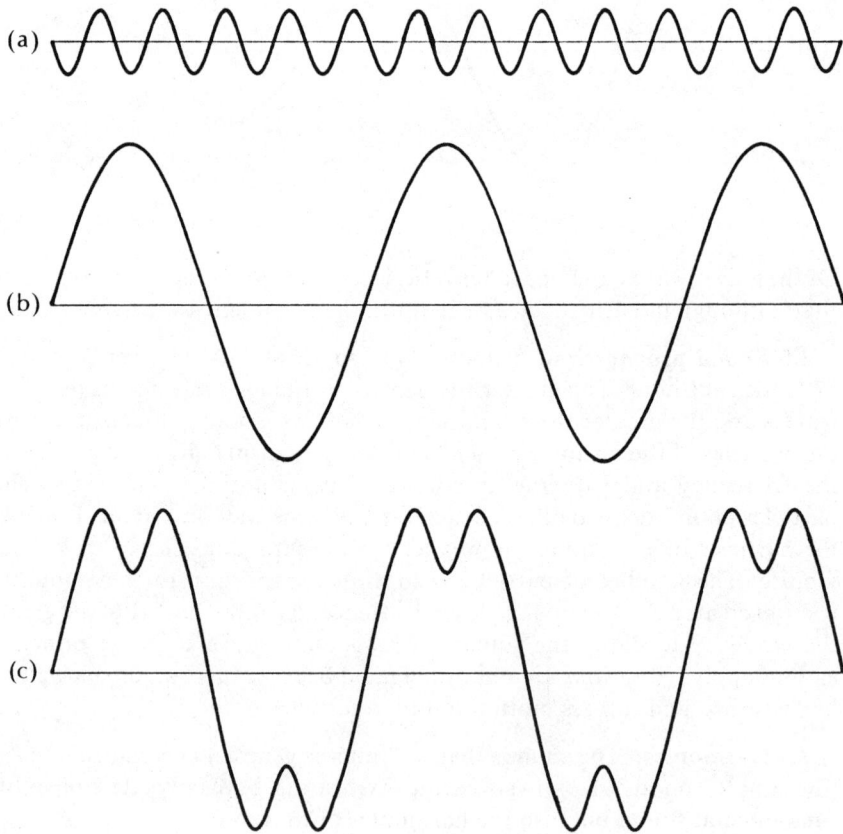

All simple waves are periodic but not all periodic waves are simple. Some periodic waves are compound waves, as are those of Figures 2.4 and 2.5.

Figure 2.5 Wave shape of the vowel sound in *vase*. (The distance between A and B, B and C, etc., is a period.)

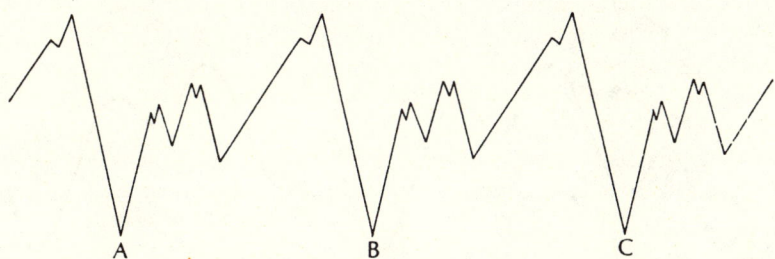

Aperiodic wave shapes do not show the relative regularity found in the vowel sound of *vase*. They represent 'noise'. The wave shapes in Figures 2.4 and 2.5 are progressively complex. A French mathematician, Joseph Fourier, showed that all nonsinusoidal (complex) curves are reducible to a number of sinusoidal (simple) curves. Conversely, complex sounds can be made out of simple sounds. For several decades now, speech scientists have been able to combine simple sounds to create speech sounds. They do it with machines called speech synthesizers. Early synthesizers were hardly comprehensible. The most commonly known stage of development is that which corresponds to what people identify as computer speech. Recently, synthesized speech has become so sophisticated as to be easily confused with human speech (see Flanagan 1972).

2.8 Resonators. We have seen that cavities, like strings or tuning forks, have specific frequencies. When a sound wave reaches the volume of air of a cavity, it creates a certain disturbance. If the frequency of the incoming sound wave is the same as that of the cavity, the motion of particles of air is multiplied and the resulting sound is louder. A cavity acts as a resonance chamber (resonator). The frequency of a cavity is not always the same as that of incoming sound waves. If it is not, the amplitude of the incoming wave is damped: the cavity does not function as a resonator. If the volume of a cavity changes, then different frequencies are damped and amplified. Water falling from a spigot onto the ground or into a sink will make a certain noise. But if the water falls into a bottle under the faucet, then a vastly different noise is heard. These sounds are amplified by the resonance chamber which the bottle constitutes. As the water rises, this resonance chamber changes volume and shape. Consequently, it amplifies and damps different frequencies. When the pitch of the sound in the bottle reaches a certain height, people know from experience to turn off the faucet.

12 / 2 The nature of sound

This chapter has introduced a few concepts of the physics of sounds. Most examples examined were taken from man-made instruments but the concepts discussed apply equally to the human body.

2.9 Questions

1. The following diagrams represent recordings of what kind of sounds? Describe the difference.

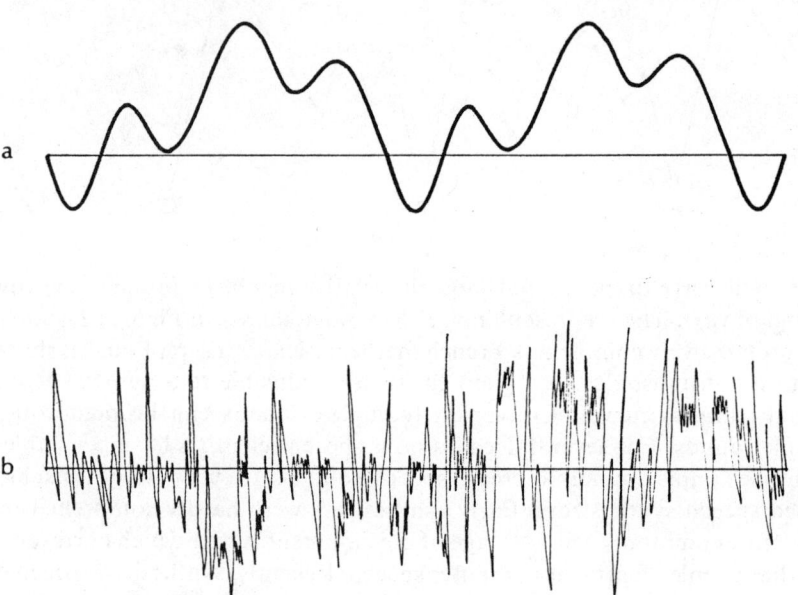

2. Consider the following diagram. If vibrations A and B are combined, the result is C. What can you conclude about the resulting sound (about its frequency and its amplitude)?

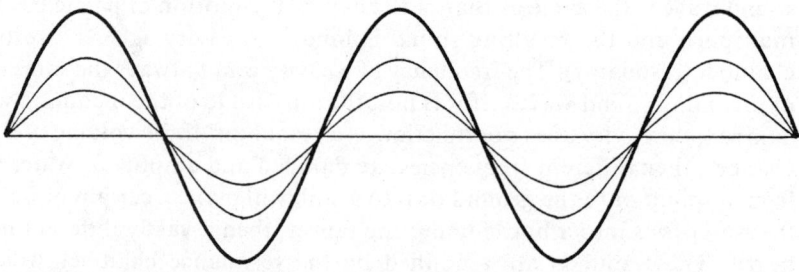

3. If you pluck a guitar string and then press down at the center, what modification will you have brought to the pitch? Explain this in terms of frequencies of vibrating bodies.

4. Describe the speed of sound in air in feet/second. In your opinion will sound travel slower or faster in water than in air? Why?

5. Compare the production of sound by a violin with that of a person talking. Start from the energy source and proceed to the ear of the listener. Make sure to include vibrating bodies, resonators, modes of transmission, and the like.

6. Compare the bugle and the clarinet in terms of vibration source, resonator opening and size, and musical range.

7. In what way is the bagpipe different from other wind instruments?

Chapter 3
The organs of speech

3.1 A superimposed system. The respiratory system of man comprises organs which are used for the purpose of inspiration and expiration. The digestive system has organs which are used for the purpose of breaking down food and digesting it. Some organs seem destined to perform only one task: the heart pumps blood, the kidneys filter blood, the stomach breaks down food, etc. Other organs have a primary purpose (found in many animal species) and the added use of speech production. So, to speak of these organs as the speech organs is a slight misnomer; but in practice phoneticians refer to them as such anyway, just to avoid the longer circumlocution 'organs used in the production of speech'.

3.2 The bellows. Inspiration and expiration, like the pumping action of the heart, are physical activities of which we are not constantly conscious. Unlike the action of the heart or the digestion of meals, however, respiration can be altered at will, to some degree at least. People can delay inspiration or expiration, increase their rate, and use them for purposes other than breathing. The production of speech sounds involves the infinite number of ways humans can alter the process of expiration. These ways are defined in terms of the strength of expiration, of its path from the lungs to the outside air, of the involvement of organs, muscles, cavities, and membranes which alter the flow of the air being expired.

The force responsible for inspiration and expiration comprises the diaphragm and other muscles. The diaphragm is a flat muscle which separates the chest from the abdomen. When it relaxes and the abdominal muscles contract, the abdomen moves up partly into the chest cavity, pushing out the air in the lungs. Conversely, when the diaphragm contracts, it pushes the abdomen down. This creates a vacuum in the chest and the air is sucked in. The chest cavity is enclosed within the rib cage, which is lined with muscles capable of enlarging or diminishing the chest cavity. In short, air is inhaled and exhaled through the well-coordinated interaction of three muscles or sets of muscles: the abdominal muscles, the diaphragm, and the chest muscles. The chest cavity and these muscles can be viewed as the bellows of the most natural of wind instruments: the human speech mechanism.

3.3 Speech production. In speech production the air is forced out of the chest cavity, as just seen. It travels through the wind pipe or trachea which leads it to the larynx or voice box, where it causes the vocal cords to vibrate. The sounds produced by the vocal cords are damped or reinforced by three cavities in ways yet to be examined. These cavities are the pharynx, the nose (or more properly, the nasal cavity), and the mouth or oral cavity.

3.4 The larynx. When people breathe normally, the air flowing out makes little audible sound. In particular, the air does not cause the vocal cords to vibrate. Take a very big breath and hold it, keeping your lips apart. You may have felt a valve closing in your throat. That valve is the glottis. Embedded in the larynx, the glottis remains wide open during normal breathing. The glottis can be wide open, closed, or partially open (see Figure 3.1).

Figure 3.1

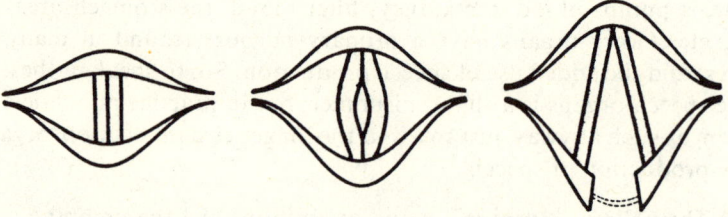

When the glottis is partially open, the membranes which line this valve are caused to vibrate. This vibration is heard as voice. The membranes are known as the vocal cords or, more appropriately, the vocal folds. The vocal cords are attached to the thyroid cartilage (Adam's apple) in the front part of the larynx and to the arytenoid cartilages in the back part. The opening and closing of the glottis is controlled by muscles which move the arytenoids apart or together.

The larynx functions as a valve. It can be closed to allow pressure to build in the chest cavity, as happens when people make physical efforts such as lifting heavy objects. In this case, the vocal folds seal the glottis. Another way of closing the larynx is to cover it with the epiglottis, a pear-shaped muscle which deflects food into the esophagus and keeps the trachea free of foreign bodies. When a person swallows, the epiglottis teams with the vocal folds to shield the trachea, directing the incoming food or liquid to the stomach via the esophagus.

3.5 The vocal tract. The part of the speech mechanism which lies past the larynx as the air is expired is called the vocal tract. It consists of the pharynx, the oral cavity, and the nasal cavity. The shape of the vocal tract, and therefore its resonance (cf. Section 2.8) can be altered by the interaction of all its parts. The ways in which speakers open and close their lips, allow air to flow through their nose, shape and place their tongue, make their pharynx wide or narrow, and so on, determine the sounds that they make, i.e. determine their articulation.

3.5.1 The pharynx. The tube connecting the larynx to the mouth and nose is called the pharynx. The shape of the pharynx during speech determines some of the frequencies of speech sounds. The pharynx acts as a resonator and creates one of the frequencies of speech sounds.

Figure 3.2 Comparison of the size of the pharynx for two French vowels.

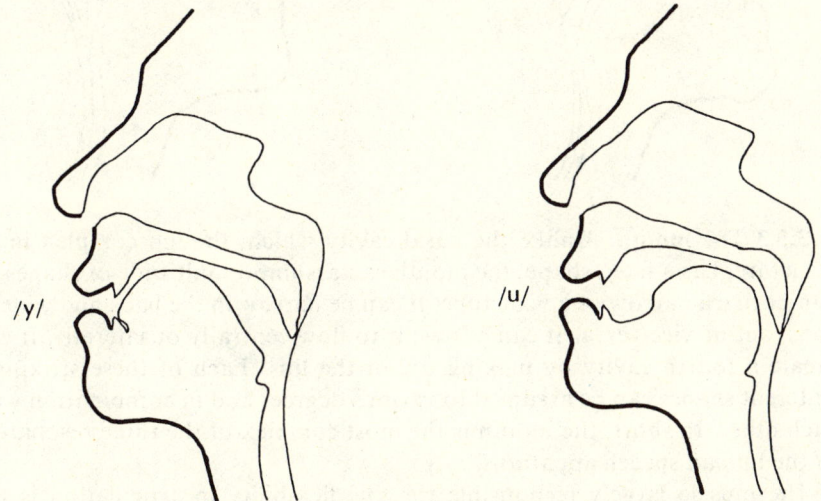

Some languages have pharyngeal sounds, that is, sounds produced by a constriction of the pharynx. Arabic is one such language. English and French do not have pharyngeals (but see Delattre 1969).

3.5.2 The nose. The shape of the nasal cavity, unlike that of the pharynx, cannot be altered at will. Participation of the nasal cavity in the speech act is determined by whether air is allowed to flow through the nose. The opening of the nasal cavity is guarded by the soft palate or velum. When the velum is lowered, air can flow through the nasal cavity. When the velum is raised, the entrance to the nasal cavity is blocked and air must flow from the pharynx to the mouth only (cf. Figure 3.3). In short, air and the vibrations it carries from the larynx and the pharynx can flow through the nose only (if the lips are closed), through the mouth only (if the velum is raised), or through both

16 / 3 The organs of speech

resonating chambers. The shape of the nasal cavity is highly complex. Many of its linings are membranes which add a particular quality to its resonance.

Figure 3.3

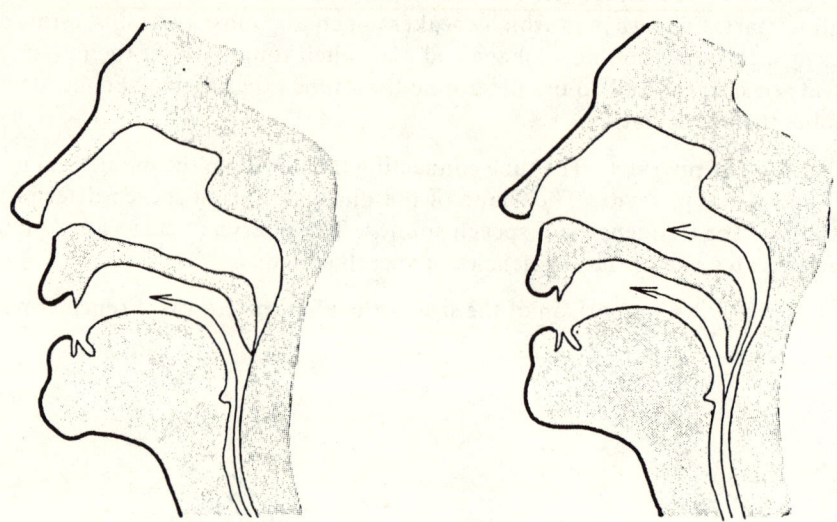

3.5.3 The mouth. Unlike the nasal cavity which, though complex in its structure, has a fixed shape, the mouth can assume a multitude of shapes. It can be like a narrow or a wide tube. It can be narrow in the back and wide in the front or vice versa. It can allow air to flow centrally or laterally. It can create a fourth cavity by making use of the lips. Each of these strikingly different shapes can be assumed to various degrees and in combination with each other. In short, the mouth is the most complex of the three resonators of the human speech apparatus.

The muscle largely responsible for this flexibility in articulation is the tongue. But the tongue is by no means the only muscle at work in the mouth. It is assisted by the muscles used to open and close the mouth, to smile, to pucker, to swallow, etc.

The physical structure of the mouth can be best examined by pictorial illustration (as in Figure 3.4). For the purpose of phonetic study, the roof of the mouth is generally divided into three parts: the teeth ridge (alveoli), the hard palate (palatum), and the soft palate (velum). The back end of the soft palate is a pointed appendix called the uvula. The tongue is also conventionally divided into three parts. The part which, in the neutral position (to be defined in Chapter 5), lies opposite the velum is the back of the tongue. The one which, in the neutral position, lies opposite the palate is called the body of the tongue. The part of the tongue which, in the neutral position, lies opposite the alveolar ridge (or teeth ridge) is the blade of the tongue. The tip of the tongue, also known as the apex, is considered to be a part of the blade.

3.5.3 The mouth

Figure 3.4 The oral cavity.

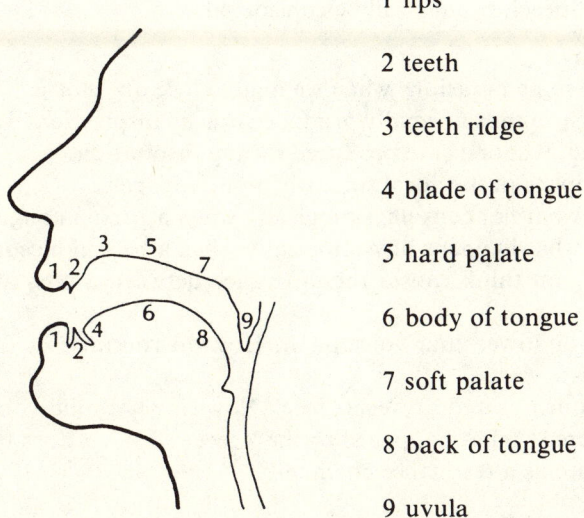

1 lips

2 teeth

3 teeth ridge

4 blade of tongue

5 hard palate

6 body of tongue

7 soft palate

8 back of tongue

9 uvula

The teeth and the lips also take part in speech production in ways to be described in Chapter 4. When referring to articulation, it is customary to refer to these areas of the mouth by their adjectival forms. Sounds made with the lips are called labial sounds; with the teeth, dental sounds; with the teeth ridge, alveolar sounds; with the hard palate, palatal sounds; and with the velum, velar sounds.

The mouth, more than any other element of the speech apparatus, has been associated with language and has even been viewed as language in the layman's conception of linguistic phenomena. It is not surprising that, because of this misconception, many languages use the word for tongue, the adjective referring to the mouth (oral) and the like, to refer to language. There are in English and French expressions like *au bout des lèvres, closed-lipped, on the tip of one's tongue, tongue-tied, foul-mouth, son nom est dans toutes les bouches, to pay lip service, le don des langues*, and all the derivatives of the Latin word *lingua*, such as *language, langage*, and, quite obviously, *linguistics*.

The expression *word of mouth*, like any of the foregoing, is quite telling not only in the sense just illustrated but more importantly in that it does seem to disregard the rest of the linguistic aspect of human communication. These apparently trivial remarks are of importance not, of course, as a complaint about the layman's failure to understand language better, but because they point to a need often left unfilled in books on general phonetics and on the phonetics of particular languages. It is important to realize that the sound system of a language is itself but one component of an even greater system, the grammatical system of that language. In other words, the study of speech sounds should not be done in a vacuum. That was the message of the first chapter and it is the message of the second and third parts of this book. In the next chapter, however, only the mechanisms involved in the production of speech sounds will be considered.

3.6 Questions.
1. What are some occasions when we might close our glottis?
2. Are speech sounds normally produced during inspiration? Why or why not? What kind of sounds are produced during inspiration?
3. What happens in the vocal tract when one whispers?
4. Describe what happens physiologically when a person coughs.
5. Describe what happens physiologically when a person hiccoughs.
6. What do you think causes the difference between a bass and a tenor voice?
7. How do you lower your voice pitch? How do you raise it? Explain this physiologically.
8. Spread your lips and say 'eeeeeeeee'. Now slowly round your lips until they are puckered. What happened to the 'eeeeeee'? What does this tell you about the mouth as a resonance chamber?

Chapter 4
Articulatory properties of French sounds

4.1 Articulation. Of the speech organs and muscles, those located above the trachea are known as articulators. Some articulators can move, others cannot. Of the movable articulators, the most mobile is, of course, the tongue. In Chapter 1, we saw the extent to which this complex muscle has been identified with human verbal communication. Raised or lowered, bunched toward the front or back of the mouth, made concave or convex, it can change the shape, and therefore the resonance, of the oral and pharyngeal cavities. Other muscles participate as movable articulators in the production of French speech sounds by rounding the lips, spreading them or pressing them together, raising and lowering the soft palate (velum), opening and closing the glottis, etc. Some fixed articulators are the upper lip, the upper front teeth, the alveolar ridge, the palate. The way in which the articulators participate in the production of speech constitutes the subject of this chapter. To be examined here are the two parameters of articulation (point and manner), the vowels, and the other sounds (consonants, nasals, liquids, and glides).

4.2 Manner of articulation. The sounds of a language are produced with or without voicing, with the jaws more or less apart, with the lips rounded or spread, with the velum raised or lowered, with the tongue in one of its many possible shapes. The different ways of positioning or moving the organs of speech determine the manner of articulation of sounds. A given sound, or segment (cf. Chapter 1), produced with vibrating vocal cords, is said to be voiced; with no complete closure of the vocal tract, it is a continuant (cf. Chapter 5); with a lowered velum, it is nasalized, etc. These are the manner of articulation features of that sound. The manner of articulation features of a sound (to be examined in more detail in Chapter 5) provide one set of characteristics for a sound segment. Another set of characteristics for a segment is provided by the segment's point(s) of articulation.

4.3 Point of articulation. The point of constriction of the vocal tract for a particular sound is the point of articulation of that sound. The constriction may be a complete closure (as of the lips in producing the first sound of *police*) or a degree of aperture (the amount of opening of the mouth) for a vowel. There may be more than one point of constriction for a particular sound, and consequently, that sound has more than one point of articulation.

The rest of this chapter is an elaboration of the concepts of point and manner of articulation as they apply to vowels, consonants, liquids, nasals, and glides. It also provides illustrations of these possibly novel terms.

4.4 Vowels (syllabic sounds). The vowels of French may be oral or nasal, depending on whether the velum is raised or lowered. If it is raised, they are oral; if it is lowered, nasal. The last sound in *plein* is a nasalized vowel; the last sound in *plaie* is an oral vowel. The vowels of French can be high, mid, or low, depending upon whether the tongue is near the roof of the mouth, moderately far from the roof of the mouth, or farther yet from the roof of the mouth. The last sound in *ami* is high, the last sound in *été* is mid, and the first sound in *être* is low. In pronouncing these sounds successively, one can feel the difference in tongue height. The vowels of French can also be front, central, or back, depending upon the relative placement of the tongue toward the front or back of the mouth. The last sound in *feu* is front, and that of *chaud* is back. The vowels of French can be rounded or spread (unrounded), according to the shape of the lips. All back vowels in French are rounded. Front vowels can be rounded, as in the vowel sound of *cru*; or unrounded, as in the vowel sound of *cri*. The vowels of French can be tense or lax, depending on the degree of muscular effort used. If there is muscular effort, the sound is tense; if not, it is lax (nontense). The vowel /a/ in *pas* is tense; but the second vowel in *entretient*, /ə/, is lax.

In considering the vowels of French, it is useful to keep in mind the parameters just mentioned. These parameters are used to compose the chart in Figure 4.1. This blank chart is provided for those who wish to pencil in the vowels that are introduced in the text. Figure 4.2 serves as verification.

4.4.1 Oral vowels. The front unrounded vowels are /i/, /e/, and /ɛ/, as in *si*, *ses*, and *sept*. They differ from each other in that /i/ is a high vowel, /e/ is

Figure 4.1

	Front		Central		Back
	Unround	Round	Tense	Lax	(Round)
High (oral)					
Mid (oral)					
Low (oral)					
(nasal)					

a mid vowel, and /ɛ/ is a low vowel. The front rounded vowels of French are /y/, /ø/, and /œ/, as in *su, ceux,* and *seul,* respectively. They differ from each other in the same way as the unrounded vowels differ: /y/ is high, /ø/ mid, and /œ/ low. Entered in the vowel chart, these sounds fit in the leftmost box of Figure 4.1, in two columns.

French has two central vowels: the second vowel of *autrefois,* /ə/, and the vowel in *part,* /a/. Both are low vowels. Some phoneticians claim that there are two distinct *a*'s in French, but evidence from speaker to speaker and sometimes within the speech of a single speaker is too contradictory to give empirical support to this claim. Here, only one *a* sound is assumed. The vowel /a/ is distinguished from /ə/ in that it is tense whereas /ə/, generally called schwa, is lax. The back vowels of the oral vocalic system of French are /u/, /o/, and /ɔ/, as in *pou, peau,* and *port*. These vowels are also distinguished on the basis of tongue height: /u/ is high, /o/ is mid, and /ɔ/ is low. This rounds out the oral vowel system of French.

4.4.2 Nasal vowels. The oral vowels have no resonance in the nasal cavity. They are produced with a raised velum. Their nasalized equivalents are produced with a lowered velum, which accounts for the air passing through the nasal cavity, and the ensuing resonance. These are /ɔ̃/, /ã/, /ɛ̃/, and /œ̃/, as in *long, lent, lin,* and *l'un,* respectively. The French nasalized vowels are generally described as low vowels. It will be shown later that the back /ɔ̃/ tends to be raised to /õ/ in the speech of most speakers. For our present purposes it is described here as low.

Rounding is more acutely perceived and produced in high vowels than in low vowels. This accounts in part for why some dialects of French fail to distinguish /ɛ̃/ from /œ̃/ and /ɔ̃/ from /ã/. No French dialect, however, fails to distinguish /i/ from /y/ or /y/ from /u/.

French, as can be seen from Figure 4.2, has more front vowels than back vowels. This imbalance in the vocalic system is one reason why French speakers appear to pronounce primarily with their lips. This imbalance in the vocalic system and the fact that French has front rounded vowels are reasons why actors imitating French speakers tend to speak with their lips protruding.

Figure 4.2 The vowel system of Standard French.

	Front		Central		Back
	Unround	Round	Lax	Tense	(Round)
High Oral	i	y			u
Mid Oral	e	ø			o
Low Oral	ɛ	œ	ə	a	ɔ
Nasal	ɛ̃	œ̃		ã	ɔ̃

4.4.3 Summing up the vowels. The vowels of French, and, in fact, vowels in most languages, share a number of features: voice (i.e. vibrations of the vocal folds), continuance (as opposed to noncontinuance in some consonants), sonorance, and syllabicity, to mention a few. Leaving aside the others (to be examined in Chapter 5), consider the feature syllabic. To say that a segment is syllabic is to say that each occurrence of that segment corresponds to a syllable. The number of syllables in a line is of importance in French poetry for a number of reasons, two of which should be mentioned here. The number of syllables identifies the type of verse employed in a piece of poetry: the poetic line par excellence in French is the 12-syllable alexandrine. The number of syllables also helps us scan a poem, i.e. identify the meters of each line.

In French there is a one-to-one correspondence between the syllable and the vowel, except for certain cases of mute *e* to which attention is given in the third part of this book. The sentence *Où veut-il aller?* has five vowels (u, ø, i, a, e) and, therefore, five syllables. The exclamation *Comme il fait chaud!* has four vowels (ɔ, i, ɛ, o) and, therefore, four syllables. In French, segments other than vowels are nonsyllabic. So, *extra* /ɛkstRa/ and *état* /eta/ have the same number of syllables because they have the same number of vowels. There are languages which have syllabic segments which are not vowels. English is such a language. The last segment of *little* is a syllabic *l*, that of *marxism* is a syllabic *m* (cf. Chapter 15).

4.5 Consonants (nonsyllabic sounds). The nonsyllabic sounds of French are the consonants, nasals, liquids, and glides. They are distinguished from vowels by the feature syllabic. Chapter 5 indicates which features distinguish each of these sets of nonsyllabic segments from the others. In the remainder of this chapter, the nonsyllabic segments of French are given and their articulatory parameters stated, proceeding in terms of their points of articulation, from the lips toward the glottis.

4.5.1 Bilabials. The lower and upper lips pressed together can close the flow of air. Three French consonants are produced upon release of the lips: they are the first sounds in *pelle, belle,* and *mère*. These three sounds are distinct from all others in that they are 'bilabial'. Like other sounds with complete closure, /p/ and /b/ are called 'stops'. They are bilabial stops. The sound /m/ is different from /p/ and /b/ in that it is produced with a lowered velum, allowing resonance in the nasal cavity. It is a bilabial nasal. The sounds /p/ and /b/ are not nasals. They are produced with a raised velum. They are different from each other in that /b/ is voiced and /p/ is voiceless. Voicing is produced by the vibration of the vocal folds. The vocal folds vibrate for the production of /b/ but not for /p/. They also vibrate to produce /m/: in fact, all French nasals are voiced. As with the vowels, a grid is provided in Figure 4.3, into which the reader may wish to enter the sounds discussed.

Figure 4.3

	Bilabial	Labio-dental	Dental	Alveolar	Alveo-palatal	Palatal	Velar
Stops vl							
vd							
Fricatives vl							
vd							
Nasals (vd)							

4.5.2 Labiodentals. If the point of articulation of a sound is where the lower lip and the upper teeth meet, then the sound is known as a labiodental. French has two labiodental consonants. The first sounds in *philosophe* and *ville* are labiodentals. The former, /f/, is voiceless; the latter, /v/, is voiced. They are distinct from all other sounds on the basis of their point of articulation. Unlike /p/ and /b/, /f/ and /v/ are not stops, but fricatives. They are produced with constriction, but the flow of air is not interrupted. There is constriction but not closure.

4.5.3 Dentals. French has three dentals, /t/, /d/, and /n/: the first sounds of *toi*, *doigt*, and *noix*. The blade of the tongue against the upper front teeth makes a complete closure of the oral cavity; then the air is released with or without voicing to produce /d/ and /t/, respectively. In the case of /n/, there is voicing and the velum is lowered, allowing the air to resonate in the nasal cavity during oral closure. Strictly speaking, /n/ is not a dental, but a dento-alveolar. The difference between a dental /n/ and a dento-alveolar /n/ is too small to be perceived by an untrained ear. If /n/ were reported as a dento-alveolar, it would have to be placed in a separate column, like /R/. There are good reasons for not placing /n/ in a separate column, not the least of which is the fact that, together with /t/ and /d/, it forms a natural class. (Natural classes are discussed in Chapter 7.) In strict articulatory terms, then, /n/ differs from the other two dental segments; but from the point of view of their behavior, the three segments are alike.

The English equivalents of these segments also fall into one natural class. Their behavior also supports their being classified together. Furthermore, even the strict articulatory description of English /t/, /d/, and /n/ supports this classification. All three are alveolars.

4.5.4 Alveolar fricatives. The point of articulation of alveolar fricatives is a point of constriction between the blade of the tongue and the teeth ridge behind the upper front teeth. The French alveolar fricatives are /s/ and /z/, the last sounds of *tresse* and *treize*, respectively. These two fricatives differ from each other in that /s/ is voiceless and /z/ is voiced.

4.5.5 Alveopalatals. The two alveopalatals of French, the first sounds in *choix* and *joie*, are represented by /ʃ/ and /ʒ/, respectively. They are produced with the blade of the tongue pressing against the sides of the hard palate, constricting the passage of air at a point between the hard palate and the teeth ridge. The French alveopalatals are thus fricatives. One, /ʒ/, is voiced; the other, /ʃ/, is voiceless.

4.5.6 Palatal nasal. One palatal segment of French is the nasal /ɲ/, the last sound of *montagne*. It is produced with a lowered velum, with the body of the tongue released from the hard palate. It is very similar to /n/ except that it is palatal instead of dental. The other palatal segments are the front vowels and their corresponding glides (cf. Section 4.5.10).

4.5.7 Velar stops. French has two velar stops, /k/ and /g/. They occur as the first sounds in *coup* and *goût*, respectively, and differ in that the former is voiceless and the latter is voiced. The velar stops are produced by making a closure at the soft palate (velum) with the body of the tongue and releasing the air under pressure. There are other velar segments: the back vowels and their corresponding glide (cf. Section 4.5.10).

The symmetry between oral stops and the nasals is broken with the velars. Whereas there is a nasal corresponding to the bilabial and dental stops, there is none corresponding to the velars in French. The reason why /ɲ/ is not placed in the velar column, whereas /n/ was placed with the dentals, is made clear in Chapters 7 and 13.

4.5.8 Consonantal system. French utilizes a 15-consonant system, in which 3 consonants are nasal and the other 12 oral. There are 6 stops and 6 fricatives. Most of the French consonants, 10 of the 15, are produced with a point of articulation anterior to the palatoalveolar region. These facts appear graphically in Figure 4.4.

4.5.9 Liquids. French has two liquids, the first sound in *latéral*, /l/, and the first sound in *roule*, /R/. The liquid /l/ is produced by pressing the tip of the tongue against the alveolar ridge as for a stop, but allowing the air to

Figure 4.4

	Bilabial	Labio-dental	Dental	Alveolar	Alveo-palatal	Palatal	Velar
Stops vl	p		t				k
vd	b		d				g
Fricatives vl		f		s	ʃ		
vd		v		z	ʒ		
Nasals (vd)	m		n			ɲ	

flow on each side of the tongue, i.e. laterally. English speakers should take note that the last sound of French *latéral* is similar to the first sound in the same word. This contrasts with English, where the first and last sounds of English *lateral* are different, the first sound being nonsyllabic while the last sound is syllabic. In French, both /l/'s are nonsyllabic.

French speakers can have one of two *r*'s. Speakers of Standard French have a back /ʀ/. Many speakers of French in rural areas use the alveolar /r/ produced by one or more vibrations of the tip of the tongue against the teeth ridge. This /r/, nonstandard in contemporary usage, was popular in the court of Louis XIV. The other /ʀ/ is produced in a number of ways, ably described in DeLattre (1969), the most generally known of which is a trill produced by vibrations of the uvula, the tip of the velum.

4.5.10 Glides. Glides resemble vowels in articulation but are not themselves syllabic, as vowels are. Glides, unlike vowels, are marginal elements in the syllable. They must be supported by a vowel. In principle, they may occur before or after the syllabic vowel which supports them, but in French they occur mainly before.

There are three glides in French, the first sounds in *hier* /jɛʀ/, *huitre* /ɥitʀ/, and *oui* /wi/. As the orthography suggests, the three glides are similar to the three high vowels.

The front unrounded glide /j/ resembles the front unrounded vowel /i/ in articulation, except that /j/ is not syllabic and has a smaller aperture than does /i/. For practical purposes, /j/ is an /i/ which has lost its syllabicity. The spelling reflects this fact, as /j/ is usually represented by the letter *i* (*hier* /jɛʀ/, *pied* /pje/) but note also that in *paille* /paj/ it occurs in word-final position and is represented in spelling by *-ille*.

The front rounded glide /ɥ/ resembles the front rounded vowel /y/ in articulation, except that /ɥ/ is not syllabic and has a smaller aperture than does /y/. For practical purposes, /ɥ/ is an /y/ which has lost its syllabicity. The spelling reflects this fact, as /ɥ/ is represented by the letter *u* (*nuage* /nɥaʒ/, *Suède* /sɥɛd/, *nuit* /nɥi/).

The back rounded glide /w/ resembles the back rounded vowel /u/ in articulation, except that /w/ is not syllabic and has a smaller aperture than does /u/. For practical purposes, /w/ is an /u/ which has lost its syllabicity. The spelling reflects this fact, as /w/ is usually represented by the letters *ou* (*Louis* /lwi/, *mouette* /mwɛt/, *noir* /nwaʀ/).

This relationship between vowels and glides can be represented in the form of a chart, as in Figure 4.5.

Figure 4.5

	Front		Back
	Unround	Round	(Round)
Glides	j	ɥ	w
High vowels	i	y	u

Whereas the unique point of articulation of stops, for example, is clear-cut, the area of constriction of glides like /ɥ/ and /w/ is a less straightforward matter. These two glides differ in that the former is front (palatal) while the latter is back (velar). But these constrictions are accompanied in both segments by another constriction in the labial area, namely, rounding. Some phoneticians refer to that constriction as labialization, which they see as a parallel of palatalization (discussed in 7.6.2) and velarization (not discussed here). In such cases phoneticians conclude that there are two points of articulation, one primary, the other secondary. This is the perspective adopted here.

In this context, /w/ is a glide whose primary point of articulation is the velum and whose secondary point of articulation is the rounding of the lips. In other words, /w/ is a labialized velar glide. By the same token, /ɥ/ is a labialized palatal glide. On the other hand, /j/, also a palatal glide, is not labialized, since no lip rounding is involved in its articulation.

4.6 Summary. Figure 4.6 summarizes the presentation of the French segments arranged in terms of their aperture.

This chapter has been concerned with the interplay of manner and point of articulation. This interplay is the subject matter of the area of linguistic study known as articulatory phonetics. In connection with the glides, it has been shown that there can be secondary articulation. The type of secondary articulation discussed here (labialization) is not limited to glides, as can be seen in Figure 4.5. Some vowels and some glides form a natural class in French in that they are labialized. In other languages, other segments can be labialized: the liquid /r/ of English, for example, is labialized in word-initial position. Young speakers of English seem to acquire this secondary articulation first. Consequently, their *r*'s sound like *w*'s: *Wayne* for *rain*, *wun* for *run*, *west* for *rest*, etc. Another type of secondary articulation which was exam-

4 Articulatory properties of French sounds

Figure 4.6
The anterior/posterior continuum (lips to glottis)

Aperture continuum (closed to open)

	B	LD	D	A	AP	P	V	U
Stops	p/b		t/d				k/g	
Nasals	m		n			ɲ		
Fricatives		f/v		s/z	ʃ/ʒ			
Liquids[1]				l				R
Glides[2]						j/ɥ	w	
Vowels: High						i/y	u	
Mid						e/ø	o	
Low: oral						ɛ/œ a/ə ɔ		
nasalized						ɛ̃/œ̃ ã ɔ̃		

B: Bilabial
LD: Labiodental
D: Dental
A: Alveolar
AP: Alveopalatal
P: Palatal
V: Velar
U: Uvular

[1] Liquids do not seem to be bound to a particular aperture, as can be ascertained by pronouncing *lit/la* or *riz/rat*. They change aperture depending on their environment. Delattre (1951) suggests the /ɲ/ and the liquids have the same aperture, which seems plausible. On the other hand, Chomsky and Halle (1969) argue that the degree of aperture of liquids is the same as for fricatives. Since some of their terms are adopted here, it will be simpler to adopt also their claim about the aperture of liquids.

[2] Vowels belong together on the aperture scale.

ined but not identified as such is nasalization. Nasalization, the lowering of the velum to open the nasal cavity, can apply to some stops and to low vowels in French as a secondary articulation. The same process happens in Spanish and English but, in these languages, nasalization is limited to stops.

Although the sounds of French were divided here into classes, there is evidence that the divisions between these classes are not ironclad. In fact, there is evidence that classes are formed on the basis of whether or not segments undergo certain phenomena (labialization or nasalization, for example). The next chapter shows how vowels, consonants, glides, nasals, and liquids can each be decomposed into a relatively small number of features. The second part of this book illustrates how these features come into play in creating other classes of sounds characterized by various linguistic phenomena.

4.7 Questions.

1. What do the first sounds of *port*, *tort*, and *corps* have in common? In what way are they different?
2. How are glides vowel-like? How do they differ from vowels?

3. Does French have any pharyngeal segments? Does English? How far back in the vocal tract are sounds produced in these two languages?

4. Describe the following segments in terms of voicing, point of articulation, and manner of articulation: /ʃ g t p s ʒ n ɲ/.

5. How can a sound have two points of articulation? Explain.

6. Given the phoneme on the left, apply the change stated in the middle column, and write the answer in the column at the extreme right of the page.

/f/	voice	/v/
/g/	make bilabial	/ /
/s/	palatalize	/ /
/b/	nasalize	/ /
/y/	velarize	/ /
/j/	syllabicize	/ /
/ø/	velarize	/ /
/n/	palatalize	/ /
/i/	labialize	/ /

7. In what ways do the French and English *r* differ? In answering this question, think of distribution and articulation (point and manner).

8. Why is it more natural for voiceless stops to be aspirated than for voiced stops?

9. Why is there no aspiration after fricatives?

10. Count the syllables in the following lines:

> 'Ses purs ongles très haut dédiant leur onyx,
> L'angoisse, ce minuit, soutient lampadophore,
> Maint rêve vespéral brûlé par le Phénix
> Que ne recueille pas de cinéraire amphore
> Sur les crédences, au salon vide: nul ptyx,
> Aboli bibelot d'inanité sonore . . .'

Chapter 5
The atomization of segments

5.0 Introduction. In Chapter 4, it was assumed that segments are the smallest entities of speech. Classes formed by segments of various sorts were referred to, but the question of whether segments themselves can be subdivided into smaller units was not raised. The present chapter answers this question. Some of these units, called features, have already been alluded to. They are now examined along with other features.

There are parameters which relate the acoustic and articulatory components of speech sounds. These parameters, however, are not clearly delineated for all segments and features. Consequently, this book follows the example of Chomsky and Halle (1968), from whom most feature definitions are taken, and refers mainly to articulation when examining the components of French sounds. Where clear-cut cases come to mind, the articulatory and acoustic properties of sounds are shown to be parallel.

There are various sorts of features, labeled generally according to their functions. There are manner of articulation features, like voice or continuant; point of articulation features, like back or high; prosodic features, such as length or stress; and major class features, which distinguish between the major classes of sounds, i.e. consonants, liquids and nasals, glides, and vowels.

5.1 Major class features. Three features are used in identifying major classes of segments: consonantal, syllabic, and sonorant. It has been seen that there is a continuum in the degree of aperture from the most constricted articulation (closure of the stops) to the most open articulation (low vowels). The consonantal feature is defined on an aspect of the aperture continuum.

5.1.1 Consonantal. 'Consonantal sounds are produced with a radical obstruction of the midsaggital region of the vocal tract: nonconsonantal sounds are produced without such an obstruction' (Chomsky and Halle 1968).

The aperture of this obstruction must be as narrow as that found in fricatives, and furthermore, the obstruction must be located on the midsaggital line. Of these two conditions, the first makes stops and fricatives consonantal, but not glides and vowels. It also makes /R/ a consonantal segment because the constriction of /R/ at the point between the back of the tongue and the vibrating uvula is the same as for fricatives. The second condition (i.e. that nonconsonantal sounds are produced without a radical obstruction of the midsaggital region) makes /l/ also consonantal because even though the air flows freely laterally, there is contact (potential closure) between the blade of the tongue and the palate. Hence, all vowels and glides are nonconsonantal, while all consonants, nasals, and liquids are consonantal.

5.1.2 Sonorant. 'Sonorants are produced with a vocal tract cavity configuration in which spontaneous voicing is possible; obstruents (nonsonorants) are produced with a cavity configuration that makes spontaneous voicing impossible' (Chomsky and Halle 1968).

The details of exactly how spontaneous voicing comes about are beyond the scope of this book. It is sufficient to know that there is a point which distinguishes between vowel-like and consonant-like sounds in terms of spontaneous voicing. That point separates the stops and fricatives, the true consonants, from the liquids, glides, nasals, and vowels of French. The feature sonorant splits into two distinct groups the set of sounds referred to in Chapter 4 as consonants: /p t k b d g f s ʃ v z ʒ/ are nonsonorant, while /m n ɲ/ are sonorant. In other words, the features consonantal and sonorant can combine to distinguish between classes of sounds, as shown in Figure 5.1. In this and subsequent figures, the plus (+) and minus (−) signs are to be understood as specifying a given feature positively or negatively. For example, the minus sign (−) at the intersection of the sonorant column and the consonant row means that consonants are nonsonorant. Conversely, the plus sign (+) at the intersection of the sonorant column and the vowels and glides row means that vowels and glides are sonorant.

Figure 5.1

	Sonorant	Consonantal
Vowels and glides	+	−
Liquids and nasals	+	+
Consonants (obstruents)	−	+

5.1.3 Syllabic. Along with consonantal and sonorant, there is another feature which distinguishes between major classes of sounds. This feature is syllabic. In Chapter 4, the feature syllabic was shown to distinguish between the vowels of French and all the other sounds of the language.

A syllable is composed of at least a syllable peak, which is a vowel. Each syllable peak may be accompanied by other segments, which are not vowels and do not count as syllable peaks. The feature syllabic distinguishes between those segments which are syllable peaks and those which are not. In French, consonants, liquids, and glides cannot be syllable peaks; vowels always are. (This statement will be qualified in Chapter 15.) Consequently, consonants, liquids, and glides are nonsyllabic and vowels are syllabic.

The features sonorant, consonantal, and syllabic are necessary and sufficient to distinguish between four major classes of sounds, as can be seen in Figure 5.2.

Figure 5.2

	Sonorant	Consonantal	Syllabic
Vowels	+	−	+
Liquids, nasals	+	+	−
Glides	+	−	−
Consonants	−	+	−

5.2 The neutral position. 'A number of features are defined in terms of the particular configuration of the vocal tract known as the neutral position' (Chomsky and Halle 1968). It is known from work in experimental phonetics using X-ray motion pictures that immediately prior to speech production, the vocal tract assumes the characteristic shape known as the neutral position. In the neutral position the velum is raised so as to close the nasal cavity (open during normal breathing), the body of the tongue is slightly higher and more forward than for normal breathing, and the glottis is slightly more closed than for normal breathing. It is important to note the position of the tongue in order to understand the configurations of the various articulations which will now be discussed. The body (not the blade) of the tongue is raised to a level slightly higher than that of the vowel of *uh* (the sound produced when one hesitates in English), but the tip of the tongue touches the lower front teeth.

5.3 Features defined in terms of resonators.

5.3.1 Anterior. Anterior sounds are produced with an obstruction located in front of the alveopalatal area; nonanterior sounds are produced without such an obstruction.

Consequently, vowels, which have no obstruction, are nonanterior. Note that glides, which correspond to high vowels, are also excluded. They have no obstruction and their primary constriction is in back of the alveopalatal area. Alveopalatal, palatal, velar, and uvular obstruents are also nonanterior because their obstruction is at, or in back of, the alveopalatal area. The anterior sounds of French are /m n p t b d f s v z l/.

5.3.2 Coronal. 'Coronal sounds are produced with the blade of the tongue raised from the neutral position; noncoronal sounds are produced with the blade of the tongue in the neutral position' (Chomsky and Halle 1968).

It is important to note that coronal affects only the blade, not the rest of the tongue. So, any sound which is not articulated with the blade will be noncoronal. Vowels are not articulated further front than the palatal region, and they involve the body of the tongue. Consequently, they are noncoronal, as are the glides. For the same reason, palatal, velar, and uvular sounds are noncoronal. They are too far back to be coronal. Bilabials and labiodentals are noncoronal because they are too far front (i.e. their point of articulation is more anterior than that of sounds produced with the blade of the tongue). The coronal sounds of French are dental, alveolar and alveopalatal: /n t d s ʃ z ʒ l/. Figure 5.3 summarizes the foregoing features and relates them to the segment chart in Chapter 4.

5.3.3 Low. 'Low sounds are produced by lowering the body of the tongue below the level it occupies in the neutral position; nonlow sounds are produced without such a lowering of the body of the tongue' (Chomsky and Halle 1968).

It is important to note that low, high, front, and back are features associated with the body of the tongue only. Other portions of the tongue are not specific to these features. There are no low consonants in French. All French consonants, glides, and liquids are nonlow. The liquid /R/ is nonlow because it articulates with the uvula and the root, not the body of the tongue. High and mid vowels are also nonlow. In French, the feature low identifies / ɛ ɛ̃ œ œ̃ a ã ə ɔ ɔ̃/.

Figure 5.3

		Anterior				Nonanterior			
		B	LD	D	A	AP	P	V	U
Stops		p/b		t/d				k/g	
Fricatives			f/v		s/z	ʃ/ʒ			
Nasals		m		n			ɲ		
Liquids					l				
Glides							j/y	w	ʁ
Vowels: High							i/y	u	
Mid							e/ø	o	
							ɛ/œ	ɔ	
Low	oral						a/e		
	nasalized						ɛ̃/œ̃	ã	ɔ̃

| Noncoronal | Coronal | Noncoronal |

B: Bilabial
LD: Labiodental
D: Dental
A: Alveolar

AP: Alveopalatal
P: Palatal
V: Velar
U: Uvular

Cns: Consonantal
Ncns: Nonconsonantal
Son: Sonorant
Nson: Nonsonorant

32 / 5 The atomization of segments

5.3.4 High. 'High sounds are produced by raising the body of the tongue above the level it occupies in the neutral position; nonhigh sounds are produced without such a raising of the tongue body' (Chomsky and Halle 1968).

Clearly, the high vowels are high, as are the glides, which correspond to the high vowels. The French liquid /R/ is nonhigh because it does not involve the body of the tongue. The bilabials, labiodentals, and dentals are also nonhigh. Alveopalatals, palatals, and velars are high. Hence the feature high is a component of /i y u j ɥ w k g ʃ ʒ ɲ/.

5.3.5 Front. When front sounds are produced, the body of the tongue is located more to the front than in the neutral position; when nonfront sounds are produced, the body of the tongue does not assume that position. The vowels /i e ɛ ɛ̃ y ø œ œ̃/, the glides /j ɥ/, the palatal nasal /ɲ/, and the alveopalatals /ʃ ʒ/ are front. All the other sounds are nonfront.

5.3.6 Back. 'Back sounds are produced by retracting the body of the tongue from the neutral position; nonback sounds are produced without such a retraction from the neutral position' (Chomsky and Halle 1968).

The feature back is a component of the vowels /u o ɔ ɔ̃/, of /w/, of the consonants /k g/, and of the liquid /R/. All other sounds are nonback.

Figure 5.4 shows the use of the features front, back, high, low, and nasal to distinguish between all the vowels of French. Note that the mid vowels are both nonhigh and nonlow, and that central vowels are characterized by both the features nonback and nonfront. Not used in this chart but easily understood, are the features round and tense.

Figure 5.4

		front		nonfront		
nonlow	high	i/y			u	nonnasal
	nonhigh	e/ø			o	
		ɛ/œ	a/ə		ɔ	
low		ɛ̃/œ̃	ã		ɔ̃	nasal
		nonback		back		

5.3.7 Round. 'Rounded sounds are produced with a narrowing of the lip orifice; nonrounded sounds are produced without such a narrowing' (Chomsky and Halle 1968).

The rounded vowels of French are /y ø œ œ̃ u o ɔ ɔ̃/. Also rounded (i.e. labialized) are the glides /w ɥ/. In these two segments rounding is a secondary feature (see Section 5.5). French has no labialized consonants or liquids.

5.4 Features determined by the manner of articulation.

5.4.1 Continuant. 'In the production of continuant sounds, the primary constriction in the vocal tract is not narrowed to the point where the air flow past the constriction is blocked' (Chomsky and Halle 1968). Noncontinuant sounds are produced with a closure.

The six stops and the three nasals of French are excluded from the class of continuants. This is because stops and nasals are produced with a closure. On the other hand, all vowels, glides, fricatives, and liquids are continuants.

5.4.2 Strident. 'Strident sounds are marked acoustically by greater noisiness than their nonstrident counterparts' (Chomsky and Halle 1968).

In strident sounds the turbulence of the flowing air causes the noise. Excluded from stridency by their very nature are vowels, glides, and liquids, which produce no turbulence to speak of. Also excluded are the stops because they block the air flow. The fricatives /f s ʃ v z ʒ/ are the only strident sounds of French. Note that the affricates of English and Spanish, as in *church*, *judge*, and *chiquita*, respectively, are also strident sounds.

5.4.3 Tense. 'Tense sounds are produced with a . . . gesture that involves considerable muscular effort: nontense sounds are produced rapidly and somewhat indistinctly' (Chomsky and Halle 1968).

All French sounds are produced with considerable effort in the larynx except one: /ə/, the only nontense (lax) sound in the whole language.

5.5 Features defined by secondary articulation

5.5.1 Nasal. 'Nasal sounds are produced with a lowered velum which allows air to escape through the nose; nonnasal sounds are produced with a raised velum so that the air flowing from the trachea can escape only through the mouth' (Chomsky and Halle 1968).

The nasal sounds of French are the consonants /m n ɲ/ and the vowels /ɛ̃ ã œ̃ ɔ̃/. All the other sounds are produced with a raised velum.

5.5.2 Lateral. 'Lateral sounds are produced by lowering the mid section of the tongue at one or both sides, thereby allowing air to flow out of the mouth in the vicinity of the molar teeth; in nonlateral sounds no such side passage is open' (Chomsky and Halle 1968).

The feature lateral applies to only one French sound: /l/.

5.6 A glottal feature

5.6.1 Voice. A sound is voiced if the vocal folds vibrate during its production; nonvoiced sounds are produced without vibrating vocal folds.

All vowels are voiced in French, though there are languages with voiceless vowels. Glides are also voiced. Liquids can be voiced or nonvoiced (voiceless), depending on their position. In isolation and in word-initial position they are always voiced. It is best, therefore, to consider them voiced and to specify a rule to make them nonvoiced. Nasal consonants are also voiced. The other consonants are split into two equal groups, one voiced and one nonvoiced. The voiced consonants are /b, d, g, v, z, ʒ/ and their voiceless equivalents are /p, t, k, f, s, ʃ/.

5.7 Diacritic features

5.7.1 Aspirated. Aspirated sounds are produced with less muscular effort in the larynx than nonaspirated sounds. This feature applies only to consonants.

In English, initial nonvoiced noncontinuants (i.e. /p, t, k/) are produced with aspiration. In French, phrase-final nonvoiced noncontinuants can also be aspirated. Aspiration is the letting out of a puff of air. Aspiration is explained by the fact that the speaker relaxes his larynx and allows the 'puff of air' associated with aspirated plosives to eject. In phonetic transcription, aspiration of a stop is represented with an apostrophe ('). So English *pat* is transcribed [p'æt], while French *patte*, which is pronounced [pat'] is generally transcribed /pat/, without the indication of aspiration on the final stop. In English, /h/ is an aspirated segment, distinguishing between *hair* and *air*.

5.7.2 Length. Some sounds are produced for a longer period of time than others. Length of segments is determined relatively. In French, length is predictable: the /o/ of *rose* is long but the /ɛ/ of *sec* is short. In phonetic transcription the colon is used to mark length. Consequently, *rose* is transcribed /ʀo:z/ and *sec*, /sɛk/. This is discussed in 11.3.2.

5.7.3 Stress. Some sounds are produced with more force than others: stress is relatively determined. In general, three and even four different degrees of stress are found. French has only two: strong and weak. There is also a form of strengthening of some segments known as contrastive stress, as in *Elle a huit enfants*. When stress is shown in phonetic transcription, it is represented by the conventional accent aigu (´) and is placed over the stressed vowel: /ɛlaɥítãfã/. The stress mark is not used in this book because stress is predictably on the last syllable in French. It is simply assumed on the last syllable.

The marks used to identify aspiration, length, and stress are not inherently features of segments. They are added to some segments under specific circumstances. These diacritics are often referred to as suprasegmental. The imagery of this technical term is obviously drawn from the realm of transcription, where diacritics are placed above, as additions to segments.

5.8 The distinctive features of French. Once all segments of French are assigned their distinctive features, they can be represented in the form of a chart like that in Figure 5.5. Each segment is therefore composed of a bundle of features which is unique to that segment.

5.9 The components of segments. A distinctive feature can be viewed as a dividing line between groups of sounds. Together with other features, it can form a bundle of features which are the components of that sound. All

5.9 The components of segments / 35

Figure 5.5 The distinctive features of Standard French.

	i	e	ɛ	ɛ̃	y	ø	œ	œ̃	a	ã	ə	u	o	ɔ	ɔ̃	j	w	ɥ	m	n	ɲ	p	t	k	b	d	g	f	s	ʃ	v	z	ʒ	l	R
Consonantal	-	-	-	-	-	-	-	-	-	-	-	-	-	-	-	-	-	-	+	+	+	+	+	+	+	+	+	+	+	+	+	+	+	+	+
Sonorant	+	+	+	+	+	+	+	+	+	+	+	+	+	+	+	+	+	+	+	+	+	-	-	-	-	-	-	-	-	-	-	-	-	+	+
Syllabic	+	+	+	+	+	+	+	+	+	+	+	+	+	+	+	-	-	-	-	-	-	-	-	-	-	-	-	-	-	-	-	-	-	-	-
Anterior	-	-	-	-	-	-	-	-	-	-	-	-	-	-	-	-	-	-	+	+	-	+	+	-	+	+	-	+	+	-	+	+	-	+	-
Coronal	-	-	-	-	-	-	-	-	-	-	-	-	-	-	-	-	-	-	-	+	+	-	+	-	-	+	-	-	+	+	-	+	+	+	-
High	+	-	-	-	+	-	-	-	-	-	-	+	-	-	-	+	+	+	-	-	+	-	-	+	-	-	+	-	-	-	-	-	-	-	-
Low	-	-	+	+	-	-	+	+	+	+	-	-	-	+	+	-	-	-	-	-	-	-	-	-	-	-	-	-	-	-	-	-	-	-	-
Front	+	+	+	+	+	+	+	+	-	-	-	-	-	-	-	+	-	+	-	-	-	-	-	-	-	-	-	-	-	-	-	-	-	-	-
Back	-	-	-	-	-	-	-	-	+	+	+	+	+	+	+	-	+	-	-	-	-	-	-	+	-	-	+	-	-	-	-	-	-	-	+
Round	-	-	-	-	+	+	+	+	-	-	-	+	+	+	+	-	+	+	-	-	-	-	-	-	-	-	-	-	-	-	-	-	-	-	-
Continuant	+	+	+	+	+	+	+	+	+	+	+	+	+	+	+	+	+	+	-	-	-	-	-	-	-	-	-	+	+	+	+	+	+	+	+
Strident	-	-	-	-	-	-	-	-	-	-	-	-	-	-	-	-	-	-	-	-	-	-	-	-	-	-	-	+	+	+	+	+	+	-	-
Nasal	-	-	-	+	-	-	-	+	-	+	-	-	-	-	+	-	-	-	+	+	+	-	-	-	-	-	-	-	-	-	-	-	-	-	-
Lateral	-	-	-	-	-	-	-	-	-	-	-	-	-	-	-	-	-	-	-	-	-	-	-	-	-	-	-	-	-	-	-	-	-	+	-
Voice	+	+	+	+	+	+	+	+	+	+	+	+	+	+	+	+	+	+	+	+	+	-	-	-	+	+	+	-	-	-	+	+	+	+	+
Tense	+	+	+	+	+	+	+	+	+	+	-	+	+	+	+	+	+	+	+	+	+	+	+	+	+	+	+	+	+	+	+	+	+	+	+

segments can be characterized by a relatively small number of features. The number of features needed to characterize a segment is dependent upon the articulatory nature of that segment and on the number of similar segments from which it must be differentiated. In the case of French /œ/, the features [+syllabic], [−consonantal], [+sonorant], and, say, [+round] do not suffice to distinguish it from all other sounds of French. The vowel /œ/ must be distinguished from other round vowels in terms of the features [low] and [front] and from nasal vowels in terms of the feature [nasal]. In other words, if the sound /œ/ is to be referred to unambiguously in terms of features, then the following must be stated: [+syllabic], [−consonantal], [+sonorant], [+round], [+low], [+front], [−nasal]. On the other hand, the feature [+lateral] alone is sufficient to identify /l/.

Under the heading of major class features, the liquids and nasals were not distinguished. The feature [nasal] is necessary and sufficient for that purpose.

5.10 Why features? Linguists assume that, since some form of linguistic expression is shared by all normal human beings, there is an innate ability on the part of people to distinguish between sounds. This ability is reflected in a small inventory of distinctive features, most of which are retained, some of which are not used, depending on the language. The feature [aspirated], for example, is a distinctive feature in the stops of some languages but in English and French stops, it is predictable whether they are aspirated or not. Hence since this feature is predictable, it is not distinctive.

The processes which affect phonological systems are generally not limited to one segment but rather apply to sets of segments. These sets of segments are easily identified in terms of features. A rule that applies to segments /u o ɔ/ applies to [+back] vowels; a rule that must refer to /i y u/ can be stated in terms of [+high] vowels; clusters of segments like /kstʀ/, /sm/, etc. include stops, liquids, fricatives, nasals, but can be referred to with one feature: [−syllabic]. In short, features allow the linguist to state natural classes.

Thus segments can be atomized, i.e. split into smaller components. These components can serve as referents for segment classes. These classes of segments are often natural classes, experiencing influences of different sorts, as shown in the second and third parts of this book.

5.11 Questions.
1. Specify the feature distinctions between

/a/ and /ə/	/k/ and /g/	/a/ and /ɛ/
/ɥ/ and /y/	/e/ and /ø/	/w/ and /j/
/u/ and /y/	/ø/ and /o/	/ɛ/ and /j/
/y/ and /i/	/e/ and /i/	/d/ and /g/
/d/ and /n/	/e/ and /ɛ/	/ɛ/ and /œ/

2. Why cannot the feature high distinguish between /œ/ and /ø/?

3. What is the difference between the first segment of *cas* and the last segment of *parc*? State the difference in terms of features. What feature distinguishes between the first segment of English *park* and French *parc*?

5.11 Questions / 37

4. What feature do the English affricates in *charity* and *jail* have in common with French fricatives in *charité* and *gel*? What feature do they not have in common?

5. Identify, with as few features as possible, the class to which the following belong: /p t k b d g m n ɲ ʀ/.

6. Identify /p t k f s ʃ/ with as few features as possible.

7. Identify /w j ɥ/ with as few features as possible.

8. Imagine a language which can have only the following word-initial clusters of consonants: /st/, /sk/, and /sp/. State in features the only permissible sequence in question.

9. Using a single feature, identify all the vowels of French. Using a second feature, exclude schwa. Now formulate in your own words the rule that assigns stress to French words.

10. To represent segments in terms of features, the vertical arrangement illustrated in (10a) is used. Following this model, state the features needed to identify the classes and single segments listed in (10b) through (10h).

(10a) /u o ɔ/ is represented by $\begin{bmatrix} +\text{syllabic} \\ -\text{nasal} \\ +\text{back} \end{bmatrix}$

(10b) /i y e ø œ ɛ ɛ̃ œ̃/ is represented by [ ]

(10c) /ʀ/ is represented by [ ]

(10d) /m n ɲ/ is represented by [ ]

(10e) /e ø o/ is represented by [ ]

(10f) /f s ʃ v z ʒ l ʀ/ is represented by [ ]

(10g) /p t k/ is represented by [ ]

(10h) /œ̃ ɔ̃ ã ɛ̃/ is represented by [ ]

11. The features [front] and [back] were pictured in Figure 5.4, distinguishing among vowels. Since they also apply to consonants, make them fit into Figure 5.3.

Part Two.
Phonology: Influences, reactions, and consequences in the society of sounds.

This second part of *The Sound System of French* is concerned with what one might refer to very loosely as the sociology of sounds. In Part One, the physics of sound and the physiology of sound production were examined. A mini-census of the sounds of French was taken and the segments of French were dissected into their components, the features. This second part is concerned with the ways in which sounds behave around other sounds. Chapter 6 shows how strong sounds become even more important and weak sounds become less significant, or even disappear. Chapter 7 is concerned with the ways in which sounds change to resemble their neighbors, how some sounds blend together into one, or otherwise alter some of their features.

Chapter 6
The rise and fall of segments

6.0 Introduction. This first of two chapters on regular phenomena of language deals with the factors which strengthen or weaken phonological segments. The results of these factors are processes of insertion, deletion, reduction, or diphthongization. The purpose of this chapter is to explain these processes.

The phonological system of a language, like all linguistic systems, is interdependently constructed. In other words, the components of that system support one another. If, for whatever reason, a segment undergoes a change, then the repercussions of that change are felt in the neighboring segments. One such repercussion can be observed in the syllable structure.

The deletion or insertion of a segment can affect the syllable structure of a word. French, like many other languages, favors the sequence Consonant-Vowel (CV). So, French syllables are said to be of the CV type. The rules of the language conspire to make syllables conform to the CV structure.

Another effect that phonological segments undergo is that of weakening. A segment can be weakened by reduction. The opposite effect is strengthening. Diphthongization is a case of strengthening. Diphthongization and reduction are often dependent on the placement of stress in a word. Some stressed vowels are diphthonigized; some unstressed vowels, particularly when located near the stressed vowel, can be reduced or deleted.

The so-called principle of least effort is responsible for a number of sound processes. If it is relatively difficult to produce a particular sequence of sounds, then that sequence of segments is likely to be simplified. This simplification may take the form of segment deletion or insertion, or both. This principle, that of syllable structure, and other processes to be discussed in this chapter, are all interdependent. Syllable structure, the forces at work in weakening and strengthening, and the principle of least effort comprise a network of factors which, among others, are typical of the interdependency of linguistic units in all languages.

This chapter is organized as follows: (1) the rules for the insertion and deletion of segments whether vowels (6.1, 6.2) or consonants (6.3, 6.4) are discussed and (2) instances of diphthongization (6.5) and reduction (6.6) examined from the viewpoint of both synchronic or contemporary and diachronic or historical evidence.

6.1 Vowel insertion. The easiest way to see why vowels are inserted is to look at words which have large clusters of consonants. Typically, people find that some words of foreign origin are difficult to pronounce. One reason is that these words may contain too many consonants clustered together. The way to resolve problems with complex consonant clusters is to make the difficult sequence conform to a sequence familiar to the speaker. This is done by inserting a vowel or deleting one or more consonants.

This process of vowel insertion has fascinated language students for many centuries, as the nomenclature of our inherited linguistic terminology which corresponds to that process testifies. Greek names for various types of vowel insertion are *prothesis*, *epenthesis*, *anaptyxis*, and *paratyxis*, and there is also a Sanskrit word for this phenomenon: *svarabhakti*.

In Spanish, a vowel is inserted word initially if the word begins with /s/ followed by a consonantal segment. Spanish speakers support the first segments of an initial cluster with an epenthetic vowel, /e/. They say /espesjal/, /eskwela/, and /estudio/ (and, in fact, they write these words with the epenthetic vowel: *especial*, *escuela*, *estudio*) for the equivalents of English *special*, *school*, and *study*. When Spanish speakers learn a language like

English or French they tend to apply the rule of epenthesis to English or French words. They do so in a subconscious attempt to simplify a cluster of consonants. The result of this subconscious 'hispanization' of cluster is so systematic that it has become characteristic of a Spanish accent, as can be observed on the stage and screen, or in cartoons.

The cases of vowel insertion just examined in terms of Spanish have parallels in French: German /ʃnapan/ 'highwayman' has become /ʃənapã/, *chenapan*, as can be seen in *ils étaient neuf chenapan*, where the inserted schwa must be pronounced. Arabic /tbēb/ has become French /tubib/, *toubib* 'medic, doctor' as in *Fais venir le toubib*! Also, Arabic /dʒbəl/ has become French /dʒebɛl/ *djébel* 'mountain'.

English inserts a vowel when forming the plural of certain words. *Horse* /hoːrs/ made plural becomes /hoːrsəz/, *edge* /edʒ/ becomes /edʒəz/. The vowel insertion before the /z/ of plural has only one purpose: to break up the clusters /sz/ and /ʒz/, which are unacceptable to the language. In the plural of *cow*, /kawz/, no supporting vowel is inserted because none is needed.

The history of French has a few interesting cases of vowel insertion. Words like *affable*, *visible*, *possible*, which come, respectively, from Latin *affabilis*, *visibilis*, and *possibilis*, developed final /ə/ after the fall of the last two /i/ to support the last segment of the /bl/ cluster. This piece of historical evidence is mirrored by the contemporary facts. Since French speakers relate forms like *possible* and *possibilité*, the rules which delete the two /i/ and the rule which inserts /ə/ are also rules of Modern French, just as they are rules of the development of the language. Further support of this insertion of /ə/ can be adduced from the way that adverbs are derived from these adjectives. There is no question that /ə/ must be added after /bl/ in *affablement* and *visiblement*, because */viziblmã/ and */afablmã/ are unacceptable pronunciations.

6.2 Vowel deletion. In considering cases of vowel insertion in the previous section, cases of vowel deletion were observed: the last two /i/ which can be found in *visibilité* and *possibilité* were deleted in the derivation of *visible* and *possible*. Schane (1968) proposes a rule called Nonlow Vowel Deletion which drops mid and high vowels in posttonic position. ('Posttonic' means after the word stress.) Historically, Latin *affabilis*, *possibilis*, and *visibilis* were stressed as shown in the transcription: /afábilis/, /posíbilis/, /visíbilis/. The loss of the nonlow posttonic vowels contributed to the development of /afablə/, /posiblə/, and /visiblə/, respectively.

Schane's rule is written as a description of Modern French. That it reflects the historical development of the language is a coincidence, a happy coincidence. The rule is only meant to reflect the claim that French speakers relate the members of pairs like *affable/affabilité*, *aimable/amabilité*, *visible/visibilité*.

6.2.1 Apocope. The deletion of a posttonic vowel, a process known as 'apocope', is a fairly common phenomenon. It is found, for example, in some Spanish nouns and adjectives in the singular. Consider the data in Table 6.1.

Table 6.1

Type 1		Type 2		Type 3	
Forms ending in: unstressed /e/		other vowels		/s/	
papele	-s	casa	-s	lunes	-s
razone	-s	café	-s	crisis	-s
útile	-s	bueno	-s	análisis	-s
fácile	-s	comodo	-s		

The *s* at the end of each word is the mark of plural in Spanish.

After the insertion of the plural marker, words of Type 3 undergo a rule of contraction (to be discussed later). The words of Type 1 and Type 2 are different in that those of Type 1 occur in the singular without the final *e*: *papel, razón, útil, fácil*, while those of Type 2 retain their final vowel in the singular. The claim that *papel* and *papeles* are derived from *papele* finds support of various types. First, the rule for pluralization can be stated simply in terms of adding *s*. Second, the rule of stress assignment can also be stated more simply than otherwise: all the words of Spanish which are stressed on the final syllable can be regularized and made to conform to the general rule which stresses the next to last syllable. The rule which deletes the final *e*, yielding the proper singular forms, is known as apocope. Spanish apocope deletes posttonic /e/ in form-final position (cf. Harris 1970).

The case of apocope best known to students of French is that which drops final /ə/ in word-final position in most styles of expression except in highly formal situations. Hence, *chétive* /ʃetivə/ becomes /ʃetiv/, *travaillent* /tRavajə/ becomes /tRavaj/, i.e. pronounced like *travail*.

6.2.2 Elision. Elision is another case of vowel deletion. It is discussed in greater detail in Section 15.3.1. For now, it suffices to say that elision, like other cases of vowel deletion, applies to unstressed vowels. This rule deletes a word-final /ə/ or /a/ when the following word begins with a vowel. In the following paired examples, the second member of each pair illustrates elision: *un autre compagnon/un autre ami, de semblables coups/semblable à la précédente, je vois/j'entends, nous la voyons/nous l'entendons.*

Very similar to elision is the vowel deletion which takes place in colloquial styles in English: a rule sometimes called 'aphesis' changes the first member of the following pairs into the second: *I am/I'm, he will/he'll, you would/you'd.*

6.2.3 Syncope. Syncope is yet another type of vowel deletion. Like apocope, it applies to posttonic vowels. In syncope, a vowel is deleted in a word when it occurs after the stress and before another vowel. (See Appendix 3 for a complete statement of syncope.) In English, the words *poplar* (etymologically, 'the tree of the people') and *people* come distantly from the Latin word *populum*/pópulum/. Syncope, which applied to Latin (cf. Spanish *pueblo* and French *peuple*), deleted the /u/ of the middle syllable. Note that in *poplar* the consonant cluster (/pl/), which resulted from the application of syncope to Latin, is retained. In the case of *people*, epenthesis has applied in English to insert /ə/ and break up an impossible final cluster, resulting in /pijpəl/. Alternatively, the final /l/ is analyzed as syllabic. (For more on this alternative, cf. Section 15.2.)

In connection with the nature of apocope and syncope, note that the Nonlow Vowel Deletion proposed by Schane is, in fact, a case of these two processes combined. The first /i/ of /amábili-/ can be deleted by syncope and the second by apocope. Schane combined these two processes into one rule because he found no evidence in Modern French for two different rules.

By way of conclusion about vowel insertion and vowel deletion, some observations must be made about these processes and the nature of the syllable. It was noted earlier that vowels are syllable peaks. As the nucleus of the syllable, a vowel should be in a position of enough importance to prevent deletion. Yet, from all the evidence amassed here, it appears that vowels are deleted and even that some are inserted. Both processes clearly change the syllabic structure of words. Is there a contradiction, a discrepancy, an explanation possibly? There is, but only a partial one. All vowels which are candidates for deletion are weakened vowels; they are generally posttonic. Also, those which are inserted are never inserted as tonic vowels. Weak vowels are often found near tonic vowels. In fact, they are weakened in contrast with their stress-bearing neighbors. This interplay of vowels bobbing up like fishing corks and the reasons for their behavior can be explained in terms of the factors at play in the systematic structure of a phonological system. The principle of least effort is at work when epenthesis provides a vowel to help pronounce an otherwise difficult consonant sequence. Weakening sets up vowels for the axe of deletion. Deletion, which affects syllable structure, and the principle of least effort conspire to bring about insertion. Together they participate in the constant rise and fall of segments.

6.3 Consonant deletion

6.3.1 Final consonant deletion. The rule of Final Consonant Deletion is fairly well known to students of French as it relates to orthography. The student is familiar with the fact that the final /t/ of *petit* is not pronounced at the end of an utterance although it may be pronounced if followed by a vowel (liaison). Similarly, the final consonants are deleted in Column A of Table 6.2, but not in Column B, where they are retained for various reasons.

6.3.1 Final consonant deletion

Table 6.2

A	B
du drap	un drapier
dans le champ	le garde-champêtre
un plomb	le plombier
ce chat	cette chatte
qu'il est grand	qu'elle est grande
c'est un escroc	c'est de l'escroquerie
un nerf	je suis nerveux
sans elles!	elles arrivent!

Column B shows that the consonants in question must be included somehow in the words of Column A because they are pronounced under some circumstances. Column A is a set of words in which the final consonant may not be pronounced. This suggests a deletion rule.

The deletion of final consonant is a common process in language. This deletion rule seems to obey the general tendency that favors syllables of the CV type over those of the CVC type.

Final Consonant Deletion can be found at work in Latin, which lost its final /k/ quite early. Thus Latin *sic* becomes Old French *si*, *hic* becomes *y*, *illac* becomes *la*, etc. Similarly, the final *m* (accusative case) and *n* also were dropped in the vernacular. By the time of the conquest of Gaul, Caesar's soldiers probably did not pronounce final *m* or *n* in polysyllabic words. The liquids and the other stops also tended to fall.

There is in Caribbean Spanish a tendency to drop final /s/. Hence, a sequence like *Vienen los otros* 'The others are coming' is pronounced as if it rhymed with the singular *el otro* 'the other'.

There are, of course, exceptions to the French Final Consonant Deletion rule. Some cases in point are the numerals *cinq* /sɛ̃k/, *six* /sis/, *sept* /sɛt/, *huit* /ɥit/, *neuf* /nœf/, *dix* /dis/; borrowed vocabulary like *idem*, *snob*, *gang*, *kirsh*; neologisms like *gaz* (created by a physicist); acronyms like *IFOP*; and simple French words like *serf*, *neuf*, *sud*, *cep*, *sec*, *chic*, *os*, *bal*, *bol*, *net*, *bar*, *coq*, *œuf*, *sens*, all monosyllabic.

Throughout the discussion of final consonant deletion, consonants which are followed by an *e* in spelling, that is, a deleted /ə/ phonetically, have not been considered. These cases deserve consideration.

Given that final /ə/ is deleted in most styles, what is to prevent Final Schwa Deletion from applying first to an adjective like *petite* in the sentence *elle est petite*, preparing the ground for Final Consonant Deletion? If the latter rule applied, the result would be the incorrect /pəti/ which is homophonous with *petit* (masculine). Clearly, these two rules of French must be prevented from yielding such incorrect sentences as *Elle est petit* /ɛlepti/. Suppose that it was a principle of French that Final Consonant Deletion must apply before Final Schwa Deletion. If that ordering were established, Final Consonant Deletion would not apply to /pətitə/ since the last segment is not a consonant. Then, Final Schwa Deletion would apply and the result would be correct: /pətit/. Because this order of application of rules works for French, it will be hypothesized (1) that rules may have to be ordered with respect to each other, and (2) that in French, Final Consonant Deletion must precede Final Schwa Deletion. (For a more precise account of Final Consonant Deletion and Final Schwa Deletion, and their order of application, cf. Appendix 3, where the rules are listed.)

6.3.2 Cluster simplification. Another type of consonant deletion is the one which results from the relative difficulty encountered with borrowed (often technical) vocabulary. English has many such examples. For instance, all Greek words beginning with a /ps/ cluster are simplified to an /s/ e.g. *psyche*, *psoriasis*, *psychiatrist*, whereas French retains the Greek cluster e.g. *psyché* /psiʃe/, *psoriase* /psɔʀjaz/, *psychiatre* /psikjatʀ/. Similarly, of the Greek clusters /pn/ and /mn/ English drops the first of the two clustered consonantal segments, e.g. *pneumonia* /nəmownjə/, *mnemonic* /nə-manɪk/, whereas French retains both, e.g. *pneumonie* /pnømɔni/, *mnémonique* /mnemɔnik/.

There are cases of consonant deletion in French but they are seldom found in the technical vocabulary borrowed from Greek. Instead, one finds such everyday words as *biftek* from English *beef steak*, or *école* from Latin *scola*, which became *escola* (yielding Spanish *escuela*) via epenthesis, and eventually *école* by dropping the *s* from the cluster. French orthography marks many words with a circumflex accent to indicate the loss of an *s* before another consonant: *nostrum* > (*le*) *nôtre*, *pastellage* ~ *pâte*, *asinaire* ~ *âne*.

6.3.3 Failure to link. The phenomenon of linking (liaison) can be viewed as a case of compliance with the tendency to keep as close as possible to the CV syllable. Liaison occurs when the last segment of a word combines with the first segment of the next word to form a /CV/ syllable. As is the case in all processes, linking is governed by a set of constraints of various types, some syntactically conditioned, others dependent on individual words, still others triggered by the register of the conversation. The details of these constraints are taken up later in this book. What is of interest here is that for liaison to take place, there must be a word-initial nonconsonantal segment which combines with the word-final consonantal segment at a word boundary. If the word-initial segment is not nonconsonantal, then liaison does not take place and, automatically, the word-final consonant, which is no longer supported, is deleted. Failure to link causes a consonant deletion. This deletion is strikingly similar to the final consonant deletion just examined. Table 6.3 illustrates and summarizes what has been said about consonant deletion in French.

Table 6.3

	Before a vowel (*homme*)	Before a glide (*oiseau*)	Before a consonantal segment (*pain*)	At phrase boundary (##) (*il est . . . ##*)
grand	grãtɔm	grãtwazo	grã pẽ	grã
gros	grozɔm	grozwazo	gro pẽ	gro
petit	ptitɔm	ptitwazo	pti pẽ	pti
sans	sãzɔm	sãzwazo	sã pẽ	sã

6.4 Consonant insertion

6.4.1 Liaison mal à propos. 'Liaison mal à propos' is a name given to unjustified consonant insertions. When most nouns and adjectives are pluralized the plural suffix /-z/ is inserted if the next word begins with a vowel. But there are semantically plural words, like the numerals *vingt* 'twenty', *cent* 'hundred', *mille* 'thousand', which are not marked plural by this process. No /-z/ is inserted after them; they are exceptions. When a speaker incorrectly inserts the /-z/, this process is called 'liaison mal à propos'.

There are also humorous imitations of such errors, e.g. *les quatre Arts* /llekatzaʀ/, or *les Dupont et les Durand* with a /-z/ liaison between *Dupont* and *et*.

Historically, similar errors in linking developed quite generally. In the inversion of subject and verb for the purpose of interrogation, there developed a liaison between the verbs of the third group (which have a /t/ in final position in the third person) and the following pronoun. This is still the case in Modern French: *que fait-il? que sait-il? que dit-il?* Following this model, verbs of other groups also developed a /t/ in this position. This is mirrored in the spelling and is now not only accepted, but obligatory: *A-t-il lu cet article? Va-t-il sortir à temps? Pour qui chante-t-elle?*

While examples of liaison unmotivated by the structure have cropped up at different points in time, only those which are of some logical importance have been accepted. Some grammarians claim that the generalization of the /t/ to the verb system is motivated in that it avoided hiatus, but there are many other cases where vowels come together without shocking even the most sensitive ears. One thing is clear. The error of yesteryear is the norm of today, while the error of today is simply an error. Time makes right.

6.4.2 Homorganic consonant insertion. The cases of consonant insertion discussed so far are all analogically conditioned. There is an attempt to construct *B* to make it conform with *A*. There are also cases of consonant insertion conditioned by a phonological environment. In Table 6.4, which lists examples taken from Classical Latin and Modern French, one can observe some striking modifications, both in terms of the number of syllables and in the consonants found in the cited forms.

Table 6.4

númerum	nombre
trémore	trembler
cámera	chambre
cínerum	cendre
pónere	pondre

The syncope of the weak vowel which comes immediately after the word stress creates clusters of consonants composed of a nasal and a liquid (NL). Commonly, a NL cluster develops into a NCL cluster, where C is a stop. The Romance languages followed that rule. It is easy to see how such a development can occur if one thinks of nasals as stops. As the cluster NL is produced, the velum, which is lowered for the production of the nasal, is raised in anticipation of the liquid. This produces a stop whose point of articulation is the same as the nasal's. Thus /b/ is produced after /m/ and /d/ after /n/: they correspond in point of articulation. This process is called homorganic consonant insertion, where the term 'homorganic' means 'having the same composition'.

6.5 Diphthongization. Stressed vowels have a tendency to be further marked by lengthening. One way of marking a strongly stressed vowel is to load it, so to say, with additional phonological material. This is done by creating a diphthong, i.e. by placing a glide before the stressed vowel. The process that adds a glide before a vowel for the purpose of strengthening that vowel is called 'diphthongization'. Examples of diphthongization are shown in Table 6.5.

Table 6.5

A	B
céleste	ciel
pédicure	pied
chenil	chien
nous venons	il vient

The stem vowel in the words of Column A in Table 6.5 is not in a position of stress; it occurs in a nonfinal syllable. On the other hand, the equivalent sound(s) in Column B are in word-final position, which is always stressed, so the process of diphthongization has taken place, yielding the sounds /je/, /jə/, or /jɛ̃/, depending on the phonological context.

Diphthongization can be a process of the language in its contemporary form or it can be a historical process. The examples in Table 6.6, given as an illustration of a contemporary rule, can also be used to illustrate the historical process.

Table 6.6

A	B
caelum	ciel
pedem	pied
canem	chien
venet	il vient

The words of Column A in Table 6.6 are the Latin equivalents of the French words in Column B. There was no diphthong in the Latin words. At one point in the development of French, the stressed vowel /e/ was diphthongized.

Diphthongization is discussed in more detail in Chapters 9 and 12.

6.6 Reduction. Reduction is a process by which a vowel is changed to a schwa. This change occurred historically in the feminine ending of Latin: /a/ became /ə/ in Modern French, as Table 6.7 shows.

Table 6.7

Latin	French
rosa	rose
alba	aube
scola	école
folia	feuille
via	voie
harpa	harpe
auricula	oreille

This rule applies even when /a/ is not a marker of the feminine, as in the masculine nouns, shown in Table 6.8.

Table 6.8

Latin	French
poeta	poète
problema	problème
nauta 'sailor'	(astro)naute
papa	pape
pirata	pirate

Reduction is a process that took place during the historical development of French; it is also one characteristic of Modern French phonology. This is so because there are pairs like *feuille/(dé)foliation, école/scolarité, problème/problématique, pape/papauté*.

Reduction is also important to English speakers learning French. Consider the examples of reduction in English shown in Table 6.9.

6 The rise and fall of segments

Table 6.9

A		B	A		B
able	~	ability	ejbəl	~	əbílə ti
happy	~	happily	hǽpi	~	hǽpəli
major	~	majority	méjdʒər	~	mədʒárəti
proper	~	propriety	prápər	~	prəprájəti

When a sound is near the stressed segment it is often reduced. Change the stress (as happens between Column A and Column B) and the reduction occurs in other segments.

English speakers learning French have a tendency to transfer this rule to their spoken French. As a result, the sequence of sounds they produce when attempting to say the French words in Column B resembles that of their English cognates in Column A of Table 6.10.

Table 6.10

A		B	
/əbílətɪ/	ability	/abilté/	habileté
/mədʒárətɪ/	majority	/maʒɔRité/	majorité
/prəprájətɪ/	propriety	/pRɔpRieté/	propriété
/fətágrəfí/	photography	/fɔtɔgRafí/	photographie

This chapter examined a few of the rules which are affected by the general tendencies of syllable structure, weakening and strengthening, and the principle of least effort. Syllable structure and the principle of least effort are also at work in assimilation processes, the topic of Chapter 7.

6.7 Questions

1. Compare the syllable breaks in the first two columns with what happens in the third. What does liaison seem to do to the syllable structure of the words in the third column?

vieux	amis	vieux amis
grand	animal	grand animal
gros	orteil	gros orteil
beaux	enfants	beaux enfants

2. The *Appendix Probi*, a manuscript of spelling mistakes in Medieval Latin, offers the following corrections:

speculum	non	speclum
masculum	non	masclum
articulus	non	articlus
calida	non	calda
viridis	non	virdis

What process was taking place in the examples given in the right column? Reconstruct where the stress must have been in the left column.

3. It is said that the final e in words like *petite*, *saine*, *grande*, marks the preceding segment 'to be pronounced'. How does this relate to the statement that Final Consonant Deletion precedes Final Schwa Deletion?

4. What happened to the /a/ found in the second syllable of the Latin words (Column A) as French (Column B) developed?

A	B
ornamentu	ornement
pergamenu	parchemin
bachalare	bachelier
Alamania	Allemagne

5. How do you know that, in fast speech, the /t/ which precedes *elle* in *Pour qui chante-t-elle?* has been inserted? Why is it not the case that such a /t/ is the last sound of *chante*?

6. Identify the rules which are needed to explain the changes from the items in the left column to those in the right.

scola	école
specie	épice
spina	épine
stábula	étable
strángulat	(il)étrangle
scríbere	écrire

7. Consider these phonetic transcriptions involving *h*-muet and *h*-aspiré.

Aspiré:	Muet:
le héro /ləero/	l'homme /lɔm/
les héros /leero/	les hommes /lezɔm/
une honte /ynəɔ̃t/	une humanité /ynymanite/

Note that neither Liaison nor Elision applies in the so-called aspirated examples. Give two possible explanations for these facts, one phonological and the other morphological. Then, compare the merits of each of these solutions.

8. You have read that, historically, *numerum* became *nombre*. Explain how that happened, making sure to refer to an intervening rule.

9. Transcribe in sequence the numbers 20-32. When that is done, answer the following questions.
   (a) Is 28 a case of liaison? Why or why not?
   (b) Compare 28, 38, and 88 in terms of word-final phenomena.
   (c) Compare 25, 35, and 85 in terms of word-final phenomena.
   (d) What can you conclude about the word-final consonant of 20? Answer in terms of regularity.

Chapter 7
Birds of a feather

7.0 Introduction. This chapter is concerned with the ways in which sounds cause one another to alter their feature composition. The most common of the processes to be discussed is assimilation.

7.1 Assimilation. Assimilation is a process by which a segment becomes similar to (sometimes identical with) an adjacent segment. A segment assimilates with another segment if it acquires one or more features of that segment. Generally, assimilation is limited to one of two types. In a sequence of segments $X_1 X_2$, where X_2 influences X_1 (i.e. X_1 assimilates to X_2), the feature copied from X_2 onto X_1 regresses by one segment. This is called regressive assimilation. In a sequence $X_1 X_2$, where X_1 influences X_2 (i.e. X_2 assimilates to X_1), the feature copied from X_1 onto X_2 progresses by one segment. This is called progressive assimilation. Evidence of assimilation can be found both in the history of the French language and in data which reflects the current state of the language.

7.1.1 Voicing assimilation. 'Voicing assimilation' is a technical term referring to the addition or deletion of the feature voice by assimilation with adjacent material. 'Devoicing' is a term applied to the deletion of voice; 'voicing' applies to the addition of voice. In rapid speech, voiced obstruents have a tendency to become devoiced if followed by a voiceless consonant.

(1) valet de chambre /valɛtʃɑ̃bʀ/
    une robe sale /ynʀɔpsal/
    rouge foncé /ʀuʃfɔ̃se/
    je te crois /ʃtəkʀwa/

Contrast (1) with (2), where devoicing does not occur.

(2) valet de madame /valɛdmadam/
    une robe jaune /ynʀɔbʒo:n/
    rouge-gorge /ʀuʒgɔʀʒ/
    Quand je vous vois /kɑ̃ʒvuvwa/

Voiceless obstruents can also become voiced if followed by a voiced consonant, as in (3).

(3) Voiced: Voiceless:
    avec Jean /avɛgʒɑ̃/   avec Paul /avɛkpɔl/
    prince des ténebres /pʀɛ̃zdetenɛbʀ/   prince charmant /pʀɛ̃sʃaʀmɑ̃/
    un passe boule /œ̃pazbul/   passe partout /paspaʀtu/
    la tête dure /latɛddyʀ/   la tête carrée /latɛtkaʀe/

7.1.1 Voicing assimilation / 51

The examples in (1) through (3) show that obstruents are subject to voicing assimilation. Using the feature system of Chapter 5, one can formulate the following rule.

>RULE. VOICING ASSIMILATION (preliminary version): In fast speech, a word-final nonsonorant segment agrees in voicing with the first segment of the next word, if that segment is consonantal.

This rule as stated is more general than the foregoing evidence would suggest. It predicts that nasals and liquids, which are also consonantal, cause preceding obstruents to assimilate in voice. That prediction proves to be correct with respect to /m/, /n/, and /l/ (see (4)). In 7.1.2, /R/ is shown to be excluded from this conditioning environment.

(4) avec moi /avɛgmwa/
    cette nigaude /sednigod/
    avec la tête /avɛglatɛt/

Voicing Assimilation is not limited to word boundaries. It also applies word-internally, but evidence is not clear-cut. The reason why it is difficult to find word-internal evidence is that there are very few alternations involving Voicing Assimilation word-internally. One such alternation is found in the pair *médecin/médical*. The noun *médecin* and the adjective *médical* belong to the same word family. To prove that these forms are related, a rule must be shown to exist which explains the variations between these two words.

The rule of Voicing Assimilation provides that explanation. In *médecin*, the voiced dental stop /d/ is devoiced before the consonantal segment /s/. Note that the vowel which separates them in *médical* is dropped in *médecin*. There are dialects of French which do not drop this vowel. In those dialects the dental stop remains voiced, /medøsɛ̃/, pronounced like *mes deux seins*. The alternation with *médical* and these facts from nonstandard French provide evidence that the /t/ of /mɛtsɛ̃/ is a devoiced /d/. Words like *sauvetage*, *oisiveté*, *disgrace* are also cases of voicing assimilation within a word. They alternate with *sauver*, *oisive*, *distraction*. In (5), the /v/ of *sauvetage* and *oisiveté* and the /s/ of the prefix /dis/ are shown to alternate.

(5) sauvetage /softaʒ/ sauver /sove/
    oisiveté /wazifte/ oisive /waziv/
    disgrace /dizgRas/ distraction /distRaksjɔ̃/

In the light of this word-internal and word boundary evidence, it is now possible to improve upon the form of the rule of Voicing Assimilation.

>RULE. VOICING ASSIMILATION (improved version): In fast speech, an obstruent agrees in voicing with an immediately following obstruent or nasal or /l/ at word boundaries or word-internally.

Other words may appear to be cases of voicing assimilation but are not. Words like *obscur* and *observateur* are pronounced /opskyʀ/ and /opsɛʀvatœʀ/, respectively, although their spelling suggests voiced stops. Unfortunately, spelling is not a reliable source of data, especially with regard to languages with a long literary tradition. Writing systems are, of course, echoes of sound systems; but orthography is often an archaic reflection (e.g. the *m* of *condamner*) or even an incorrect reconstruction (e.g. the *g* of *vingt*) of actual sounds. The best way to provide supportive evidence for a rule, here Voicing Assimilation, is to demonstrate that an alternation exists which the rule in question can account for. Since there is no alternation between *obscur* or *observation* and words with equivalent voiced segments, these two words cannot be viewed as cases of Voicing Assimilation.

7.1.2 /ʀ/-Devoicing. The segment /ʀ/, which is inherently voiced, becomes voiceless in the environment of voiceless nonsonorants. /ʀ/-Devoicing takes place whether /ʀ/ precedes or follows the environment.

Table 7.1

	Voiced	Voiceless
Before consonants:	ardu barbe verve	alerte harpe cerf
After consonants:	fibre tigre ouvre	chiffre apre autre
Before and after consonants:	ordre arbre	tertre tartre

/ʀ/-Devoicing is a rare rule, combining both progressive and regressive assimilation.

/ʀ/ also devoices in word-final position, as can be seen in Table 7.2.

Table 7.2

Voiced	Voiceless
paternel	père
mairie	maire
épicerie	épicière
circularité	circulaire

Devoicing in final position is a fairly common type of sound change. For example, in German all consonantal segments devoice in final position.

Since the data in Tables 7.1 and 7.2 show a change of the same type, one might want to collapse the two processes into one rule. Before collapsing these rules, however, it might prove useful to look at further data, in particular at the behavior of /R/ at boundaries.

(6) Voiced   Voiceless

    le père Lachaise   le père travaille
    une peur bleue   une peur soudaine
    ma soeur Marie ⎫   ma soeur Cécile
    ma soeur Anne ⎭
    c'est pour Robert   c'est pour Cécile

The data in (6) illustrate two points: the left column shows that word-final devoicing does not take place if the next word in the phrase begins with a voiced segment. The right column shows that there is regressive devoicing of /R/ across word boundaries when the environment is a voiceless stop or fricative.

At word boundaries /R/ occurring word-initially is also devoiced by progressive assimilation if a voiceless stop or fricative precedes it.

(7) Voiced   Voiceless

    la grande route   la petite route
    la bonne route   la fausse route
    nous sommes rendus   un service rendu
    une seule rayure   une grosse rayure

All these facts can be accounted for by the following rule.

> RULE. /R/-DEVOICING: /R/ is devoiced (1) in phrase-final position, or (2) by assimilating progressively and regressively to a voiceless obstruent, within words and at all boundaries.

Now consider the relationship between Voicing Assimilation and /R/-Devoicing. It should be clear that /R/ is too unstable a segment to cause other segments to assimilate. Whenever /R/ occurs in the environment of a voiceless segment, it will assimilate to that segment. With /R/-Devoicing ordered before Voicing Assimilation, /R/-Devoicing excludes from the input of Voicing Assimilation any environment involving /R/. Consequently, it is not necessary to exclude from the environment of Voicing Assimilation any occurrence of /R/ and the rule can be stated generally.

> RULE. VOICING ASSIMILATION: In fast speech, an obstruent agrees in voicing with an immediately following consonantal segment both at word boundaries and word-internally.

7.1.3 Some remarks. The scope of Voicing Assimilation in French is far more complex than the foregoing discussion would suggest. Some readers may find that they do not voice or devoice segments as stated in the rule which has been given here. This can be explained. Many rules have differing scopes, depending on regional or social differences. Schools combat certain tendencies of sounds to change. For example, children are often told to pronounce the *s* in words ending in *-isme* not as a /z/ but as an /s/. However, the rule of Voicing Assimilation suggests that the French who tend to pronounce it as /z/ are following a natural process.

Another factor not examined thus far stems from the question: 'How rapid is rapid speech?' Clearly, rapid speech forces the speaker to make segment-to-segment transitions shorter and less distinct, setting the scene for less distinctly produced segments and a greater likelihood for certain features to be carried over. At what point in an increasingly rapid progression of speech is it determined that speech is rapid? These questions are extremely complex and cannot be considered, let alone answered, within a broad study like this one.

In voicing assimilation, consonantal segments acquire features from one another. There are cases of assimilation where consonants acquire features from vowels, cases where vowels acquire features from other vowels, and cases where vowels acquire features from consonants. An example of assimilation where consonants acquire features from vowels is palatalization (7.2), mentioned briefly in the next section. Assimilation of vowels can take the shape of vowel harmony, as in some West African languages, like Twi, and in Turkish, or can look like umlaut, as in many Germanic languages. There is in French a tendency toward vowel harmony on the basis of aperture. For example, the unstressed vowel /ɛ/ of *prête*, also found in *prêtons* /pʀɛtɔ̃/, assimilates in aperture with the stressed /e/ in the past participle *prêté* and in the infinitive *prêter*, both of which are pronounced /pʀete/. Finally, assimilation by which vowels acquire features of consonants is best illustrated by nasalization (7.3) which is discussed after palatalization (7.2).

7.2 Palatalization. This is a phonological process by which a front (i.e. palatal) vowel or glide causes an adjacent consonant to become palatal. It is a case of assimilation in point of articulation between a consonantal and a nonconsonantal segment.

There are no examples of palatalization in French deriving from contemporary evidence alone except very indirectly. Good contemporary evidence can be found in all Slavic languages word internally and in English at word boundaries. For example, people with names like *Bruce Young* or *Lois Yates* tend to palatalize the final /s/ of their first name when giving their names. These cases of English palatalization are probably the clearest because of the tendency many people have to slur rather than clearly enunciate their names. Thus the /s/ of *Bruce* and that of *Lois*, which in isolation are clearly alveolar, become palatal (i.e. /ʃ/) by assimilation with the point of articulation of /j/. Along the same line, English and French can be shown to differ. Latin words with the suffix *-tionem* lost the *-em* ending long before English borrowed them from French. As students of French know, these words are pronounced with /sjɔ̃/. Contrast *nation, potion, élection, permission* with

English, where the /s/ is palatalized, yielding /ʃ/. (See Shaw's spelling for *fish* (1.2).)

An example of palatalization in French can be adduced in comparing the pronunciation of the letter *c* in *médical* and *médecin*, *musical* and *musicien*, *vocal* and *vociférer*. The change from /k/ to /s/ before front vowels is directly related to the process of palatalization.

7.3 Nasalization. Nasalization is also a very common type of assimilation. In English, for example, the vowel /æ/ in *cat* is different from the vowel of *can* in that the latter is nasalized while the former is not. The vowel of *can* is nasalized because it assimilates in nasality with the following nasal. This is a case of regressive assimilation. The velum is lowered in anticipation of a nasal consonant before the articulation of the preceding segment is completed.

All nasalized vowels are former oral vowels that assimilated with a nasal. Some languages, French and Portuguese in particular, have nasalized vowels which are not followed by nasals. Those cases are less clear than the English example just given; but they too are subject to assimilation with a nasal. Nasalization in French and Portuguese takes place if a vowel precedes a nasal which precedes either a word boundary or a consonantal segment. This explains why the /i/ of *vigne* and *fine* is not nasalized while the vowels of *vent*, *cinq*, and *fondue* are nasalized. In the former, the nasal is followed by a nonconsonantal segment, /viɲə/, /finə/, while in the latter it is followed by a consonantal sound or by a word boundary.

7.4 Contraction. Contraction, or coalescence, is a process of language which unites as one single sound two otherwise separate sounds. In (7) items in the left column have two segments (italicized) which become one in the corresponding words in the right column (also italicized).

(7a) comp*réhen*sion   comp*ren*dre
(7b) app*réhen*sible   app*ren*dre
(7c) b*el* (/ɛ + l/)   b*eau*
(7d) ch*aleur*   ch*aud*
(7e) m*agi*stral   m*aî*tre
(7f) p*aci*fique (pacis facere)   p*ai*x

The /e/ and /ã/ of items (7a) and (7b) contracted to /ã/, the /ɛ/ and /l/ of *bel* and the /a/ and /l/ of *chaleur* contracted to /o/, and the /a/ and /i/ of items (7e) and (7f) contracted to /ɛ/.

Generally, when two sounds coalesce to form a single sound, the resulting sound is long. This is believed to be a universal tendency. In languages where length is conditioned by the environment, as is the case in French, the segment resulting from coalescence is further changed by a delengthening rule where appropriate. Contraction can occur to all types of segments. In (7a) and (7b), vowels are subject to contraction. In (7c) and (7d), contraction involves a vowel and a liquid. In (7e) and (7f), a low and a high vowel (which became a glide historically) also coalesce. In (7.6.3) consonants which coalesce are classified under the heading of total assimilation.

7.5 Glide formation. When a high vowel precedes a vowel, there is a strong tendency for the high vowel to lose its syllabicity, thus changing into a glide. Evidence of this type of alternation between high vowel and glide can be observed in verb paradigms, doublets, or in the derivation of one word from another. In such instances, it happens that the phonological environment of a high vowel is altered, and this alteration causes the sound in question to become a glide. In (8), the words in the left column contain vowels which are not in the environment of other vowels, while the words in the right column contain vowels which immediately precede another vowel. The predictable result (barring exceptions not discussed in this chapter) is that the items in the right column are pronounced with a glide, while the corresponding sounds in the left column are full vowels.

(8) je sue   nous suons
    il lie   vous liez
    je scie   il faut scier
    les nues   les nuages
    la roue   un rouage
    fugitif   fuite

In some regional dialects, the items in the right column (except *fuite*) may or may not be glided (i.e. the vowel is retained).

7.6 Historical evidence. The concept of assimilation was first understood in the context of linguistic studies relating to the history and development of languages. The great steps made in the area of historical (diachronic) linguistics enabled linguists to identify similar 'changes' in synchronic studies. In Section 7.6.1 the symbol for 'becomes' (>) is used to mean 'changes over time'.

7.6.1 Voicing assimilation and Nasalization. These very common linguistic phenomena are found not only in the contemporary context in which they were introduced (7.1.1) and (7.3), respectively, but also in the historical development of many languages. In fact, the linguistic phenomena found at any period of time are often but reflections of the history of the language or languages in which these phenomena are found. Such is the case for word-internal voicing assimilation and for nasalization.

Historically, the /t/ of *médecin* /mɛtsɛ̃/ was derived from the /d/ of Latin *medicinum*. Reduction of the first /i/ in *medicinum* to /ə/ was the first of these steps. After reduction to /ə/, deletion of /ə/ became possible, setting the stage for Voicing Assimilation, which made the contiguous obstruents /ds/ agree in voicing. This three-step process makes for a certain regularity.

Similarly, the /ɛ̃/ of *médecin* /mɛtsɛ̃/ was derived from the /in/ of *medicinum*, but not before the rule which deletes posttonic vowels and consonants (i.e. those that occur after the stress) did in fact delete /um/. Without this prior deletion, Nasalization would have been inapplicable. That is precisely what happened in the case of many feminine nouns and adjectives. The posttonic final /a/, unlike all other vowels, is not deleted but reduced. In words like Latin *fina* and *bona*, final /a/ weakened to /ə/ and prevented the application of Nasalization.

Consequently, Latin *finam* and *bonam* > French *fine* and *bonne*, while their masculine equivalents, Latin *finum* and *bonum* > French *fin* and *bon*, respectively.

Other cases of assimilation can be found in the history of French. Palatalization is one of the most complex of these.

7.6.2 Palatalization.[1] Historically, it is hypothesized that the velars /k/ and /g/ were palatalized when they occurred before /i/, /e/, and/ surprisingly, /a/.[2] The development of the /s/ of *cime* /sim/ from the Latin form *cyma* /kima/ of the Greek word (*y* was pronounced /i/ in Latin) requires the prior formation of /j/. The first step is /kima/ > /kjima/. Similarly, the following Latin words create a palatal glide.

cera /kera/ > /kjera/
placere /plakere/ > /plakjere/

Then a vowel-raising rule effected the following changes:

/kjima/ remains the same because /i/ is already a high vowel,
/kjera/ > /kjira/,
/plakjere/ > /plakjire/.

That was the second step. The third step is metathesis, a rule which permutes two items: /kj/ > /jk/, if preceded by a vowel. The same permutation is needed to derive *maison* from *ma(n)sione* (/masjone/ > /majsone/), *aire* from *area* (/arja/ > /ajra/), and *paire* from *paria* (/parja/ > /pajra/). Hence:

/kjima/ remains because /k/ is word-initial,
/kjira/ remains because /k/ is word-initial,
but /plakjire/ > /plajkire/.

In the fourth step, /k/ becomes /ts/ if it is followed by a front vowel or glide (/i/, /e/, /j/). This is palatalization.

---

[1] This analysis of the development of the palatal consonants of French is adapted from Loy (1970).
[2] The palatalization of a velar before a low central vowel (*campum* > *champs*, *carrum* > *char*, *cantare* > *chanter*, etc.) remains an unexplained fact of the development of French.

/kjima/ > /tsjima/,
/kjira/ > /tsjira/,
/plajkire/ > /plajtsire/.

In the fifth step, intervocalic consonants are voiced.

/tsjima/ does not change,
/tsjira/ does not change,
/plajtsire/ > /plajdzire/.

Finally, /ts/ and /dz/ become /s/ and /z/, final /a/ becomes /ə/, final /e/ drops, and /aj/ becomes /ɛ/, yielding the words *cime*, *cire*, and *plaisir*.

This whole development of /k/ to /s/ and /z/ is dependent on one critical step: palatalization of the velar /k/ (i.e. /k/ > /kj/ and /kj/ > /ts/). In both cases, the palatalization of a segment is a case of assimilation of a velar consonant to a palatal vowel or glide.

That is precisely why the development of French *chant* from Latin *cantum* is odd. The vowel which causes palatalization and also makes the stop /k/ into a continuant /ʃ/ is itself not a palatal but a low central vowel. One has to conclude either that /k/ > /ʃ/ before /a/ is not a case of assimilation (which is an unnatural explanation) or that a /j/ was inserted (for no known reason) between /k/ and /a/, a solution for which there is no historical evidence and no logical reason.

7.6.3 Total assimilation. Fouché (1966:802-803) shows clusters of consonants which assimilated totally. Hence all of the following are cases of regressive assimilation.

/eksagiu/ > /esɛ/	*essai*	ks > ss > s
/ruktare/ > /ʀote/	*roter*	kt > tt > t
*/adrestare/ > /aʀete/	*arrêter*	dr > rr > ʀ
/rupta/ > /rotta/ > /ʀut/	*route*	pt > tt > t
/tepidu/ > /tjevde/ > /tiedde/ > /tiɛd/	*tiède*	vd > dd > d
/ad satis/ > /assatis/ > ase/	*assez*	ds > ss > s

7.7 Questions

1. Words are given in the first column. Transcribe them in the other two.

Orthography	Careful speech	Fast speech
Ex: à jeter	/aʒte/	/aʃte/
(a) haut de forme		
(b) clavecin		
(c) oisiveté		
(d) rejeton		
(e) rez-de-chaussée		
(f) dynamisme		
(g) transvasez-les		
(h) une pauvre femme		
(i) disgrace		
(j) chauve-souris		

2. Identify the type of assimilation.
   Ex: /kudbɔt/ ~ /kutpje/   regressive-voicing..........
   (a) /fʀap/ ~ /ilfʀabbjɛ̃/   ....
   (b) /ʒibje/ ~ /ʒipsjeʀ/   ....
   (c) /sæk/ ~ /sæŋ/ (English)   ....
   (d) /sovele/ ~ /softwa/   ....
   (e) /sijts/ ~ /sijdz/ (English)   ....
   (f) /pan duro/ ~ /pam bweno/ (Spanish) ....
   (g) /ʀəʒet/ ~ /ʀəʃtɔ̃/   ....
   (h) /səgɔ̃a/ ~ /zgɔ̃d/   ....

3. Is French basically a regressive or progressive assimilating language?

4. What is the difference between 'nasal' and 'nasalized'? Are the following segments nasalized or are they nasals? /ɑ̃ ɔ̃ œ̃ ɛ̃/ Why?

5. What is the difference between nasalization in French and in American English? Specify the conditions for French nasalization and state what would block its application.

6. With contraction, the resulting sound is generally longer than either of the two sounds which coalesced. However, there are in French cases where the resulting sound is short, yet we know that contraction has taken place (example: *bel* > *beau*). What has happened? On what does vowel length depend in French? Give other examples of contraction.

7. What kind of assimilatory processes have taken place between the two (or three) forms given?

   /rupta/ > /rotta/ 'route'   /ʀut/ 'route'
   /leny/ 'les nues'   /lenɥaʒ/ 'les nuages'
   /fin/ 'fine'   /fɛ̃/ 'fin'
   /sove/ 'sauver'   /softaʒ/ 'sauvetage'
   /avɛkpjeʀ/ 'avec Pierre'   /avɛgʒɛʀmɛn/ 'avec Germaine'

8. The last segment of the truncated form of *quatre*, /kat/, occurs as /d/ in *quatre veaux gras* /kadvogʀa/. What rules are needed to derive /kadvogʀa/ from /katʀəvogʀa/ and in what order do they apply?

9. If someone told you that *Alsace, Alsacien, balsa, balsamine* (all pronounced with /lz/) are cases of progressive voicing assimilation, what proof would you demand before accepting that claim? In what way are words like *absent, abstention, observer, obscur* likely to induce one to make the same error? How are they different from *Alsace*, etc.?

10. What would be the consequence of the following order of application: Voicing Assimilation first, then /ʀ/-Devoicing?

Part Three.
French phonological rules:
The forces that shape the main traits of the French sound system.

Part Three draws heavily on all that has been discussed in Parts One and Two, and constitutes the nucleus of the description proper. Here the vocabulary of French is divided into its phonologically relevant classes, phonological rules that bear on the most important French vowel system are examined, and a number of the processes discussed in Part Two are examined in detail.

Chapter 8
It's what's up front

8.1 Fronting. Although the title of this chapter seems to limit the discussion to fronting, one of the strongest tendencies of the phonology of French, an equally important set of facts is developed here regarding the division of French vocabulary into structurally definable groups of words. Fronting and the rules associated with that process are developed on the basis of phonological correspondences found in vowel alternations.

8.1.1 Tonic/pretonic vowel alternations: /a ~ ɛ/, /ɔ ~ œ/. French exhibits vowel alternations in tonic and pretonic position in pairs of related words. This complementary distribution suggests that the alternating segments are one and the same. These alternations apply both to rounded and unrounded low vowels.

(1) /a/ alternates with /ɛ/
    s*a*linité   s*e*l

c*a*rnivore   ch*ai*r
sensu*a*lité   sensu*e*l
form*a*lité   form*e*l
scol*a*rité   scol*ai*re
(2) /ɔ/ alternates with /œ/
 fav*o*ritisme   fav*eu*r
 *o*vipare   *oeu*f
 profess*o*ral   profess*eu*r
 édit*o*rial   édit*eu*r
 s*o*litude   s*eu*l

The forms in the left column, which are learned vocabulary items, do not contain either of the two front vowels exhibited in the right column of (1) or (2). In the left column the italicized vowels always occur in pretonic position, while in the right column the italicized vowels are stressed and also front. The italicized vowels of the left column are nonfront. A way of relating these segments is to assume that a rule changes one into the other. Here it is assumed that a nonfront vowel becomes front when it occurs in tonic position. In other words, the underlying representation of the words in the right column contains not /ɛ/ or /œ/, but rather the same vowel as that italicized in the corresponding words in the left column. A rule which changes /a/ to /ɛ/ and /ɔ/ to /œ/ when these vowels are in stressed position yields the stressed vowels in the right column. For example, the word *sel* is derived by such a rule from an underlying representation /sal/.

8.1.2 Defining Fronting. It is easy to see that the vowels /ɛ/ and /a/ differ by only one feature, namely, [front] (cf. Figure 5.5). The segment /ɛ/ is [front] while /a/ is nonfront. For the nonfront vowel /a/ to become front, the only feature change needed is to make nonfront [front]. In other words, a fronted /a/ is in fact /ɛ/. Similarly, /ɔ/ is different from /œ/ in that /ɔ/ is nonfront while /œ/ is front. The feature change which accounts for the shift of /ɔ/ to /œ/ is also nonfront to front. It is true that /ɔ/ is also [back] and [round] but neither represents a problem. Since [front] and [back] are mutually exclusive by definition (cf. Chapter 5), then the change of [nonfront] to [front] entails a loss of backness. Since both /ɔ/ and /œ/ are [round], roundness plays no role in the fronting of /ɔ/ to /œ/; it simply distinguishes /œ/ from /ɛ/.

The fronting of these two nonfront vowels could be stated in two separate rules, but a generalization is captured simply by referring in the rule to a class of sounds which includes /a/ and /ɔ/, rather than to refer to each vowel separately. Since /a/ and /ɔ/ are low segments and /ɛ/, the only other low segment, is already [front] and therefore not affected by Fronting, then Fronting can apply to all low segments. Hence, the following (tentative) formulation.

Rule. Fronting (tentative version): Low segments in tonic position are fronted.

This rule applies to /a/ and /ɔ/, making them /ɛ/ and /œ/. It also applies to /ɛ/, making it [front]. Since /ɛ/ is already [front], Fronting applies vacuously to /ɛ/. When a rule applies vacuously to a segment, that segment undergoes no observable change.

8.1.3 Another round vowel alternation: /œ ~ u/. Besides the alternation between /œ/ and /ɔ/ just examined, there is another between /œ/ and /u/.

(3) /œ/ alternates with /u/

peuvent	pouvons		
veulent	voulons	(volonté)	/vɔlɔ̃te/
meurs	mourons	(mort)	/mɔRt/
douleur	douloureux	(endolori)	/ɑ̃dɔlɔri/

The alternation /œ/ ~ /u/ is not independent of alternation /œ/ ~ /ɔ/, as is shown by the words in parentheses. This alternation suggests that /œ, ɔ, u/ need to be related by rule. The case for relating them is particularly strong in light of the fact that *meurs*, *mourons*, and *mort* are but different forms of the verb *mourir*. One of the rules relating /œ/ and /u/ is Fronting, which relates /ɔ/ and /œ/, as seen in Section 8.1.2. The other rules are discussed in Section 8.3 and in Chapter 10.

8.1.4 An alternation with schwa: /ɛ ~ ə/. Alternations in (3) are characteristic of round vowels. When a nonround vowel alternates with a pretonic vowel segment, that segment is schwa. This is illustrated in (4) for /ɛ/ and is illustrated again in Chapter 9.

(4) /ɛ/ alternates with schwa

hôtel	hôtelier	(hospitalité)
graine	grenier	(granulation)
frêle	freluquet	(fragile)
mènent	menons	

In (4) one can see a threefold alternation at play. A stressed /ɛ/ corresponds to an unstressed schwa and an unstressed /a/. From what is known of the feature composition of /a/ and schwa, one would expect that they are related. Other than [tense], which separates /a/ and /ə/, only one more feature, [front], separates /ə/ and /ɛ/. With this in mind and the alternations illustrated in (4), one can conclude that the examples in (1)-(4) are all illustrative of Fronting.

8.2 Basic classes of French morphology

8.2.1 Two kinds of alternations. Since the complex vowel alternations illustrated in Sections 8.1.3 and 8.1.4 are not exceptional (cf. Chapter 9), then we must conclude that there are two sets of pretonic vowels and one set of tonic vowels. In the case of the round vowels (cf. (3)), the sole member of tonic vowels is /œ/ and the members of the two sets of pretonic vowels are /u/ and /ɔ/. In the case of the unrounded vowels (cf. (4)), the sole member of the set of tonic vowels is /ɛ/ and the members of the two sets of pretonic vowels are /a/ and /ə/. Therefore, one set of pretonic vowels includes /a/ and /ɔ/, while the other set includes /u/ and /ə/, as shown in Table 8.1.

Table 8.1 Alternating stem vowels.

	Tonic	Pretonic Set 1	Set 2
+ round	œ	ɔ	u
- round	ɛ	a	ə

Within the fairly restricted vocalic system examined so far, the vowels of Set 1 are underlying segments. They alternate with fronted vowels and with reduced or displaced vowels. The fronted vowels are tonic vowels, the other vowels are members of Set 2. In these alternations, the forms containing the vowels of Set 1 are found in learned French vocabulary. Those containing the vowels of Set 2 are found in native French vocabulary.

8.2.2 Native and learned forms. The distinction made between native and learned words is based strictly on their underlying form and the rules that apply to them. Some rules apply to both native and learned forms. Final Schwa Deletion does so. Some rules apply only to native forms; others only to learned forms.

In English, for example, rules which derive *subliminal* from *sublime*, *residence* from *reside*, apply only to learned forms. Similarly, the French rule which raises /ɛ/ to /e/ to yield *bénédiction*, *céleste*, *pédale* (cf. Chapter 9) also applies to learned forms exclusively. Reduction, on the other hand, applies to French pretonic vowels in native vocabulary only.

There are general guidelines that suggest which French forms are native and which are learned. Forms can be identified on the basis of their affixes. Words suffixed in *-ité*, *-ation*, *-isme*, as are *mortalité*, *coloration*, and *favoritisme*, are typical of learned vocabulary. Forms in *-age*, *-ment*, or not suffixed at all, such as *ouvrage*, *seulement*, and *œuf*, are typical of native vocabulary. Not all affixes, however, provide a clear distinction between learned and native vocabulary. The suffix *-té*, for example, which is generally considered a native suffix, yielding *beauté*, as opposed to *pulchritude*, *joyeuseté* with a fronted /ø/, should also yield *claireté*; but instead, the proper word is *clarté*. The suffix *-iste*, generally regarded as learned, should yield *floriste*, but *fleuriste* is the proper word. These guidelines are therefore subject to exceptions.

8.2.3 Derivational and inflectional classes. Another distinction made in French phonological studies is that between derivational and inflectional morphology. When two words are related derivationally, one is derived from the other. For example, *bonté* is derived from *bon*, *clarté* from *clair*, *aimable* from *aimer*, *difficilement* from *difficile*. A derived form is generally of a different syntactic class than its formative (i.e. the word from which it is derived). *Bonté* is a noun but *bon* is an adjective, *aimable* is an adjective but *aimer* is a verb, etc. These class changes are due to affixing of nominalizing, adjectivizing, or adverbializing suffixes.

By contrast, inflectionally related words belong to the same (inflectional) class. *Menons* and *mènent*, *mourons* and *meurent*, *cheval* and *chevaux*, *fermier* and *fermière*, are inflectionally related. What is different between them is not that one has a suffix that the other does not have but rather that each shows a different suffix. The contrasts of meaning indicated by these contrasting inflectional suffixes relate to person, number, gender, and sometimes case.

8.3 Some rules

8.3.1 Pretonic Vowel Raising. A shift from /ɔ/ to /u/ is needed in order to relate the members of the pairs *mort*/*mourir*, *endolori*/*douloureux*, etc. Two rules are used to raise /ɔ/ to /u/. One raises /ɔ/ to /o/. The second rule, to be discussed later, completes the shift to the high back /u/. The first rule can be stated in terms of only one feature change: [low] to [nonlow].

> RULE. PRETONIC ROUND VOWEL RAISING (preliminary version): In native vocabulary, pretonic low rounded vowels become nonlow.

8.3.2 Pretonic Vowel Reduction. The reduction of /a/ to /ə/ is also characteristic of native vocabulary. This rule is needed to account for words like *menotte* and *grenier* as related to *main* and *grain*. The relation between /ə/ and /ɛ/ is determined by the placement of stress: /ə/ is the pretonic equivalent of tonic /ɛ/. The relation between /a/ and the tonic /ɛ/ is determined by the native vs. learned distinction; /a/ is found in learned and /ɛ/ in native vocabulary. Phonetically, /ə/ and /a/ are distinguished by the feature [tense], whereas /ə/ and /ɛ/ are distinguished by [tense] and [front]. The Pretonic Vowel Reduction rule accounts for these facts by detailing the reduction of /ɛ/ and /a/ to schwa.

> RULE. PRETONIC VOWEL REDUCTION (preliminary version): In native vocabulary, pretonic unrounded vowels become nontense and nonfront.

To this point, Fronting and its satellite rules have been stated in strict phonological terms. Unfortunately, this apparent regularity has not taken into account complicating factors which are now to be considered.

8.4 Fronted vowels in pretonic position. The fronted forms in the right column of examples (5) and (6) are derived via Fronting. This becomes evident when one considers alternations like *seul/solitude, feuille/foliation, implorer/pleure, aime/amant, aile/alaire*. Examples in the left column of (5) and (6) also show fronted vowels. These vowels, however, are in pretonic position. Because they are clearly related to their equivalents in the right column, they too must be derived via Fronting. But, if Fronting is to derive nontonic vowels along with tonic vowels, the rule cannot be restricted to tonic vowels, as was assumed earlier. An alternate condition must be imposed on the rule. Consequently, Fronting applies not only to stressed vowels but also to others yet to be defined.

(5) Pretonic /ε/   Tonic /έ/
    aileron   aile
    aimable   aiment
    abaissement   abaissent
    craignons   craignent

(6) Pretonic /œ/   Tonic /œ́/
    seulette   seule
    feuillage   feuille
    pleurons   pleurent
    veuvage   veuve

As another consequence of having Fronting apply to nontonic vowels, the grammar of French must distinguish between two types of pretonic vowels: those which are subject to Pretonic Vowel Reduction and Pretonic Round Vowel Raising, and those which are subjects to Fronting. If Pretonic Round Vowel Raising were to apply to fronted vowels, words like *feuillage, pleurera, peuplement, veuvage* would incorrectly have /ø/ in their first syllable rather than the expected /œ/. While there are words like *heureusement, peuplier*, which allow either /ø/ or /œ/, Pretonic Round Vowel Raising is not the rule which can account for these fluctuations. Similarly, if Pretonic Vowel Reduction were to apply to forms in (5), the following incorrect forms would be derived: */kʀəɲɔ̃/ instead of /kʀɛɲɔ̃/, */əmabl/ instead of /ɛmabl/, etc. It is therefore imperative that the class of words whose pretonic vowels are subject to Fronting not be subject to Pretonic Round Vowel Raising and Pretonic Vowel Reduction.

8.5 Divisions in French vocabulary. For lack of a better terminology, let us distinguish between these two sets of vowels by marking them as strong if they undergo Fronting and weak if they undergo Pretonic Vowel Raising or Pretonic Vowel Reduction. This marking is a mere mnemonic device. The two classes are in fact solely defined in terms of their members. Rules that apply to classes so defined are known as morphologically conditioned rules.

In the division proposed, both subsets of French stem morphology fall in the category of the marked vocabulary. Forms with stems whose vowels are not so marked fall in the unmarked stem class, as illustrated in the Venn diagram in Figure 8.1.

Figure 8.1

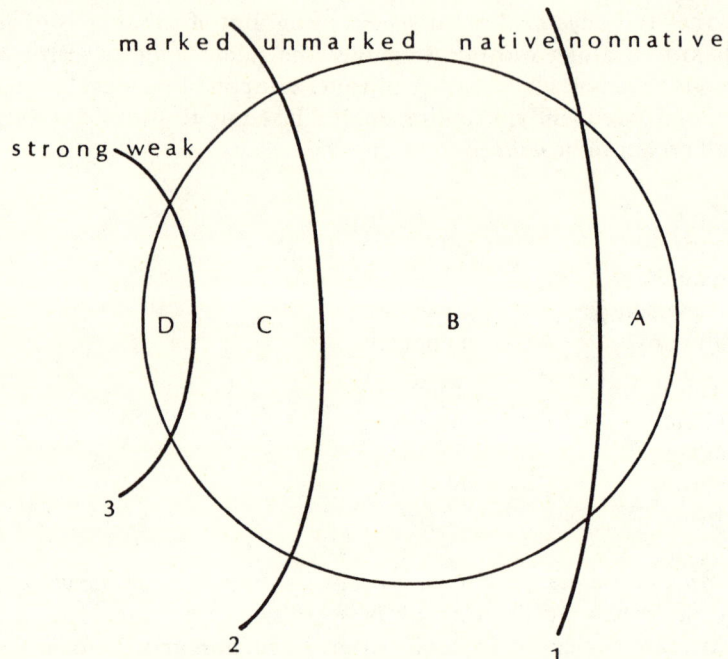

The vocabulary of French is represented by the circle in Figure 8.1. It is divided into several classes. The lines labeled with Arabic numbers define positively in their concave configuration and negatively in their convex configuration. Line 1, therefore, cuts across the vocabulary of French in such a way as to include native vocabulary on the left side of the arc, and to exclude nonnative vocabulary on the right side. The figure formed by the circle and line 1, to the right of line 1 (namely, *Class A*), represents learned and foreign words. Line 2 divides native forms into a marked and an unmarked class. The unmarked class, a set represented by the circle as bisected by lines 1 and 2, comprises the bulk of French vocabulary. Line 3 further divides the marked class into two *Classes*: *C* and *D*. Forms of *Class C* are characterized by a stem vowel marked weak. Forms of *Class D* are characterized by a stem vowel marked strong. In other words, line 3 defines strong forms positively and weak forms (nonstrong) negatively.

To take a concrete example, the *grain*-family is divided as follows: *grain, graine, grainetier* belong to *Class D*, in which the stem vowel, marked strong, undergoes Fronting; *grenier, égrener* belong to *Class C*, whose members are subject to Pretonic Vowel Reduction and Pretonic Round Vowel Raising; *granule, granulation, granite* belong to *Class A*: they are learned words. No member of the *grain* family belongs to *Class B*. No example of *Class B* should be expected because this chapter deals with word families in which stem vowels are marked, while *Class B* is comprised of words whose stem vowels are not marked.

8.6 The rules with morphological conditioning. With the foregoing classification in mind, we are now ready to state the rules discussed in this chapter. Each of them is modified to some degree in later chapters; but for the moment, they constitute our conclusion on the ideas and problems raised in Chapter 8.

RULE. VOWEL FRONTING (to be relabeled in Chapter 10): Low vowels become front if they are marked strong.

RULE. PRETONIC VOWEL REDUCTION (tentative version): Pretonic unrounded vowels become nontense and nonfront if they are marked weak.

RULE. PRETONIC ROUND VOWEL RAISING (tentative version): Pretonic low round vowels become nonlow if they are marked weak.

There is no need to indicate that these rules apply only to native vocabulary because marked forms are members of *Class C* and *Class D*, which are both proper subsets of French native vocabulary.

In this chapter, the effect of Fronting on French vocabulary has been examined and, as a result of that effect, a classification has been established. It has been decided that French word stems fall into at least four stem classes. This classification is further documented in Chapter 9.

8.7 Questions
1. Indicate whether the following are related inflectionally or derivationally.

été ~ estivant   pied ~ piéton
travail ~ travaux   aile ~ alaire
peignent ~ peint   beau ~ beauté
bouche ~ bouchée   faille ~ faut

2. Decompose the following words into their stems and affixes.

illumination   sidérurgie
décomposition   inimitable
accouchement   cinéraire
inhumanité   militarisme

3. Determine whether the segments with the italicized vowels belong to Set 1, Set 2, or whether they are tonic vowels.

c*o*rdial   m*a*ritime
ils se m*eu*vent   nous f*ai*sons tout

nous v*ou*lions solitude
rien à f*ai*re sa s*œu*r

4. In a number of dialects of French, both central vowels are pronounced as shown in the following words:

sac /sæk/, ça /sæ/ where /æ/ is the vowel of English words like *rat*, *fat*, and *bat*

vous entreriez /vuzãtRœRje/

What tendency do you see in this pronunciation? Is a speaker with these forms likely to pronoune *politesse, occident, mort, Languedoc* as /pœlitɛs/, /œksɪdã/, /mœR/, and /lãgdœk/? Why?

5. When speakers of English (or any other language, except French) wish to imitate the speech of the French, how do they pronounce the vowels? Give facts from French phonology, more specifically from this chapter, which support your answer. Show how Peter Sellers' portrayal of Inspector Clouseau carries this to the extreme, the humoristic extreme.

6. Below are two columns of words in transcription. State which rule or rules, if any, are needed to relate the word pairs in each line. Limit your answer to the italicized vowels.

/s*o*lityd/	/sœl/
/sk*o*larite/	/skɔlɛR/
/dul*œ*R/	/dul*u*Rø/
/ot*ɛ*l/	/otəlje/
/kRɛɲ/	/kRɛɲɔ̃/
/s*œ*l/	/sœlet/
/p*œ*v/	/p*u*vɔ̃/
/m*ɛ*n/	/mənɔ̃/

7. In this chapter, a distinction has been made between learned and native vocabulary. Why? In answering this question, assume that no distinction was made. What would be the consequences?

8. What distinct ways of fronting are there in French?

Chapter 9
The more it changes

9.0 Introduction. Diphthongization and the rules related to it pattern just like Fronting and its satellite rules. Hence, this chapter parallels the previous one in a number of ways: vowel alternations yield rules quite similar to the ones relating to vowel fronting and the divisions advocated for the vocabulary of French in the previous chapter are further motivated. The proper ordering of application of the rules discussed in this and the previous chapter are also demonstrated.

9.1 Pretonic/Tonic vowel alternations. French exhibits alternations between tonic and pretonic vowels in pairs of related words. These alternations can be of a fronting type, as shown in the preceding chapter, or they may involve diphthongization.

(1) /e/ alternates with /jɛ/:

céleste	ciel
bénédiction	bien
fébrile	fièvre
lévrier	lièvre

(2) /e/ alternates with /wa/:

légalité	loi
réception	reçois
crédulité	croire
sérénité	soir

The forms in the left column, which belong to the learned vocabulary of French, do not exhibit front rounded or diphthongized vowels. Diphthongs appear only in the right column, in tonic position. Diphthongs, then, are good candidates for being derived from the unrounded vowel /e/ via Diphthongization, since this rule applies generally to stressed vowels. Deriving both diphthongs from the same vowel, however, is not possible because these diphthongs are distinct. Their alternation with the same vowel at the observable level of structure is due to a fact not directly related to the process of diphthongization. For now, /ɛ/ is arbitrarily chosen as the underlying vowel of the segment /jɛ/ and /e/ as the underlying vowel of the segment of /wa/, leaving until later the motivation for this choice.

The word 'diphthong' is borrowed from the Greek and means 'two sounds'. Cast in the terminology of this book, it means bisegmental. Diphthongization, a strengthening process, changes a single segment into two, or more precisely, adds a specific segment to a tonic or otherwise strong vowel. The segment generally added is a glide. In the cases illustrated in (1) and (2), the glides are, quite obviously, /j/ and /w/. The former is added to the low vowel and the latter is added to the nonlow vowel.

> RULE. DIPHTHONGIZATION (preliminary version): Insert a glide before a stressed nonhigh front vowel. The nonlow vowel occurs with the round back glide; the low vowel occurs with the nonround front glide.

9.2 Alternations with schwa. Besides the alternations shown in (1) and (2), there are also some tonic/pretonic vowel alternations with schwa. The examples in the right column of (3) and (4) are cases of reduction, just like the ones discussed in connection with Fronting (cf. Chapter 8).

(3) /j/ alternates with schwa:
    viennent   venons
    tiennent   tenons
    palmier   palmeraie

(4) /wa/ alternates with schwa:
    poil   pelé
    déçois   décevons
    foin   fenil
    poids   pesant

The diphthongs (/jɛ/, /wa/) and the front unrounded low vowel (/ɛ/) form a class. This class is characterized by an alternation with schwa, which is derived via Pretonic Vowel Reduction. Pretonic Vowel Reduction, then, is a rule that can apply to three different underlying segments (that of /jɛ/, that of /wa/, and that of tonic /ɛ/) to reduce them to schwa.

On the basis of the alternations illustrated in (1)-(4), one can conclude, as in Chapter 8, Table 8.1, that the vowels under consideration are divided into three sets. One set, composed of the tonic vowels, shows the two diphthongs. The other two sets are composed of pretonic vowels. One has schwa as its sole member. The other set, composed of /e/ and /ɛ/, corresponds to the underlying segments of the two diphthongs. This parallels exactly the distinctions made in the preceding chapter, as can be seen in Table 9.1.

Table 9.1 Alternating stem vowels.

Tonic	Pretonic	
	Set 1	Set 2
wa	e	ə
je	ɛ	ə

Some similarities must be noted between the data of Chapters 8 and 9. Underlying vowels are referred to as Set 1, the reduced vowels as Set 2. Alternations which involve Set 1 vowels (the underlying set) occur between pairs of words which are derivationally related (see examples (1) and (2)). Alternations which involve Set 2 vowels (the reduced ones) occur both between derivationally related and inflectionally related forms (see examples (3) and (4)). This categorization also parallels the one shown in the preceding chapter. Furthering the parallel, we distinguish between derivational and inflectional morphology, and between native and learned vocabulary. But, as was also the case in Chapter 8, these categories are not sufficient because they do not account for pretonic phenomena (see 8.4-5 and 9.5).

9.3 A more complex alternation. Beside the alternations examined in (3) and (4), there is another alternation involving the diphthong /wa/.

(5) /wa/ alternates with /i/

poil	épiler
foi	fidélité
boire	biberon
froid	frigorification
voir	vision

This alternation suggests that there is a rule which relates the /i/ found in the right column and the /e/ of which /wa/ is the diphthongized equivalent. That rule provides strong support for the analysis just proposed.

9.4 Some rules

9.4.1 High Vowel Lowering. The alternation between /i/ and /wa/ is accounted for by means of a lowering rule, High Vowel Lowering. Suppose that /i/ is lowered to /e/ via High Vowel Lowering. Suppose further that this lowering rule applies to stressed /i/ in native forms. Then, *poil* can be derived from /pil/ via (1) High Vowel Lowering and (2) Diphthongization, in that order. *Pelu* is derived from /pilu/ via (1) High Vowel Lowering and (2) Pretonic Vowel Reduction, in that order. *Epilons*, however, is not subject to High Vowel Lowering.

> RULE. HIGH VOWEL LOWERING (preliminary version): A high front vowel becomes nonhigh in stems of certain native forms if it is stressed.

9.4.2 Pretonic Vowel Raising. Earlier in this chapter, in connection with the rule of Diphthongization, the source of the /e/ was brought up. It was noticed that both /jɛ/ and /wa/ alternate with /e/ but that these diphthongs could not be derived from the same vowel. If they were, the words diphthongized in /jɛ/ would be related to the words diphthongized in /wa/. Yet, there is no such relation. To avoid this pitfall another vowel was chosen. At the time, no justification was given for why /e/ would correspond to /wa/ and /ɛ/ to /jɛ/.

The reason for the choice of /ɛ/, alternant of /jɛ/, as the underlying low vowel and not /e/, alternant of /wa/, is that the alternant of /wa/ must be nonhigh and nonlow, in order for the /e/ issued from /i/ via High Vowel Lowering to merge with /e/ and be diphthongized. This merging is necessary for a systematic relation between the members of pairs like *pisiforme/pois, fidèle/ foi, épilons/poil*. Under the other analysis considered here, the rule which lowers /i/ would have to effect the lowering more distantly than does the preferred analysis, and would, in fact, have to do so across /e/. It is clear that this is less desirable than the simple shift from /i/ to /e/. Consequently, /e/ is the underlying segment for /wa/ and /ɛ/ underlies /jɛ/. The diphthongs /wa/ and /jɛ/ are derived via Diphthongization, a rule which is restricted later. Some /ɛ/ to which Diphthongization does not apply are subject to Pretonic Vowel Raising, the purpose of which is to provide the appropriate height to front vowels in the forms *céleste, pédestre, pédicure*.

RULE. PRETONIC VOWEL RAISING (final version): In open syllable, in learned vocabulary, pretonic low front segments become [non-low].

9.4.3 /wa/-Adjustment. Diphthongization changes /e/ to /we/, but not to /wa/. Another rule must lower /we/ to /wa/. The shift from /e/ to /wa/ in two steps is needed because nasalized diphthongs undergo only one of the two rules: Diphthongization. If Diphthongization made the shift in one fell swoop, then there would be no way to account for *foin* /fwẽ/. Instead, the incorrect */fwã/ would be generated.

RULE. /wa/-ADJUSTMENT (final version): The diphthong /we/ becomes low and nonfront (e.g. /we/ becomes /wa/).

Nasalized vowels are [low]. There are some nasalized vowels alternating with nonlow vowels. Since these nasalized vowels are derived from nonlow vowels, an adjustment rule is needed which lowers vowels that have been nasalized.

RULE. NASALIZED VOWEL LOWERING (final version): All nasalized vowels become [low].

This rule applies vacuously to low vowels. Note that /wa/-Adjustment and Nasalized Vowel Lowering are both lowering rules, but they apply to different segments and serve different purposes. The interrelation of these two rules is illustrated by the derivations for *foin* and *loi* displayed in Table 9.2.

Table 9.2 Derivations of *foin* and *loi*.

After the ... rule has applied:	... results.	
Diphthongization:	/fwen/	/lwe/
Nasalization and /N/-Deletion:	/fwẽ/	...
/wa/-Adjustment:	...	/lwa/
Nasalized Vowel Lowering:	/fwẽ/	...
	foin	*loi*

9.5 Diphthongized vowels in pretonic position. The cases of diphthongization examined so far are limited to tonic vowels. There are cases of diphthongization in pretonic position as well. The same was shown in the preceding chapter with regard to fronting. This phenomenon is now examined with respect to Diphthongization.

The forms in (6) and (7) do not exhibit vowel alternations.

(6) /j/ tiédeur   tiède
         piéton   pied
         mieleux   miel
         assiégeons   assiègent

(7) /wa/ froideur   froid
          poivron   poivre
          poirier   poire
          soirée   soir
          voyons   vois

When considering the fact that the diphthongs in (6) and (7) exhibit no alternations, one might wonder whether there is any reason to have these diphthongs derived from vowels via Diphthongization. That they are indeed derived via Diphthongization is made evident by alternations in pairs of words such as *mielleux/mellification* 'honey production', *piéton/pédale*, or *soirée/serein* 'evening bird'. In other words, there are pretonic diphthongized vowels which alternate with pretonic nondiphthongized vowels. It follows that Diphthongization cannot be restricted to vowels in tonic position. A condition must be placed on its application. That condition is the same as the one stated for Fronting: the rule applies only to vowels that are marked 'strong'. The justification for this decision will be discussed shortly. It is possible now to state the rule of Diphthongization in a way that covers both the tonic and pretonic vowels. It is not, however, stated in its final form because other factors related to the domain of application of that rule are discussed in Chapter 12.

> RULE. DIPHTHONGIZATION (nonfinal version): Strong nonhigh front vowels are strengthened by the addition of a glide: the low vowel gets a /j/, and the nonlow vowel gets a /w/.

9.6 More on vocabulary divisions. The stems of French native vocabulary are either marked or unmarked. If they are unmarked, as are *fil*, *cil*, *sec*, *fer*, *port*, *bord*, they do not alternate. Those that are marked contain vowels that alternate with vowels in one or both of two subgroups: learned forms or other marked forms.

French has a condition which causes a marked stem to lose its markedness if that stem occurs in a learned form. For example, the stem of *vois* (/vis/ in its underlying representation) is marked for alternation but if it occurs in a learned word, it loses its markedness. Put another way, it moves from *Class D* to *Class A* (8.5) under the influence of the characteristically learned suffix *-ible*. Consequently, the stem of *visible* is not subject to Diphthongization. Furthermore, the division established for Fronting is shown to be needed independently for Diphthongization. The same shift in classes applies to *imprévisible, conductible, dégustation, épilation, foliation*. Alternations between /y/ and /u/ are taken up in Chapter 10.

Another way that the division between marked and unmarked can be justified is by showing that other processes of the language are conditioned by this division. One case in point is High Vowel Lowering. Given that in the *poil* family, the /i/ of *épilation, épiler, épilatoire* alternates with both the schwa of *pelé, pelu, pelage*, and the /wa/ of *poil, poilu* (adj.), *poilu* (n.), it follows that High Vowel Lowering must lower the stem vowels of both the strong and the weak stems, which are diphthongized and reduced, respectively. The class that includes both weak and strong stems is none other than the so-called marked class. It is therefore possible to state High Vowel Lowering in terms of the class 'marked.'

> RULE. HIGH VOWEL LOWERING (preliminary version): In marked stems high front vowels become nonhigh.

The output of High Vowel Lowering serves as input to Diphthongization and Pretonic Reduction. These facts constitute strong support for the classification proposed in Section 8.5. That classification is further supported by facts about the *soir* family.

Soir, *soirée*, *sérénade*, and *serein* are related. *Sérénade* is learned; *soir*, *soirée*, and *serein* are native and marked. The first two forms are subject to Diphthongization. They are marked strong. The third must undergo Pretonic Reduction. It is marked weak. Note that the *soir* family is not subject to High Vowel Lowering. If it were, it would constitute a problem for the proposed classification because the learned forms *sérénade*, *sérénité* contain stem vowels that are nonhigh, in contrast to the high vowel in the stem of *épiler*. The underlying representation of *soir* and its relatives is not therefore */siR/ but /seR/.

Being subject to Diphthongization and to Pretonic Reduction does not seem to depend on the derivational suffixes associated with these forms, as the alternations *poil/pelé* and *soir/soirée* demonstrate. If /e/ were a morpheme that determines the class of *soirée* and *pelé*, then both would be diphthongized or reduced. The fact that one is diphthongized while the other is reduced strongly supports the conclusion reached in Chapter 8, that the divisions between those items which undergo weakening rules and those which are strengthened must be made arbitrarily. Morphological support for this classification is only accidental, as shown in what follows.

The fact that the verb *épiler* is to be viewed as learned and therefore a member of *Class A*, does not follow from any morphological evidence. Nothing about its form makes it different from *filer*, which does not alternate and which falls into *Class B*, the unmarked class.

Another caveat is in order regarding the classification proposed here. While the members of the marked class have been shown to alternate, that does not exclude *Class D* from containing forms which do not alternate. Such is the case with *poivre*, *soie*, *veuve*, *craindre*. These forms are subject to strengthening rules which derive them from forms that contain underlying vowels corresponding to /wa/, /œ/, and /ɛ/, namely, /e/, /ɔ/, and /a/, respectively.

As for the application of Diphthongization and Fronting to forms alternating within inflectional morphology (*peuvent/pouvons*, *reçois/recevons*), French has a condition that applies to this highly limited set of verbs to mark their tonic vowels as strong. It is precisely that which makes them subject to the strengthening rules discussed in Chapters 8 and 9.

9.7 Ordering the rules.

9.7.1 Diphthongization and Fronting.
Since both Diphthongization and Fronting apply to strong segments (i.e. they have the same conditioning environment), it is possible that these rules may need to be ordered with respect to each other in order to derive the proper forms. The derivation displayed in Table 9.3 assumes that Fronting applies before Diphthongization.

Table 9.3 Incorrect derivation for *clair*, *ciel*, *fleur*.

	clair	*ciel*	*fleur*
Underlying form:	/klaʀ/	/sɛl/	/flɔʀ/
Fronting:	/klɛʀ/	/sɛl/	/flœʀ/
Diphthongization:	*/kljɛʀ/	/sjel/	*/fljœʀ/

This demonstrates that if Fronting is applied before Diphthongization the forms *clair* and *fleur* cannot be correctly derived since they would be incorrectly diphthongized.

If, on the other hand, the rule of Diphthongization is applied before the rule for Fronting, as the derivation displayed in Table 9.4 shows, then both the diphthongs and the fronted vowels can be correctly derived.

Table 9.4 Correct derivation for *clair*, *ciel*, *fleur*.

	clair	*ciel*	*fleur*
Underlying form:	/klaʀ/	/sɛl/	/flɔʀ/
Diphthongization:	. . .	/sjel/	. . .
Fronting:	/klɛʀ/	/sjel/	/flœʀ/

The derivation in Table 9.4 shows no ungrammatical forms. The forms *clair*, *ciel*, and *fleur* can be properly derived because Diphthongization applies to underlying front vowels, not to front vowels derived via Fronting. For this reason Diphthongization should be ordered before Fronting.

9.7.2 High Vowel Lowering and /wa/-Adjustment.
The purpose of High Vowel Lowering is to relate /i/ and /wa/ by lowering /i/ to /e/ in order to make it subject to Diphthongization. It follows that High Vowel Lowering must apply before Diphthongization. Indeed, one might say that High Vowel Lowering 'feeds' Diphthongization.

The rule for /wa/-Adjustment, by its very nature, must follow Diphthongization. Its purpose is to provide the second of two necessary steps in relating /e/ and /wa/. The first step, /e/ to /wa/, is provided by Diphthongization. The second step, /we/ to /wa/, applies only to oral vowels, as explained in

Section 9.4.3. As for /wa/-Adjustment, it cannot precede Fronting. If it did, Fronting would make /wa/ front, i.e. change it to */we/. Instead, if Fronting is applied before /wa/-Adjustment, the resulting order avoids /wa/ being fronted in such a way as to derive incorrect forms.

Thus, these rules obey the following ordering constraints:
1. High Vowel Lowering must precede Diphthongization.
2. Diphthongization must precede Fronting.
3. Diphthongization must precede /wa/-Adjustment.
4. Fronting must precede /wa/-Adjustment.
5. Fronting is indirectly ordered with respect to High Vowel Lowering. It must follow Diphthongization, which follows High Vowel Lowering.

These ordering requirements are satisfied if the four rules apply in the order displayed in Table 9.5 for the derivation of *poil*, *soir*, and *fleur*.

Table 9.5 Derivation of *poil*, *soir*, *fleur*.

	poil	*soir*	*fleur*
Underlying representation:	/pil/	/seR/	/flɔR/
High Vowel Lowering:	/pel/	...	...
Diphthongization:	/pwel/	/sweR/	...
Fronting:	...	...	/flœR/
/wa/-Adjustment:	/pwal/	/swaR/	...

9.8 Questions

1. Why is it more logical to assume that /e/ underlies /wa/ and /ɛ/ underlies /jɛ/ and /je/, rather than the other way around, or rather than have /e/ underlie both diphthongs?

2. If /wa/ alternates with /ə/ and /e/, how can you account for the alternation between *foi* and *fidélité*? How would you modify Table 9.1 to account for these facts?

3. Go through the derivation of: (a) *ciel*, (b) *soir*, and (c) *foi*. What is different between the derivation of *soir* and *foi*?

4. How does *foin* constitute evidence for a two-step derivation to relate /e/ and /wa/? Go through the derivation to illustrate, making sure to try both the one-step and two-step solution.

5. Given that the normal stress in Spanish is on the penultimate syllable, formulate a Diphthongization rule for Spanish on the basis of the following data:

Learned	Native	Inflectional		Derivational	
óvalo	huevo	podemos	- puedo	portal	- puerta
gélido	hielo	contar	- cuento	moblaje	- mueble
		acordar	- acuerdo		
		pensar	- piensan		
		tenemos	- tienen		
		perdemos	- pierdes		

6. Can Diphthongization apply to fronted vowels? If it does, what are the consequences? If it does not, how is that accomplished?

7. Given the learned form for each of the following entries, you are to provide the corresponding native form, the tonic vowel that corresponds to the italicized nontonic vowel in the learned form, and the rule which is responsible for that change.

Learned forms	Native forms	Tonic vowel	Rule
annu*a*lité			
sud*o*ripare			
f*a*mine			
r*é*galien			
c*a*pripède			
s*o*roraux			
vulg*a*rité			
s*é*rénade			
m*a*ritime			
p*é*destre			

8. If Round Vowel Raising and/or Pretonic Vowel Reduction applied to diphthongized segments and/or to fronted vowels, then the words in the left column would be derived as the incorrect forms which you are to record in the right column.

aimable	*/	/
feuillage	*/	/
piéton	*/	/
soirée	*/	/

Chapter 10
High vowels . . . front!

10.0 Introduction. This chapter is concerned primarily with the derivation of /y/ and /u/. It is shown here that /y/ is derived from /u/. The arguments used in support of this derivation hinge on generalization.

The chapter is organized as follows. First, the vowels which occur typically in learned vocabulary are examined (10.1). It is concluded that the learned portion of the vocabulary of French exhibits fewer vowels than the native portion, and that their arrangement is quite revealing regarding the structure of the language. Second, alternations which suggest that the fronting tendency is even greater than discussed earlier are examined and a solution is proposed (10.2). Third, a number of changes are brought to some previously discussed rules, resulting in generalizations (10.3, 10.4). Finally, the order of application of all the rules discussed in this chapter is stated (10.5).

10.1 The vowels of learned vocabulary. Learned vocabulary and native vocabulary differ in several ways. In particular, learned vocabulary is remarkably free of any pretonic nonhigh front rounded vowel, of diphthongs, or of pretonic schwa. In other words, the first vowel of *solitude* is [back], not [front] as that of *seul*; the second vowel of *épilation* is not a diphthong, as is that of *poil*; and the first vowel of *granulité* is /a/, not schwa, as is that of *grenier*. *Solitude*, *épilation*, *granulité* are learned forms; *seul*, *poil*, *grenier* are native forms. Some rules apply to the latter which do not apply to the former. In these cases, Pretonic Vowel Reduction applies exclusively to native forms; Fronting and Diphthongization do not apply to pretonic vowels in learned vocabulary. Consequently, the vowels derived by means of these restricted rules are not found in learned vocabulary.

Another vowel not found in learned forms is /u/, in whose stead the high front rounded vowel /y/ is found. The presence of /y/ and the absence of /u/ lead to a notable asymmetry, as can be seen in Table 10.1.

Table 10.1 The asymmetrical distribution of vowels which occur in learned vocabulary.

	Front	Center	Back
High	i / y		
Mid	e		o
Low	ɛ	a	ɔ

For this asymmetry to be resolved, the /y/ in Table 10.1 should be replaced by /u/ and occur in the column for the back vowels. Suppose that this were true in the underlying representation of all forms. Then, a sweeping rule which fronts /u/ could create the vocalic system illustrated in Table 10.1. This analysis is the one adopted here.

On the other hand, one might wonder why an asymmetric vowel system is found undesirable. This question is taken up in Section 10.2.1 in connection with the relative merits of a fronting or a backing analysis.

10.2 Fronting

10.2.1 /u/ and /y/ in native and learned forms. The tendency to front is not limited to the Fronting rule discussed in Chapter 8. In addition to the alternations already discussed which motivate Fronting as a rule, there are also alternations between high vowels. Some low vowel alternations are repeated here in (1) and (2). High vowel alternations which also take place between learned and native vocabulary, are shown in (3).

10.2.1 /u/ and /y/ in native and learned forms

(1) /ɔ/ alternates with /œ/:

floral	fleur
solitude	seul
majorité	majeur

(2) /a/ alternates with /ɛ/:

clarté	clair
santé	sain
salière	sel

(3) /y/ alternates with /u/:

surdité	sourd
bifurcation	fourche
pulsation	pouls
ébulition	bout
rubescent	rouge
incubation	couve
curviligne	courbe
pulvériser	poudre
buccal	bouche

In (1)-(3), a vowel in a learned word (left) alternates with a vowel in a native word (right). The three sets of forms seem to bear a striking resemblance. However, this resemblance is limited. On the one hand, the fact that the learned forms in (1) and (2) contain the vowel which underlies the equivalent vowel in native forms would suggest that /y/, which occurs in learned forms, should be the underlying representation from which /u/ is derived. On the other hand, the fact that, in (1) and (2), the nonfront vowel underlies a front vowel would suggest that /u/, a back vowel, should be the underlying vowel from which /y/ is derived. Examining (1)-(3) results, therefore, in a dilemma. This dilemma is resolved by considering the consequences of each possibility (i.e. Fronting or Backing) and deciding on the more acceptable rule by determining what consequences each would have for the rest of the phonological rules of French. The Backing Rule and its consequences are evaluated first. In other words, it is now assumed that /u/ is derived from /y/.

First, the existence of a rule that would back high vowels suggests that there is no high back round vowel in the underlying representation of French words. Such a claim is not natural because it produces an asymmetric system with back nonhigh vowels but no back high vowels, as in Table 10.1. Furthermore, in light of the discussion in Chapter 8, there are no nonhigh front rounded vowels in the underlying system of French. Yet, by the reasoning consonant with the Backing of front vowels, there would be a high front rounded vowel. This asymmetrical arrangement requires that the vowels /i/ and /y/ be distinguished in the underlying representation by the feature [round] while the roundness of /œ/ is a natural consequence of the application of Fronting. On the other hand, if /y/ were derived from /u/ via Fronting, then the roundness of the front vowel /y/ would be a natural consequence of Fronting in exactly the same way as it is for /oe/.

Second, given an alternation between front and back vowels in French, it is unnatural to expect that the high back vowel should be derived from a front vowel when phonetic and phonological evidence points unambiguously to a process of vowel fronting as characteristic of French (cf. 8.7.5, for examples).

Third, such a proposal would make the grammar more complex. A rule creating a back vowel /u/ as an alternant of /y/ could not be stated as simply as examples in (3) might suggest: there are also cases of /u/ in pretonic position.

(4) Pretonic /y/ alternates with pretonic /u/:

culpabilité	coupable
ébulition	bouillon
incubateur	couveuse
rubescent	rougeur
cursif	courir
nutrition	nourrison

Hence, a Backing rule would have to apply to both tonic and pretonic vowels. Deriving /u/ from /y/ would therefore require a more complex rule than deriving /y/ from /u/ which is stated, in 10.4, as an unrestricted and simple shift of all high back vowels. Furthermore, it is better to have two rules conspiring toward the same end than two apparently conflicting rules.

Fourth, consider the symmetrical argument discussed in 10.1. If it is assumed that there is a Fronting rule which derives /y/ from /u/, then an explanation is automatically provided for the otherwise unexplained asymmetric arrangement of the learned vowel system of French. A Backing rule would fail to show /y/ functioning as the high back rounded vowel par excellence in the learned portion of French vocabulary.

In conclusion, evidence stemming from the arrangement of the underlying system of French vowels, from the general tendency of fronting, and from the resulting simplification and general integration of the phonological rules of French, strongly supports the claim that the direction of derivation relating to alternations illustrated in (3) and (4) is from back to front.

10.2.2 Nonalternating /y/ and /u/. In addition to the set of alternating high vowels of (3), there are others which exhibit no alternations.

(5) Tonic /y/ and pretonic /y/:

mur	emmurer
dure	durons

sûr	sûreté
nu	nudisme

(6) Tonic /u/ and pretonic /u/:

trouve	trouvaille
ouvre	ouvrons
soupe	soupière
lourd	lourdeur

The fact that there are such pairs as those in (5) and (6) might be interpreted as evidence against a rule of Fronting which would apply to high vowels. The argument would be as follows: since there are high front rounded segments which do not alternate with high back rounded segments in any environment, and high back rounded segments which do not alternate with high front rounded segments, then there should be no fronting (or backing) of high vowels. On the other hand, since there are alternations, as (3) shows, between the front and back high rounded vowels, there should exist a rule relating the learned and native forms where /y/ and /u/ occur, respectively. Such a rule would front any /u/ occurring in learned vocabulary. This topic is taken up in the next section.

10.3 Generalizing rules

10.3.1 Fronting. If a high vowel fronting rule were limited so as to apply only to learned forms, then the alternations of (3) and (4) would be accounted for but the problem of asymmetry would remain. The underlying system of French would contain a high front rounded vowel, as found in (5), but no nonhigh front rounded vowels, which are derived as shown in Chapter 8. This problem can be resolved, however, by making the fronting of high vowels apply to all forms instead of restricting its application to learned vocabulary. This is the preferred analysis.

An apparent problem with this reasoning is the following. There must be a way of preventing the /u/ of (3) and (4) from becoming [front]. If these segments were fronted, incorrect forms would result: */pʀyv/ instead of /pʀuv/, */syʀ/ instead of /suʀ/, etc. The solution to this apparent problem lies in part in the generalization of High Vowel Lowering.

10.3.2 High Vowel Lowering generalized. In the preceding chapter, a lowering rule was shown to relate native and learned forms. These are reproduced here for convenience.

(7) /i/ alternates with /wa/:

pisiforme	pois
épiler	poil
fidélité	foi
frigorification	froid

The rule of High Vowel Lowering was stated in terms of high front rounded vowels in marked stems. If it were stated more generally, in terms of all high vowels in marked stems, then it would apply to /u/ as well. In other words, the /u/ in the right column of (3) and (4) would be lowered to /o/, making it no longer subject to Fronting. Fronting could, in turn, apply to all remaining high vowels, irrespective of environment.

>RULE. HIGH VOWEL LOWERING (final version): in marked stems, high vowels become nonhigh.

Generalizing Fronting and High Vowel Lowering affords a solution to the relation between /y/ and /u/ illustrated in (3). Still, the /u/ of (6) must be derived. This requires a lengthier explanation and, in particular, a review and modification of previously discussed rules.

10.3.3 Generalizing Pretonic Vowel Adjustment. In Chapter 8, the behavior of pretonic vowels was accounted for by means of two rules: Pretonic Vowel Reduction and Pretonic Round Vowel Raising. These rules were stated so as to apply to nonhigh unrounded vowels and low rounded vowels, respectively. The effect, if not the stated intent, of these rules was to lower /e/, to raise /ɔ/, and to reduce low vowels to /ə/. The purpose of this section is to state these facts in terms of an improved set of rules to replace Pretonic Round Vowel Raising and Pretonic Vowel Reduction.

Pretonic Vowel Reduction reduces /a/, /ɛ/, and /e/ to /ə/. This can be deduced from the following alternations.

(8) Various alternations with /ə/:

manuel	main	menotte
pédestre	pied	peton
...	viens	venons
sérénité	soir	serein 'evening bird'
palmature	palmier	palmeraie

The reduction of low unrounded vowels to /ə/ is more natural than that of /e/, which requires an additional feature change, i.e. from [nonlow] to [low]. If the latter change were to be effected by another rule, then reduction could be stated more naturally.

>RULE. LOW VOWEL REDUCTION (preliminary version): Pretonic low vowels marked weak become [central] and [lax].

This rule accomplishes two-thirds of what Pretonic Vowel Reduction was designed to do. It reduces /ɛ/ and /a/ but it does not lower or reduce /e/. If /e/ were lowered to /ɛ/ before Low Vowel Reduction applies, then Low Vowel Reduction would, in fact, reduce as many vowels as Pretonic Vowel Reduction does, but it would do so more naturally. The lowering of /e/ to /ɛ/ is now shown.

Pretonic Round Vowel Raising (cf. Section 8.3.1) was shown to take part in relating alternants of pairs such as those found in (9) and (10).

(9) /ɔ/ alternates with /u/:

mort	mourant
endolori	douloureux
volonté	vouloir

(10) /œ/ alternates with /u/:

peuvent	pouvons
veulent	vouloir
douleur	douloureux

These alternations motivate a rule that would shift low vowels to high vowels, not the more expected low to mid shift. But if recalling that /y/ is really a fronted /u/, it is not unreasonable to assume that /u/ is really a raised /o/. In other words, the fact that /ɔ/ alternates with /u/ is predicated by two other factors: the sweeping shift from /u/ to /y/, which empties the high back position, and a shift from /o/ to /u/ which then fills that position. The raising from low to high is therefore better justified if it occurs in two steps. The first step and its relation to other shifts is discussed first.

Now that it appears more natural to raise the low vowel to mid, it should be noted that such a shift is the complement of the one still left undone in the front unrounded system, namely, /e/ to /ɛ/. These two shifts, one up and one down, one applying to back rounded vowels and the other to front unrounded vowels, constitute a mere adjustment. This adjustment in the pretonic vowel system is a rule, Pretonic Vowel Adjustment; it replaces both Pretonic Round Vowel Raising and the shifting portion of Pretonic Vowel Reduction.

> RULE. PRETONIC VOWEL ADJUSTMENT: Pretonic vowels that are marked weak become [low] if they are [nonround], or [nonlow] if they are [round].

It is now possible to consider the second step in the raising of back vowels.

10.3.4 Back Vowel Raising. In Section 10.3.2, an argument is presented that shows that the fronting of high vowels can be generalized if it is assumed that /u/ in some stems is lowered to /o/. It was shown that this lowering rule would be more general if it applied to /u/ along with /i/, for which it was formulated in the first place. The same argument of generalization now applies to the raising of /o/ to /u/.

First, a rule is needed to raise pretonic /o/ to /u/ to account for the alternations illustrated in (9) and (10).

Second, the /o/ derived from /u/ lowered by High Vowel Lowering needs to be raised to /u/ to provide the correct phonetic result. The result should be not */sor/, but /sur/ (*sourd*); not */forʃ/, but /furʃ/ (*fourche*); not */po/, but /pu/ (*poul*).

Third, because it was decided that the fronting of /u/ is applicable to all forms regardless of the environment, forms like those of (6), where /u/ does not alternate, cannot be /u/ in the underlying representation. For the resulting form should be not */tryve/, but /truve/; not */syrdin/, but /surdin/; and so on. Consequently, the vowel of *trouve* should be [nonhigh] in the underlying representation.

For these three independent reasons, a rule is needed to raise /o/ to /u/ in all environments. This rule is Back Vowel Raising.

> RULE. BACK VOWEL RAISING (final version): All nonlow back vowels become [high].

A logical but uninformed reaction to this rule might be that it eliminates all /o/ sounds from the French sound system. Chapter 11 provides an explanation for this incorrect conclusion.

10.4 Two fronting rules. Until now, the term 'fronting' has been used to refer to both the rule stated in Chapter 8 and the seeping flow described here. The latter, as has been observed, is not restricted in any way, whereas the former applies only to strong vowels. While it would not be impossible to state both processes in just one rule, they are stated separately in order to underscore their differences with respect to their domains, and also to reflect the plurality of effects which the general tendency to front vowels has brought about in the French language. Consequently, the rule presented in Chapter 8 is henceforth called Low Vowel Fronting. It is stated here for convenience.

> RULE. LOW VOWEL FRONTING (final version): Low vowels become [front] if they are marked strong.

The fronting of the high vowel is effected by High Vowel Fronting, as shown here.

> RULE. HIGH VOWEL FRONTING (final version): High vowels become [front].

This division into two rules enables this analysis to provide for a formal distinction between rules like Low Vowel Fronting and Diphthongization, both of which are morphologically conditioned, and rules like Back Vowel Raising and High Vowel Fronting, which are not restricted to any forms. If there were a single fronting rule, these differences between rule types would be blurred.

10.5 Ordering the rules. The ordering of application of the rules just discussed must not be in conflict with the rule ordering of the previous chapter. It is not. The order shown previously was:

(1) High Vowel Lowering
(2) Diphthongization
(3) Fronting
(4) /wa/-Adjustment

Taking into account the fact that there are now two rules which front vowels, the order of the relevant rules is as shown here, where the arrows point from the preceding to the following rules.

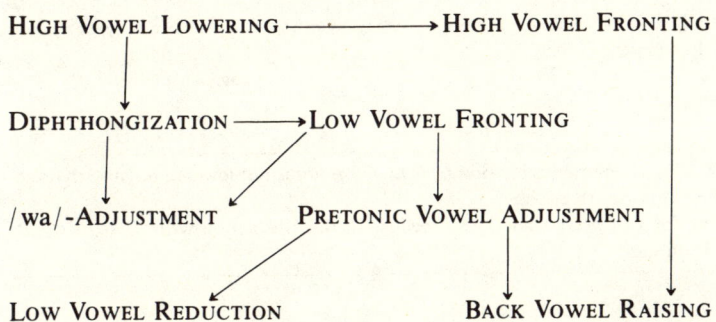

High Vowel Lowering was shown to precede Diphthongization, which it feeds. It must also precede High Vowel Fronting, which it bleeds. Pretonic Vowel Adjustment precedes Low Vowel Reduction, which it feeds. In other words, Pretonic Vowel Adjustment lowers /e/ in order to make it subject to Low Vowel Reduction. Neither of these rules is ordered with respect to Pretonic Vowel Raising, which applies to learned forms. Pretonic Vowel Adjustment must precede Back Vowel Raising, which it feeds. It raises /ɔ/ to /o/, which Back Vowel Raising shifts to /u/. Back Vowel Raising must follow High Vowel Lowering, which feeds it, and High Vowel Fronting, which it must not feed. If Back Vowel Raising preceded High Vowel Lowering, there would be words like */bojɔ̃/ instead of the correct /bujɔ̃/ (*bouillons*). If Back Vowel Raising preceded High Vowel Fronting, there would be words like */byjɔ̃/ instead of /bujɔ̃/, because High Vowel Fronting would have applied to the wrong vowel. Instead, if High Vowel Lowering applies first, followed by High Vowel Fronting and Pretonic Vowel Adjustment (which are not ordered with respect to each other), and by Back Vowel Raising, then the correct forms are produced. An illustration of this ordering is shown in Table 10.2.

10.6 Conclusion. The most important point of this chapter is that by searching for the (possibly abstract) general tendency of the language and allowing the tendency to be expressed by rules relating word families, it is possible to simplify what in previous chapters appeared to be highly complex statements. The resulting simpler statements are possible because they form

86 / 10 High vowels ... front!

a network, a system. They are discrete but interdependent rules stating relations that characterize the sound system of French.

Many more such rules exist. Some are discussed in subsequent chapters.

Table 10.2 Derivation of *pelu, poilu, sûr, surdité, sourd,* and *pouvons.*

	pelu	poilu	sûr	surdité	sourd	pouvons
Underlying representation	pilu	pilu	suR	suRdite	suRd	pɔvɔ̃[2]
High Vowel Lowering	pelu[1]	pelu[1]	...	...	soRd	...
Diphthongization	...	pwelu	...	...	...	...
High Vowel Fronting	pely	pwely	syR	syRdite	...	...
Pretonic Vowel Adjustment	pely	...	...	...	...	povɔ̃
Back Vowel Raising	...	...	...	...	suRd	puvɔ̃
Low Vowel Reduction	pəly	...	...	...	...	...
/wa/-Adjustment	...	pwaly	...	...	...	...

[1] The /u/ in the underlying representation of *pelu* and *poilu* is not lowered because the rule applies to stems of words, not to endings.
[2] The underlying form of *pouvons* has /ɔ/ because of the alternation with /œ/ (*peuvent*) accounted for by Fronting.

10.7 Questions

1. State in your own words the apparent inconsistencies which the data in examples (1)-(3) would suggest. How are these problems resolved?

2. Using a dictionary, find as many members of the *sel* family as you can. Then draw conclusions on the appropriate underlying form for *sel.*

3. What problem would result if Low Vowel Reduction were made to precede Pretonic Vowel Adjustment?

4. Why must Low Vowel Fronting precede Pretonic Vowel Adjustment? Answer negatively, that is, assume that Low Vowel Fronting is ordered after Pretonic Vowel Adjustment.

5. How is the word *douleur* derived? Is the derivation of *douleur* consistent with that of *douloureux*?

6. Why are High Vowel Fronting and Low Vowel Fronting not ordered with respect to each other? Does your answer constitute grounds for combining them into one rule? Use the rule ordering requirements of each as grounds for keeping them separate. Why are the arguments you have just presented not as strong as the ones requiring that Diphthongization and /wa/-Adjustment be different rules?

7. Find another argument why Diphthongization and /wa/-Adjustment must be kept separate. Assume that they are combined, yielding /wa/ directly from /e/. Examine the ordering established in 9.7.1. Determine how Diphthongization in its combined form can function within that ordering. State your argument why these rules must be kept apart.

Chapter 11
Other oral vowels

11.0 Introduction. The interdependency of the whole sound system of French makes it difficult to segregate clearly each group of segments into discrete classes. Rules, for example, reach across the arbitrary boundaries of chapters. Therefore it should not surprise the reader that remarks about previously discussed material reoccur in this and subsequent chapters. As the overall picture of the total sound system of French becomes clearer, some previous statements need to be modified. This is especially true in this chapter since it is a summary.

11.1 The syllable. A syllable in French is a structure composed of one obligatory vowel segment and of optional nonsyllabic segments before and after that vowel. Using V for vowel and C for nonsyllabic segment, it is possible to state that the syllables of a given language may be of the form V, CV, VC, CVC, CCV, etc. The vowel in a syllable is known as 'peak' of the syllable. C-segments to the left of the peak are called the 'onset' of the syllable; those to the right are the 'coda' of the syllable. Syllables are said to be 'open' if they have no coda, 'closed' if they have a coda. For the purposes of this chapter, this definition is slightly stretched: it is assumed here (until the notion is sharpened in Chapter 15) that both *bel* and *belle* constitute closed syllables.

11.2 Nonalternating vowels

11.2.1 /a/, /u/, /ɔ/, /y/, and /i/. In Chapters 8 and 10 rules are presented which derive vowels by shifting some to [front] and raising others to [high]. For example, /a/ was fronted to /ɛ/, /ɔ/ to /œ/, /u/ to /y/; /o/ was raised to /u/. Not all vowels, however, are subject to shifts. When they do not shift, they tend to create nonalternations. Some stem vowels are subject to a sweeping rule, like High Vowel Fronting, or Back Vowel Raising. In such cases there tend also not to be alternations.

(1) Unstressed /a/ and stressed /á/
    chevalier   cheval
    préparatifs   prépare
    lavons   laves

(2) Unstressed /ɔ/ and stressed /ɔ́/
    tonnerre   tonne
    sottise   sotte
    collons   collent

(3) Unstressed /u/ and stressed /ú/
  broutait   broute
  croûton   croûte
  poulailler   poule

(4) Unstressed /y/ and stressed /ý/
  muraille   mur
  durons   dure
  lunaire   lune

In (1) there is no alternation because Low Vowel Fronting does not apply to these words. In (3) there is no alternation because Back Vowel Raising raised all back mid vowels to [high]. In (4) there is no alternation because High Vowel Fronting applied to all high back vowels.

In Chapter 9, High Vowel Lowering, which lowers /i/ to /e/, was discussed and it was generalized in 10.3.2 to also lower /u/. Not all /i/ and /u/ segments are subject to this rule. The high round back segments which are not lowered are subject to High Vowel Fronting. They become [front] (/u/ → /y/). But the front unrounded segments which are not lowered remain unchanged. They are found in pairs of words such as those in (5).

(5) Unstressed /i/ and stressed /í/
  Niçois   Nice
  village   ville
  rions   rient
  millier   mille

The nonalternations of vowels in (1) to (5) are, therefore, due either to the nonapplication of a rule to either form of the pairs or to the application of a rule to both forms. In terms of the vocabulary classes established in Figure 8.1, in 8.5, the nonalternating vowels are found in *Class B*.

11.2.2 Vowels in unrelated words. Other nonalternations of vowels exist. For example, there are words which occur in only one form and do not appear to be related to any other: borrowed words like *képi*, *week-end*, *Gruyère*; native words like *pavot*, *pègre*, *peu*; or function words like the conjunction *et*, the adverb *presque*, and the preposition *dans*.

Some of these words are given an underlying representation exactly like their surface representation; *képi* is a good example. Other words are given the 'free ride'. For example, *Gruyère* is subject to Gliding, and *pavot* has /ɔ/ in its underlying representation in order to escape the application of Back Vowel Raising which would change /pavo/ into the incorrect */pavu/. It undergoes a rule which changes /ɔ/ to /o/ in tonic position (cf. Section 11.3). *Pavot* and *et* have no final consonants in their underlying representations, whereas *dans* has, because of sequences like *dans un panier*, where liaison takes place. The vowel /e/ is found in *képi* and *et*; /ɛ/ is in *Gruyère*, *pègre*, *presque*, and *week-end*; /i/ is in *week-end* and the /ɛ/ is nasalized to produce the /ɛ̃/ of *week-end*, which rhymes with *Les Indes*. The underlying representation of *peu* is /pɔ/. Low Vowel Fronting and a rule discussed in Section 11.3 give it its proper form.

11.2.3 Alternations with syllabic conditioning. In Chapter 9, Diphthongization was shown to apply to /e/ and /ɛ/, converting them to /we/ and /jɛ/, respectively. There are, however, words in which /ɛ/ and /e/ are not subject to Diphthongization.

(6) /e/ in open syllables alternates with /ɛ/ in closed syllables
 scellons   scellent
 cédons   céderont
 régnant   règnent
 téter   tète

(7) /ə/ in open syllables alternates with /ɛ/ in closed syllables
 levant   lève
 hôtelier   hôtel-Dieu
 recelons   recèlent
 pesons   pèse-bébé

The underlying vowel for the forms of (6) is /e/. It must be changed to /ɛ/ to account for the words in the right column. As can be seen at a glance, the change from /e/ to /ɛ/ is not dependent on stress: both tonic and atonic /ɛ/ can be found, as the right column illustrates. The alternations in (6) are accounted for by a rule which lowers underlying vowels.

 RULE. CLOSED SYLLABLE ADJUSTMENT (final version): In closed syllables nonhigh segments are made [low].

The rule needed to account for the alternations found in (7) was given in Chapter 10. It is slightly amended here to account for new information.

 RULE. LOW VOWEL REDUCTION (amended but not final version): In open syllable, pretonic low vowels marked weak become [central] and [lax].

The only difference between this rule and its earlier version is the reference to syllable structure.

11.2.4 Vowel harmony. Some pretonic low vowels in open syllables assimilate partially in vowel height with the vowel in the following syllable. For instance, the /ɛ/ of *tête* remains [low] in *têtard* but is [nonlow] in *têtu*. Table 11.1 illustrates this point. Vowel harmony is more frequent for the nonround /e/ and /ɛ/ than for the round front vowels, /ø/ and /œ/, and negligible if it exists at all for the back vowels, /o/ and /ɔ/.

French vowel harmony is achieved in terms of relative height of the conditioning vowel. Two limitations are worth noting. First, the tendency is always

Table 11.1.

/ɛ/ in CVC	/ɛ/ before low V	/e/ before nonlow V
fête	fêtard	fêtée
fesse	fesseur	fessue
serre	serrons	serrée
sommeil	sommeillons	sommeillez
bête	bêta	bêtise

/œ/ in CVC	/œ/ before low V	/ø/ before nonlow V
beugle	beuglement	beugler
abreuve	abreuvoir	abreuvée

toward closure; that is, no vowels harmonize by causing a wider opening of the mouth. For example, the following low vowel does not cause the /e/ to open to /ɛ/ in *téléphone, étang, état,* or *équerre*. Second, the raising caused by vowel harmony is only from [low] to [nonlow] and never reaches [high]. In other words, there is no raising from /ɛ/ or /e/ to /i/: the word is /fesy/, not */fisy/; /betiz/, not */bitiz/.

> RULE. VOWEL HARMONY (final version): In open syllable, word-internally, a low vowel followed by a syllable whose peak is [nonlow] becomes [nonlow].

11.3 The vowels /o/ and /ø/

11.3.1 Low vowels alternating with nonlow vowels: /œ ~ ø/, /ɔ ~ o/. When a stressed [low] [round] vowel is in an open syllable, it must become [nonlow]. It is a phonetic fact of French that stressed rounded vowels in open syllables must be [nonlow].

(8) Low and nonlow vowels in CVC and CV alternants.

sotte	sot
dévote	dévot
veulent	vœu
peuvent	peut
boeuf	boeufs

Consequently, a rule is needed that will raise /œ/ and /ɔ/ to /ø/ and /o/, respectively. It is called En-Haut.

There are also words where /o/ and /ø/ occur before a segment /z/. Although this tendency is not used by all speakers of French, it is nevertheless fairly general. See Table 11.2. This vowel raising from /ɔ/ to /o/ and /œ/ to /ø/ could be accounted for by a single rule with two environments: one in word-final position, the other before /z/. There is, however, evidence which points to these as two different processes.

Table 11.2

/øz/	/œC/*	/oz/	/ɔC/*
creuse	peur	close	clore
berceuse	berceur	prose	fort
heureuse	veuf	rose	rosse
Meuse	jeune	chose	roche

*Here /C/ does not include /z/.

First, the [nonhigh] vowel before a /z/, which may be /o/ or /ø/, is found in tonic and pretonic position. Some examples are *heureusement*, *creuset*, *deuxième*, *rosette*, *rosin*, *arroser*, *rosée*, *oser*, *poser*, *érosion*, *composition*, *préposition*, *générosité*, *gosier*. In other words, the rule raising /œ/ and /ɔ/ to /ø/ and /o/ before /z/ must apply to both tonic and nontonic vowels. The vowel raising rule, En-Haut, is restricted to stressed vowels. The environment of these two rules is therefore more distinct than first imagined.

Another factor suggesting that there are two separate rules is related to length. The segments /ø/ and /o/ in word-final position are shorter than before /z/.

Furthermore, not all speakers of French share these rules. All speakers share the final round vowel raising but a substantial number of speakers do not raise /ɔ/ to /o/ or /œ/ to /ø/ before /z/. While there is evidence that the vowel raising before /z/ is gaining ground, it is not universally distributed. For those who have only the final segment raising rule, the raising before /z/ is not an inherent part of their grammar and they are likely to learn raising before /z/ as a separate rule.

In conclusion, there are two different rules: vowel raising before /z/ or Zaizing, and the raising of final /ɔ/, called En-Haut, for obvious mnemonic effect.

RULE. ZAIZING (final version): Round vowels before /z/ become [nonlow] and [long].

RULE. EN-HAUT (final version): Stressed round vowels in open syllable position become [nonlow].

Pairs of words like *jouons*/*jeu*, *voulons*/*vœu*, *nouons*/*nœu* exhibit an alternation between /u/ and /ø/. The relation of these words is accounted for by Low Vowel Fronting, Pretonic Vowel Adjustment, Back Vowel Raising, and En-Haut, as illustrated in Table 11.3. (The inflectional morphemes are not derived, as they are not relevant to the point illustrated.)

11.3.2 /o/-adjustment rules. In contrast to the rules just discussed, which are phonologically conditioned, other rules, which are morphologically conditioned, also derive /o/ and /ø/. They are adjustment rules and apply to a handful of words.

11 Other oral vowels

Table 11.3 Derivation of some words with /o/ and /ø/: *nouer, nœu, (je) noue, (il) veut.*

	nouer	*nœu*	*(je) noue*	*(il) veut*
Underlying representation	nɔ-e	nɔ-ə	nɔ-s	vɔ-t
Low Vowel Fronting	...	nœ	...	vœ-t
Pretonic Vowel Adjustment	no-e	...	no-s	...
Back Vowel Raising	nu-e	...	nu-s	...
En-Haut	...	nø	...	vø-t
Final Consonant Deletion	...	...	nu	vø

11.3.2.1 /o/ from /ɔs/. One of these rules, /ɔs/-Adjustment, relates few alternants.

(9) /ɔs/   /o:/   /ɔ/
     costal   côte
     hospitaliser   hôpital
                        hôte   hôtesse

While there are few alternations to support a rule deriving long /o:/ from /ɔs/, other factors suggest its existence. Spelling supports the rule, as can be seen in more archaic words such as those found in place names: *Les Vosges, L'Osne,* both pronounced with /o:/. The possessives *notre* /nɔtR/ and *le nôtre* /ləno:tR/, although they do not alternate with any French word with /ɔs/ (*Nostradamus* notwithstanding), are historically derived from /nostr-/. The adjective form, *notre,* is not stressed, whereas the pronoun form, *le nôtre,* is always stressed. Another mirror of the history of these forms can be observed through the 'window' provided by the forms borrowed by English before /s/ was dropped in French.

(10) French   English
     côte   coast
     hôte   host
     hôpital   hospital

The advantage in retaining this rule is that the length of /o:/ before voiceless stops is explained. Phonetically, it should be short before /p/, /t/, /k/. The application of /ɔs/-Adjustment makes the vowel long.

> RULE. /ɔs/-ADJUSTMENT (final version): In native forms, before a consonantal segment tonic /ɔs/ becomes /o:/ and atonic /ɔs/ drops the /s/.

11.3.2.2 Coalescence: /al/ becomes /o/. Another case of /o/ in final position or before a consonant other than /z/ is found where /o/ alternates with /al/.

(11) /al/ alternates with /o/

		Underlying representation
cheval	chevaux	/ʃəval-s/
tribunal	tribunaux	/tRibunal-s/
valent (/val-ət/)	vaut	/val-t/
malédiction	maudire	/maldiR/
altruisme	autre	/altR/

In (10), forms are shown in the right column before the consonantal environment which conditions the change. In the left column, the same forms are not preceded by the consonant so they remain unchanged.

RULE. ALLO-COALESCENCE (preliminary version): In marked vocabulary before a consonantal segment, /al/ becomes /o/.

11.3.2.3 Coalescence: /ɛl/ becomes /o/. Similarly, /o/ is derived from /ɛl/ in preconsonantal position and in word-final position.

(12) /ɛl/ and /əl/ alternating with /o/

chapellerie	chapeau
bel enfant	beau gosse
batelier	bateau
châtelain	château
nouvel	nouveau chef

This alternation is rather limited. There are numerous words with /ɛl/ which do not change to /o/. Most of those retain /ɛl/: *sel, sels*; *gel, gels*; *quel, quels*; *appel, appels*; they are in *Class B*. The rule accounting for the alternation /ɛl/ ~ /o/ applies to marked forms.

RULE. ELLO-COALESCENCE (final version): In marked vocabulary, in phrase-final and preconsonantal position, /ɛl/ becomes /o/.

The scope of ELLO-Coalescence is greater than that of ALLO-Coalescence. The former applies at word boundaries (*bel enfant*/*beau garçon*), but the latter does not (*cheval vapeur*, not *chevau vapeur). Also, /al/ can occur in phrase-final position (*un angle égal*) but /ɛl/ does not (*un homme beau*, not *un homme bel). Two rules are distinguished because of these differences.

There is a third case of coalescence found in the plural formation of words ending in /aj/, but it is not discussed until Chapter 12, where it properly belongs. It is the same type of coalescence as /al/.

A number of words with stressed /ø/ and /o/ in closed syllables remain unexplained. Many of these are learned forms (most borrowed), such as *Polyeucte, octateuque, leude, hypodrome, idiome, neume, jeûne, mandole, téléosaure, thermos, therapeute, argonaute, compost*. These exceptional items can only be accounted for by being listed as exceptions. These /o/'s, for example, cannot be subject to Back Vowel Raising. Similarly, *pôle, rôle*, *drôle, tôle*, and *trône* are also exceptions. To mark their anomalous pronunciation, French orthography placed a circumflex accent on their *o*. Where no accent is used, confusion occurs: many speakers differ as to whether a [low] or [nonlow] segment should be used in *benzol, icone, amazone, alcove, veule, éteule*. Because there are more words like *sol, seul, bonne, homme*, pronounced with a [low] segment, a tendency to make the less frequent vocabulary conform has resulted. This tendency is more pronounced south of the Loire but can be detected in speakers all over France.

When there is fluctuation, as there is with the aperture of the nonhigh round vowels of French, hypercorrection is sure to follow. Names like *Paul* and *Laure* can be heard with /o:/ instead of /ɔ/, for example.

11.4 Review of the vowels. Thus far, the following vowels have been discussed. Each is listed, followed by examples, the name of the rule or rules mentioned in connection with them, and reference to the chapter where each item was described. For more specific references, consult the Chart of RULES given in Appendix 3.

(1) nonalternating /i/, *cite/citons* (Ch. 11)
(2) /i/ alternating with /wa/, *épile/poil* (Hi-V-Low., Diph.) (Ch. 9)
(3) /e/ alternating with /ɛ/, *cédons/cèdent* (Cl-Syl-Adjst.) (Ch. 11)
(4) /e/ alternating with /wa/, *légal/loi* (Diph.) (Ch. 9)
(5) /e/ alternating with /ɛ/, *têtu/tête* (V-Harm.) (Ch. 11)
(6) /e/ alternating with /je/, *pédale/pied* (Diph.) (Ch. 9)
(7) /e/ alternating with /jɛ/, *céleste, ciel* (Diph.) (Ch. 9)
(8) nonalternating /e/, *tétée, état, téléphone* (Ch. 11)
(9) /ɛ/ alternating with /ə/, *graine/grenier* (Lo-V-Frt., Lo-V-Red.) (Ch. 8, 10, 11)
(10) /ɛ/ alternating with /e/, *cèdent/cédons* (Cl-Syl-Adjst.) (Ch. 11)
(11) nonalternating /ɛ/, *Gruyère, pègre* (Ch. 11)
(12) /y/ alternating with /u/, *surdité/sourd* (Hi-V-Frt.) (Ch. 10)
(13) nonalternating /y/, *muraille, mur, emmurer* (Ch. 10)
(14) /ø/ alternating with /u/, *jeu/jouons* (Lo-V-Frt., En-Haut, Pretonic-V-Adjst., Back-V-Rais.) (Ch. 8, 10, 11)
(15) nonalternating /ø/, *feu, deux* (Lo-V-Frt., En-Haut) (Ch. 8, 11)
(16) /ø/ alternating with /œ/, *beugler/beuglant* (V-Harm.) (Ch. 11)
(17) /o:/ alternating with /œ/, *berceur/berceuse* (Zaizing) (Ch. 11)
(18) /ø/ alternating with /œ/, *bœufs/bœuf* (En-Haut) (Ch. 11)
(19) /œ/ alternating with /ɔ/, *seul/solitude* (Lo-V-Frt.) (Ch. 8)
(20) nonalternating /œ/, *leur, peur* (Ch. 11)
(21) /œ/ alternating with /ø/ (See (16) and (18) above.)
(22) /œ/ alternating with /ø:/ (See (17) above.)
(23) /a/ alternating with /ɛ/, *clair/clarté* (Lo-V-Frt.) (Ch. 8)
(24) /a/ alternating with /ə/, *grenier/granulaire* (Lo-V-Red.) (Ch. 8)
(25) nonalternating /a/, *partons/part* (Ch. 8)
(26) /ɔ/ alternating with /œ/ (See (19) above.)

(27) /ɔ/ alternating with /u/, *voulons/volonté* (Pretonic-V-Adjst., Back-V-Rais.) (Ch. 8, 10)
(28) nonalternating /ɔ/, *tonnerre/tonne* (Ch. 11)
(29) /ɔ/ alternating with /o:/, *hôtesse/hôte* (/ɔ/-Adjst.) (Ch. 11)
(30) /o/ alternating with /ɔ/, *sot/sotte* (En-Haut) (Ch. 11)
(31) /o/ alternating with /aj/, *émail/émaux* (ALLO) (Ch. 11, 12)
(32) /o/ alternating with /al/, *chevaux/cheval* (ALLO) (Ch. 11)
(33) /o/ alternating with /εl/, *peau/pelletier* (ELLO) (Ch. 11)
(34) nonalternating /o/, *joyau, îlot, auto* (En-Haut) (Ch. 11)
(35) /o:/ alternating with /ɔs/, *côte, costal* (/ɔs/-Adjst.) (Ch. 11)
(36) /o:/ alternating with /ɔ/ (See (29) above.)
(37) /u/ alternating with /y/ (See (12) above.)
(38) nonalternating /u/, *trou, chou* (Hi-V-Low., Back-V-Rais.) (Ch. 10)
(39) /u/ alternating with /ɔ/ (See (27) above.)
(40) /u/ alternating with /œ/, *pouvons/peuvent* (Lo-V-Frt., Pretonic-V-Adjst., Back-V-Rais.) (Ch. 10)
(41) /u/ alternating with /ø/ (See (14) above.)

Still to be discussed are the derivations of nasalized vowels, of schwa, and of a few remaining segments.

11.5 Questions

1. Examine the following words. aimer /e/, entier /e/, entière /εR/, soulier /e/, poker /εR/, spider /εR/, catheter /εR/, tiers /εR/, fer /εR/, fier /εR/, se fier /e/, lier /e/, cacher /e/, trier /e/, hier /εR/, geyser /εR/, manager /e/ or /εR/, mer /εR/, première /εR/, premier /e/, gangster /εR/, fermier /e/, fermière /εR/, lierre /εR/.

Is there such a rule as /εR/ to /e/? If so, how can its exceptions be stated generally?

2. In Savoie, words like *maître, bête, sel, graise, sec* are generally pronounced /metR/, /bet/, /sel/, /gRes/, /sek/. How does the grammar of a Savoyard speaker who produces these forms differ from that of a speaker who does not?

3. Vowel Harmony was stated somewhat generally in this chapter. On the basis of the facts given, as well as of additional cases of vowel harmony, determine whether the rule in question should have only front vowels as its environment.

4. Under what conditions are vowels lengthened in French? Is lengthening the result of a unitary process? Is there any way to generalize lengthening?

5. Closed Syllable Adjustment was stated without any rigor with respect to its environment. Specify what a closed syllable in French is.

6. Having found that schwa plays a prominent role in the definition of French closed syllables, state any reservations you may have about that. Think in terms of what types of segments are generally found at codas of syllables.

7. According to what has been said in this chapter, the underlying form of *fier* /fjɛʀ/ is /fɛʀ/. How does that underlying form differ from that of the word *fer*? Show the derivation of both words.

8. In answering question 7, you must have argued that *fer* enters into no alternations such as *sel/salinité* or *clair/clarté*. You must have also noted that *fierté, fier, fièrement* do not alternate with words in /ɛ/. Formulate in your own words a critique of the position adopted in this book regarding the derivation of words like *fer* and *fier*.

9. Demonstrate the proper application of rules in order to retain the /l/ of *que valent-ils?* throughout the derivation.

10. Does the set of rules proposed thus far account for the alternation /a/ ~ /ə/ in *cavalier* ~ *cheval*?

Chapter 12
To glide or diphthongize

12.0 Introduction. This chapter is a systematic study of all French glides. It is demonstrated that although there are only three glides from a phonetic point of view, the glide system of French is far more complex than a phonetic study might suggest. In fact, there are several different sources for glides and their derivations are not at all straightforward. The study of the sources and derivations of the French glides supports the major tenets put forth in this book and once again underlines the interrelationship of all phonological segments.

12.1 Glides and vowels. In Chapters 4 and 5, the three glides of French were given the same features as the high vowels except that they were kept distinct in terms of syllabicity. Vowels are syllabic, glides are not. Table 12.1 summarizes this relationship.

Table 12.1

	i	j	y	ɥ	u	w
Syllabic	+	−	+	−	+	−
High	+	+	+	+	+	+
Front	+	+	+	+	−	−
Round	−	−	+	+	+	+

Table 12.1 represents the relevant phonetic make-up of these segments. However, the phonetic features of segments are but pale echoes of the real

systematic constitution of these segments. The fronting system showed that graphically. The glide system does also.

12.2 Gliding

12.2.1 Prevocalic glides. In Chapter 9, one source of the glides /j/ and /w/ was demonstrated. Diphthongization was shown to derive /we/ and /jɛ/ from /e/ and /ɛ/, respectively. In Chapter 14, on nasalization, a similar result is shown to exist for words in /wẽ/, such as *point, joint, loin*. Both /wɛ/ and /wẽ/, as suggested in Chapter 9, are derived via Diphthongization.

In addition to Diphthongization, there are other ways in which glides are derived in French. Evidence for one such case can be found in the alternations illustrated in (1) to (3).

(1) /i/ alternates with /j/
    étudie   étudions
    mie   miette
    ris   rions

(2) /y/ alternates with /ɥ/
    sue   suons
    pue   puez
    nue   nuage

(3) /u/ alternates with /w/
    roue   rouage
    boue   boueux
    loue   louons

These alternations suggest that prevocalic glides are derived from vowels. Put another way, high vowels followed by a syllabic segment become nonsyllabic (i.e. turn into glides).

    RULE. GLIDING (preliminary version): A high vowel preceding an adjacent vowel becomes a glide.

Gliding is not used to the same degree in the speech of all speakers of French. There are speakers for whom the words in the right column of (2) and (3) retain two syllables. This reluctance to glide /u/ and /y/ is typical of Midi speakers. In poetry also, some segments which would otherwise be glides retain syllabic status. The scope of application for Gliding, then, depends on the register (style) selected by a speaker or on the speaker's geographic dialect. Even within poetry the application of Gliding is not flatly excluded (see 20.5). There are a few words which may or may not be made subject to Gliding, depending on the metric needs of the poet. This is the case most frequently with the time adverb *hier*, which is pronounced as /iɛʀ/ or /jɛʀ/ depending on whether one or two syllables are needed in the line. The extent of application of Gliding is, therefore, not very clear.

12.2.2 Ordering Gliding. Gliding must apply after High Vowel Fronting in order for the high front rounded glide, /ɥ/, to be derived from /y/ which, as shown in Chapter 10, is derived via High Vowel Fronting. It must also apply after Round Vowel Raising in order for the high back glide /w/ to be properly derived from /u/, once /u/ has been raised from /o/. In short, Gliding must apply after the high vowels have been derived, shifted, or otherwise affected by rule.

It should be noted that the aforementioned ordering of Gliding is not a blanket generalization about how all glides are derived. There are glides which are derived before High Vowel Fronting or Round Vowel Raising. These glides are derived via Diphthongization. Only glides produced by Gliding (that is, glides derived by weakening of high vowels) are derived in the order just mentioned.

Gliding must be preceded by yet two other rules: High Vowel Assimilation and /i/-Formation. Examples of words which have undergone /i/-Formation can be seen in the right column of (4).

(4) Velar stop alternating with /i/
séducteur   séduit
fructueux   fruit
conducteur   conduite
production   produit
fugitif   fuite

The underlying form of *fuite* is /fugitə/. The /i/ is deleted by Syncope and /i/-Formation applies to change /g/ to /i/. Gliding can apply only after /i/-Formation has created the second of a two-vowel sequence.

    RULE. /i/-FORMATION: In native vocabulary a velar stop followed by a dental stop becomes a high unrounded vowel.

High Vowel Assimilation, the other of the two rules which must precede Gliding, must follow /i/-Formation. High Vowel Assimilation raises /o/ to /u/, thus assimilating /o/ to the height of /i/. Vowel assimilation is generally called vowel harmony; but here the term 'vowel harmony' is not used, to avoid confusion with those cases of vowel harmony discussed in 11.2.4. High Vowel Assimilation is crucial in relating the alternants of (5).

(5) /o/ alternating with /ɥ/
octave   huit
nocture   nuit
coction   cuit

    RULE. HIGH VOWEL ASSIMILATION (final version): In native vocabulary, /o/ becomes /u/ before /i/.

This rule makes round vowels assimilate to the height of /i/. It applies to a handful of stems, where the change from /o/ to /u/ is obvious, and it applies vacuously to the /u/ underlying the forms in the right column of (4). High Vowel Assimilation is also different from Vowel Harmony (cf. Chapter 11) in that the former raises mid vowels to high while the latter raises low vowels to mid.

12.2.3 A constraint on Gliding. So far, this analysis of glides derived by means of Gliding has accounted for the occurrence of glides in words like *yatagan*, *huissier*, *ouate*, where the glide is word-initial, as well as cases such as *diable*, *réjoui*, *conduit*. On the other hand, it does not account for the fact that in a two-vowel sequence in such words as *brouette* /bʀuɛt/ and *truelle* /tʀyɛl/ the first vowel does not change into a glide. Unless constrained, Gliding generates unacceptable forms such as */bʀwɛt/ and */tʀyɛl/. To account for the facts, Gliding must be constrained in such a way as to allow the generation of words such as those found in (7) to (9), while generating words like those in the right column of (1) to (3).

(7) /u/ not /w/   (8) /y/ not /ɥ/   (9) /i/ not /j/
    troué   /tʀue/   cruel /kʀyɛl/   brioche /bʀijɔʃ/
    ébloui /éblui/   fluet /flyɛ/   pliant   /plijâ/
    cloua   /klua/   truand /tʀyâ/   crier   /kʀije/

The facts so far suggest that Gliding does not apply to vowel sequences preceded by a consonant-liquid sequence. That constraint, however, is too general, as can be seen in (10), where CL clusters are followed by GV sequences.

(10) CLGV sequences
    truite   /tʀɥit/
    fluide   /flɥid/
    fruit   /fʀɥi/

Hence, Gliding should be stated as follows.

RULE. GLIDING (final version): A high vowel (HV) preceding an adjacent vowel (AV) becomes nonsyllabic under the following conditions: (1) if HV is /i/ or /u/, then it cannot be preceded by two or more nonsyllabic segments as HV's onset; (2) if HV is /y/, then the rule is applicable even if HV has a CC onset, provided that the AV is /i/.

12.2.4 Yod-Insertion. The examples in (9) show that /j/ is inserted between /i/ and a following adjacent vowel. This insertion does not occur in (7) and (8). To account for this palatalization of sorts, the following rule is posited.

RULE. YOD-INSERTION (final version): Insert /j/ between /i/ and a following adjacent vowel.

This rule may appear unconstrained and likely to distort derivations but it is, in fact, constrained by rule ordering. Yod-Insertion applies after Gliding. If it applied before Gliding, then the words of (11), for example, which are derived from underlying representations shown in (12), would become the unacceptable forms shown in (13).

(11) dieu /djø/   sciage /sjaʒ/   avion /avjɔ̃/
(12)   /di-ɔ/   /si-aʒ/   /avi-ɔn/
(13) */dijø/   */sijaʒ/   */avijɔ̃/

These undesirable forms are not generated if the grammar insures that Gliding precedes Yod-Insertion. Given this proper ordering, Yod-Insertion cannot apply to forms that are already glided. The only forms which can be modified by Yod-Insertion are those which are not affected by Gliding, namely, forms such as those of (9), for which Yod-Insertion is needed.

12.3 The postvocalic glide. Whereas all three glides can be found in syllable onset position, only /j/ occurs in the coda. This discrepancy is shown in the form of a distributional chart in Table 12.2, where only /j/ appears in word-final position.

Table 12.2 Distribution of glides.

	Word-initial	Medial	Final
/j/	hier	étudions	paille
/w/	oui	mouette	. . .
/ɥ/	huit	conduite	. . .

The postvocalic glide is not derived from a vowel. Suppose that the /j/ of *abeille, houille*, etc. were derived from an /i/. This would require that these two words have the following underlying representations (UR): /abɛi/ and /ui/. But these are also the UR of *abbaye* and *oui*. Clearly, it would be wrong to assume that *abbaye* 'abbey' and *abeille* 'bee', or *houille* 'coal' and *oui* 'yes', which have strikingly different meanings and functions, should be stored in exactly the same way in the vocabulary list of French speakers. One is forced, therefore, to conclude that postvocalic /j/ cannot be derived from the vowel /i/ in a fashion which would parallel its prevocalic equivalent. Another reason for not deriving final /j/ from /i/ is that there are no alternations between vowels and glides in a word-final position. Instead, one finds alternations between /j/ and /l/, as in (15). These alternations suggest that one of these segments can be derived from the other. (Further support for this derivation is found also in Chapter 15.)

(15) Some speakers: Most speakers:
     millier   /mije/   /milje/
     million   /mijɔ̃/   /miljɔ̃/
     Emilienne /emijɛn/   /emiljɛn/

Furthermore, an alternation between /aj/ and /o/, similar to that between /al/ and /o/ (11.3.2.2), can be found in the words of (16).

(16) /aj/ alternating with /o/
   vitrail   vitraux
   vaille   vaut
   émail   émaux

Evidence of alternations between /l/ and /j/ in (15) and (16) indicates that /j/ is a type of /l/. Since not all /l/ alternates with /j/, it is assumed that there are two /l/ segments. One /l/ appears at the phonetic level; the other underlies /j/. The /l/ that underlies /j/ is a palatalized /l/. Basically, it is a dental /l/, like the other /l/, but it assimilates with an adjacent /i/, a palatal, to become /ʎ/, the lateral palatal.

> RULE. /l/-PALATALIZATION (preliminary version): /li/ becomes /ʎ/ in stem-final position in native vocabulary. (It becomes [nonanterior], [noncoronal], [high], and [front].)

Subsequently, /ʎ/ is converted into a glide.

> RULE. YOD-CONVERSION (final version): The lateral palatal /ʎ/ becomes [nonlateral].

In other words, Yod-Conversion creates a consonantal glide. It should be understood that not all /li/ sequences are subject to /l/-Palatalization. This rule applies only to native words. For this reason, it applies in the derivation of words like *feuille*, *feuillage*, and *défeuillaison*, which are native forms, but not in the derivation of *foliation* and *follicule*, which are learned vocabulary.

Returning to the question of whether *oui* and *houille* are distinguished in their underlying representation, it is possible to show that they are indeed distinct (cf. the derivation in Table 12.3, where *abbaye* and *abeille* are also derived, for further illustration).

Table 12.3 Derivation of *oui*, *houille*, *abbaye*, and *abeille*.

	oui	houille	abbaye	abeille
Underlying representation:	oi	olia	abɛia	abɛlia
Back Vowel Raising:	ui	ulia	...	...
/l/-Palatalization:	...	uʎa	...	abɛʎa
Posttonic Vowel Reduction:	...	uʎə	abɛiə	abɛʎə
Yod-Conversion:	...	ujə	...	abɛjə
Gliding:	wi	...	...	...

Not shown in this derivation are the deletion of final schwa or any means of accounting for the aspirate *h* in *houille*. These processes have been left aside because they are not relevant to the point at hand.

The derivation of /j/ from /li/ has been presented in two steps instead of one. No reason was given for this apparent complication. The best way to show a need for two separate rules instead of one rule is to demonstrate that an intervening rule must apply between them. That is exactly the case, as can be seen in the derivation of words like *animal/animaux*, *émail/émaux*. This point is taken up in the derivation shown in Table 12.4.

Table 12.4 Derivation of *animal*, *email*, *animaux*, and *émaux*.

	animal	email	animaux	émaux
Underlying representation:	animál	ɛmáli	animál-s	ɛmáli-s
/l/-Palatalization:	. . .	ɛmáʎ	. . .	ɛmáʎ-s
ALLO-Coalescence:	. . .	. . .	animó-s	ɛmó-s
Yod-Conversion:	. . .	ɛmáj	. . .	. . .
Final Consonant Deletion:	. . .	. . .	animó	ɛmó

/l/-Palatalization must precede ALLO-Coalescence in order for ALLO-Coalescence to apply. It could not apply if /l/ were followed by /i/, which is the case before /l/-Palatalization creates a single segment which is a lateral palatal liquid. If a single rule converted /li/ to /j/, then ALLO-Coalescence could not apply because it requires that a lateral liquid (not a glide) follow /a/ and be followed by a consonant.

The derivation in Table 12.4 provides further support for ALLO-Coalescence, a rule proposed in 11.3.2.2. It is now possible to state ALLO-Coalescence in its final form, one that accounts for the alternations between /al/ and /o/, as well as the alternation between /aj/ and /o/.

> RULE. ALLO-COALESCENCE (final version): In marked vocabulary, before a consonantal segment, /a/ and a following adjacent lateral segment coalesce to form /o/.

12.4 Glide or diphthong. In this section other glides are examined. Given that glides are generally derived either by Gliding or Diphthongization, in a particular instance one can ask which way and why.

12.4.1 An apparent counterexample. In Section 12.3, a constraint on Gliding was discussed. It was concluded that when a consonant-liquid sequence immediately precedes a two-vowel sequence where the second vowel is nonhigh, Gliding cannot apply to the first vowel. For ease of reference, that sequence is referred to as in (17).

(17) $CLGV_{nonhigh}$

This constraint placed on Gliding would predict, then, that in French there are no sequences such as (17). That, however, is not so. There are indeed sequences like (17), as can be seen in (18).

(18) trois   /tʀwa/
     croix   /kʀwa/
     groin   /gʀwɛ̃/
     employer   /ãplwaje/

The evidence provided in (18) constitutes a counterexample to what has been proposed thus far as the analysis of glides. What is now needed is an evaluation of this evidence in order to determine whether the counterexample is real or apparent, and whether any modification of the analyses of glides is needed.

12.4.2 The diphthong as a partial explanation. The word *trois* does not constitute a counterexample to Gliding because it is not at all derived via Gliding. Instead, *trois* is derived via Diphthongization. Proof that *trois* derives via Diphthongization is that there are numerous alternations of *trois* with *tri*.

(19) *trois* alternants

in /i/	in /e/
triangle	trépied
tricolore	tresse
trident	trente

In the analysis already proposed here, there are rules which can account for these alternations: High Vowel Lowering, which feeds Diphthongization and /wa/-Adjustment. This can be seen in the derivation in Table 12.5.

Table 12.5

	trident	tresse	trois
Underlying representation	tRidant	tRisa	tRis
High Vowel Lowering	...	tResa	tRes
Diphthongization	...	...	tRwes
Nasalization	tRidãt	...	...
/wa/-Adjustment	...	...	tRwas
Final Consonant Deletion	tRidã	...	tRwa
Final Schwa Deletion	...	tRes	...
Closed Syllable Adjustment	...	tRɛs	...

12.4.3 To glide or to diphthongize. Because of /i~wa/ and /e~wa/ alternations, it has been concluded that the glide of *trois* is derived via Diphthongization. Any vocalic alternation of the same nature can be explained identically. If *croix*, *groin*, and *employer* were to alternate with /i/ or /e/, the same explanation would be possible for them. Unfortunately, *croix* alternates with *crucifix*, *groin* with *grogner*, and the /wa/ of *employer* is also found in *emploi*. This would suggest that *croix*, *groin*, *employer*, and other similar words such as *moine*, which alternates with *monacal*, must be derived via Gliding. But for Gliding to apply, a sequence of two vowels is needed and Gliding is subject to constraint (17). Therefore, *croix*, *groin*, and *employer* can in no way be generated by Gliding. It appears that an impasse has been reached, where words with /wa/ and /we/ can be neither diphthongs nor glides.

104 / 12 To glide or diphthongize

12.4.4 Diphthongizing back vowels. The only explanation left is that the analysis developed thus far is either incorrect or incomplete. Supposing that the analysis is incomplete, it is possible that Diphthongization has a broader scope than suggested in Chapter 9. In particular, Diphthongization could apply to the back vowel /o/. If so, there should be alternations which support a relation between /o/ and /wa/, and a relation between /wẽ/ and /œ̃/, /ɔ̃/, or /ɔn/. A list of such alternations appears in (20).

(20) crucifier   croix
     location   loyer
     louer   loyer
     monacal   moine
     acupuncture   pointe
     jonction   joint
     vocal   voix

The rules involved in relating the members of each alternating pair are (1) High Vowel Lowering, which applies to derive all words in the right column, (2) High Vowel Fronting, which is needed to derive *crucifier* and *acupuncture*, (3) Nasalization, needed to derive *jonction* and *acupuncture*, and (4) Back Vowel Raising, which raises the round vowel of *louer* into place.

The answer to the dilemma is, then, quite simple. There are two possible sources for /wa/-diphthongs: /e/ and /o/. The examples of /wa/-diphthongs discussed in Chapter 9 are all derived from /e/, whereas those of (20) are derived from /o/. Consequently, the revised and now final version of Diphthongization must read as follows.

> RULE. DIPHTHONGIZATION (final version): Strong nonhigh vowels are diphthongized: low front vowels become /jɛ/, nonlow vowels become /we/.

12.5 Conclusion. The three glides of French are derived in a number of different ways: /ɥ/ is derived from /y/ by Gliding; /w/ can be derived from /u/ by Gliding or can be inserted by Diphthongization before mid vowels; /j/ is derived by Diphthongization, which inserts it before /ɛ/, by Yod-Insertion, which puts it between /i/ and a following adjacent vowel, by Yod-Conversion, which changes /ʎ/ to /j/, and by Gliding, where it replaces /i/.

12.6 Questions

1. Yod-Conversion is a change from liquid to glide. Check that change in terms of the features in Figure 5.5.

2. How does the analysis deriving diphthongs from /o/ support the claim made in Chapter 9 that /e/ diphthongizes to /we/ and /ɛ/ to /jɛ/, and not vice versa?

3. On the basis of the alternation *amélioration/meilleur*, determine the underlying representation of *meilleur* and write the appropriate derivation.

4. Note the following dialect differences: D_1 is most common; D_2 is North African French.

Enunciated Standard		D_1	D_2
tu es seul	/tɥesœl/	/tesœl/	/tjesœl/
ça m'a tué	/samatɥe/	/samatɥe/	/samatyɥe/
tu en veux	/tɥãvø/	/tãvø/	/tjãvø/
tu viens?	/tyvjẽ/	/tyvjẽ/	/tyvjẽ/

(a) Give names for the glide rules taking place here.
(b) In what environment do they apply?

(5) In different dialects of French, the pronoun *tu* is pronounced as shown:

Standard		North African Jews	French Canadians
tu	/ty/	/tʃy/	/tsy/
tout	/tu/	/tu/	/tu/
tué	/tɥe/	/tʃyɥe/	/tsɥe/

(a) What causes the insertion of a spirant?
(b) What can be said about the likely point of articulation of /t/ in each of these dialects?

6. As seen in question 5, North African French has such forms as /tyɥe/ ~ /tʃyɥe/ for *tué*. Consider the following:

Standard		North African
mouette	/mwɛt/	/muwɛt/
muette	/mɥɛt/	/myɥɛt/
pliage	/plijaʒ/	/plijaʒ/

Explain how the various forms are derived. State the rule needed for deriving all forms. What does that rule have in common with Yod-Insertion? From the point of view of language change, which of the two dialects considered is more natural and most evolved?

7. Both *triller* and *trier* are pronounced /trije/. What must be done in their underlying representations to distinguish between them? How are they derived? Why do they eventually merge phonetically? (Note. *Triller* alternates with *trille*, whereas *trier* alternates with *tri*, from which *triage* is derived).

8. Write the /i/-Formation rule in features. Show how the feature statement of that rule supports your conclusion in question 6.

9. As it is written, Diphthongization applies before Low Vowel Fronting and must apply to the same vowels. Does it? How is the new wording of Diphthongization able to distinguish between its domain and that of Low Vowel Fronting?

10. How must Gliding be restated in order to account for such forms as *construire*, *instruit*, *serfouis*, and *cambouis*, all of which have a glide before /i/?

Chapter 13
Three nasals from two

13.0 Introduction. At the phonetic level, French has three nasals: bilabial /m/, dental /n/, and palatal /ɲ/. It has been claimed that French also has a velar /ŋ/ in borrowed vocabulary. Not so! One should note that many French speakers confuse the string 'nasalized vowel + /ŋ/' with the string 'nasalized vowel + /g/'. They pronounce borrowed words like *smoking*, *gang*, *gong*, *pouding* with a final /g/. Few French speakers really have a /ŋ/ and where it occurs, it is totally predictable. I will therefore not discuss it further.

The interesting question raised about nasals in the context of a systematic study is whether all three nasal segments are phonetic reflexes of equivalent underlying phonemes. They are not. One of these nasals, the palatal /ɲ/, is a mere alternant of /n/ and can be predicted in all its occurrences. The other two nasal segments /m/ and /n/ have underlying phonemic status, as the rest of this chapter shows.

In the following pages /ɲ/, the palatal nasal of French, is shown to be different from /m/ and /n/ in a fundamental way. Distributionally, /ɲ/ functions not like /m/ and /n/ nor, in fact, like other single segments, but seems to function like a consonant cluster. Moreover, the segments /m/ and /n/ create homorganic stops in certain environments while /ɲ/ does not. The nature of /ɲ/ is best explained as a derived segment. This claim is supported by historical facts. In short, /ɲ/ is not a phoneme in the underlying inventory of French segments. Instead, it is derived from /n/ via a predictable palatalization rule.

13.1 Distribution. One piece of evidence showing that /ɲ/ is not a segment in the same sense as /m/ and /n/ might be found in the phonetic distribution of these three segments.

Table 13.1 Phonetic distribution of /m/, /n/, and /ɲ/.

	1 __#	2 L__	3 V__V	4 #__	5 __N N__	6 C__
/m/	dame	arme	amour	mort	somnoler	énigmatique
/n/	vanne	orner	anneau	nuage	amnésique	cad(e)nas
/ɲ/	vigne	hargne	signal	...[1]	...	...

[1] The only words which are possible candidates for this slot are *gnole* and *gnon*, popular derivatives of *oignon* 'a blow', as judged by the resulting mark on the victim. There are also the onomatopoeic *gnangnan* from child vocabulary and the word *gnocchi* borrowed from the Italian.

Table 13.1 shows that /m/, /n/, and /ɲ/ behave similarly with respect to Columns 1, 2, and 3. They can be preceded by a liquid, or can occur word-finally or intervocalically. The table also shows that /m/ and /n/ are different from /ɲ/ in that the latter does not occur in word-initial position (Column 4), never combines with another nasal (Column 5), and cannot follow a consonant (Column 6). This establishes that the palatal nasal differs strikingly from the other nasals. Further evidence of this difference is developed throughout this chapter.

13.2 The cluster argument. There are constraints on the deletion of /ə/. Among such constraints is the nature of the cluster which would result from that deletion. Thus, in *nous trainerons* /nutrɛnRɔ̃/ the schwa is deleted while it is retained in *nous trainerions* /nutRɛnərjɔ̃/. In light of this and many similar examples, one can conclude that /nəC/, where C is any nonsyllabic segment, is reducible to /nC/ under some conditions. This rule applies to *sonnerie*, *gaminerie*, *sainement*, *bonne-dame* 'plant', etc. If /m/ and /n/ do constitute a class, one might also assume that schwa can be deleted from /məC/, to yield /mC/. Indeed it can. The schwa in *gromeler*, *amenez-les*, *aimeront*, *aime-t-il*, can be deleted. Similarly, the sequence /Cəm/ can be reduced to /Cm/, as in the following adverbs: *faussement*, *nettement*, *vainement*, *sèchement*, *drôlement*. In the same fashion /Cən/ can be reduced to /Cn/, as in *soutenir*, *maintenir*, *avenue*, *prevenu*, etc.

It is therefore a fact that /m/ and /n/ can enter into the formation of nonsyllabic clusters. They can occur as the first or last segment of a two-segment cluster and do not prevent the deletion of schwa when such a deletion can yield the cluster in question.

Unlike other nasals, the palatal /ɲ/ does not allow the deletion of schwa: in other words, */ɲC/ is not a possible cluster of French. Examples which illustrate this point are *dignement*, *agnelet*, *daigneraient*, *vigneron*, *vigneture*, where /ə/ is retained. What is important here is not only that /ɲ/ is different from /m/ and /n/ with respect to how it enters into the formation of nonsyllabic clusters, but also that /ɲ/ itself functions like a cluster. Compare /ɲ/, /tR/, /kR/, on the one hand, and /n/ and /m/, on the other (cf. Table 13.2).

Table 13.2

	ɲ	tR	kR	n	m
/__m/	dignement	autrement	sacrement	vainement	extrèmement
/__l/	agnelet	entrelacer	sucre-le	annelet	gromeler
/__R/	saignera	entrera	sucrerie	sonnerie	crèmerie
	/ə/ remains	/ə/ remains	/ə/ remains	/ə/ deletes	/ə/ deletes

Table 13.2 shows that /ɲ/ functions like a consonant cluster, while /m/ and /n/ do not. Schwa may not be dropped after /ɲ/, /tR/, and /kR/, but can be deleted after /m/ and /n/. If /ɲ/ were a single segment, like the /R/ of

rarement /ʀaʀmã/, the /k/ of *traquenard* /tʀaknaʀ/ or the /n/ of *sonnerie* /sənʀi/, the schwa would be deletable in the words of the leftmost column.

The distribution of ɲ, as opposed to that of /m/ and /n/, shows that ɲ is different from /m/ and /n/. It behaves not like a single segment but rather like a cluster. In fact, /ɲ/ is different in a rather fundamental way.

13.3 The homorganic argument. Another way in which /ɲ/ differs from /m/ and /n/ can be seen in the relative ability of these segments to create homorganic stops in certain clusters. There are cases where a dental and a bilabial stop are inserted in clusters like /nʀ/ and /mʀ/, respectively. Such a rule is attested historically in the development of words like *pondre* and *chambre*, where no /d/ or /b/ was present in their Latin equivalents: *ponere* and *camera*, respectively. The same process can be found in modern French in verb forms like *prenons/prendrons, venir/viendra, moulu/moudre*, or in doublets like *semblable/similaire, ressemblance/similitude, nombre/numéro, remembrance/rémémoratif*.

Besides evidence in both derivational and inflectional morphology for an alternation supporting the existence of a process of homorganic stop insertion, there is also evidence of an alternation /n/ ~ /ɲ/ which bears in part on homorganic insertion e.g. *joindre/joignons, craindre/craignons, feindre/feignons, geindre/geignons, peindre/peignons, enfreindre/enfreignons, épreindre/épreignons, éteindre/éteignons, restreindre/restreignons, contraindre/contraignons, ceindre/ceignons, teindre/teignons, atteindre/atteignons, oindre/oignons, poindre/poignant*. All these verbs show an infinitive and several inflected forms which exhibit (1) a homorganic /d/ and (2) a nasalized vowel, while they have other inflected forms which contain no homorganic /d/ and no nasalized vowel, but rather the palatal nasal /ɲ/. It is well known that Nasalization applies to a vowel followed by a nasal only if the following segment is C or # (cf. Chapter 7). Hence Nasalization applies only if Homorganic Consonant Insertion has applied. Since a dental nasal is needed for Homorganic Consonant Insertion to insert /d/ in the appropriate forms, it follows that the phonological alternation /n/ ~ /ɲ/ is well motivated.

Another supporting piece of evidence from derivational morphology shows that a number of nouns derived from these verbs exhibit a /t/. This occurrence of /t/ can only be due to a homorganic insertion in the verb from which they are derived, e.g. *joncture, crainte, feinte, plainte, peinture, épreintes, étreinte, contrainte, ceinture, teinture, atteinte*.

Little doubt can be left that there is an alternation /n/ ~ /ɲ/ in French and that /ɲ/ is the derived segment. The contextual factors of this derivation are discussed in Section 13.4.

13.4 The source of the palatal nasal. From what is known about language in general, one suspects that a nasal becomes /ɲ/ under the influence of a palatal segment. Two possible ways of testing the claim that /ɲ/ is a palatal nasal come to mind. First, does this source of /ɲ/ explain the distributional and other restrictions already surveyed, and second, is there supporting evidence for a nasal palatalization rule in segmental alternation? The evidence surveyed in Section 13.3 shows that there are alternations in inflectional and derivational morphology. The following sections attempt a critical review of the distributional approach I have employed in Section 13.1. The question of explanation is now taken up in detail.

13.5 Distribution reviewed. Phonetic distribution has been used by many linguists in an attempt to determine similarities and differences among items for the purpose of placing these items in the same or different classes. This approach has been criticized of late. The following review of our original distribution echoes these recent criticisms.

13.5.1 Word-final palatal nasal. If it is true that the palatal nasal can occur word-finally, then the derivation suggested must be questioned. Table 13.1 suggests that word-finally there is no difference between /m/, /n/, or /ɲ/. But derivationally, my analysis of /ɲ/ requires that a palatal segment must have palatalized a /n/, yielding /ɲ/. Phonetically, /m/, /n/, and /ɲ/ have the same word-final distribution; but derivationally they differ in that the latter is derived via Palatalization. Hence, the phonetic distribution analysis fails to account for the difference. It ignores it. In contrast, the derivational analysis accounts for the facts.

Table 13.3

	dame	fine	vigne
Underlying representation:	dama	fina	vinia
Palatalization:	. . .	. . .	viɲa
Posttonic Reduction:	damə	finə	viɲə
Final Schwa Deletion:	dam	fin	viɲ

13.5.2 After a liquid. The three nasals /m/, /n/, and /ɲ/, behave similarly after a liquid (Table 13.1, Column 2). This environment in no way affects the derivation of /ɲ/ proposed earlier. Consequently, it is not an argument for or against the derivation argued for here.

13.5.3 Intervocalically. The three nasals also behave similarly between vowels (Table 13.1, Column 3). Their derivation is not affected in different ways by this environment. Because a vowel follows the nasal, the derivation of these words is the same as for those of Column 1. One might ask why /ɲ/ is derived from /n/ + /i/ before a vowel. In other words, why are there two vowels together? A brief look at lists of words with /ɲV/ shows that /ɲ/ precedes a suffix with an initial vowel, e.g. *signe/signal, hargne/hargneux, compagne/compagnon, guigne/guignol, poigne/poignet, éloigne/éloigner, règne/règner, borgne/éborgner,* and a few exceptions like *agneau, araignée, gnon, oignon* (the last two from Vulgar Latin *uni-onem*), and *champignon*

(Old French *champegneul*). These facts support the claim that /ɲ/ is derived via Palatalization. Boundaries are known to bring together various segments which interact phonologically on each other. If we did not claim that /ɲ/ is derived from /n/ and did not state the rule at morpheme boundaries, there would be no explanation for the fact that the vowel which immediately follows /ɲ/ is the initial or only segment of a suffix.

13.5.4 Word-initially. The words of Column 4 of Table 13.1 (*mort, nuage*) show that /m/ and /n/ occur in word-initial position while there are no /ɲ/ in word-initial position (but see the note in the table). This fact would be unexplained if /ɲ/ were assumed to be an underlying segment. If, on the other hand, /ɲ/ is derived, and furthermore, if /ɲ/ occurs only before suffixes, then a natural explanation is available for the distribution of the words in Column 4.

13.5.5 Before a nasal. The words of Column 5 in Table 13.1 (*somnoler, amnésique*) show that /m/ and /n/ can occur in the immediate environments of another nasal. Arguments related to Columns 1 and 3 have shown that /ɲ/ must be followed by a vowel. So, */ɲm/ and */ɲn/ are impossible sequences.

13.5.6 After a consonant. Column 6 of Table 13.1 shows that /m/ and /n/ can cluster with true consonants while /ɲ/ cannot. As is the case for the words of Column 5, there seem to be few words exhibiting this environment. Hence, the fact that in Columns 5 and 6 /ɲ/ behaves differently from /m/ and /n/ remains unexplained. It may be due to the small frequency of /ɲ/ in the language. The same is true of /ɲ/ following a nasal. There are very few sequences of two nasals in a row. None involves /ɲ/.

13.5.7 In the context of nasalization. Two more environments are of interest which were not taken up in Table 13.1: the nonoccurrence of nasalized vowels before all three nasals and the ways these nasals can trigger nasalization. These two points are really two sides of one coin. They will be taken up in the order just given.

The three nasals do not differ from one another in their inability to follow nasalized vowels.

Table 13.4

*/pɔ̃m/	/pɔm/	pomme	'apple'
*/pã n/	/pan/	panne	'trouble'
*/pɛ̃ɲ/	/pɛɲ/	peigne	'comb'

The derivations of these words are also similar to the extent that the underlying representations must contain a final /ə/ in order to prevent nasalization which, as is known, applies if the segment after the nasal is consonantal or a word boundary.

In the context of an analysis which claims that all three nasals have underlying phonemic status, the three items in question should also behave alike in terms of what elements can follow them. It should be possible, given alternations between, say, *cousin/cousine*, *an/année*, *un/une*, to find similar circumstances with /m/ and /ɲ/. There are, in fact, no such alternations as Ṽ/VN where N is /m/ or /ɲ/. The case of /m/ is unexplained and its ramifications are taken up in Chapter 14. The case of /ɲ/ is, of course, crystal clear, given our analysis, but would be unexplained in the context of an analysis which would make it an underlying segment. Indeed, our analysis, which calls for a segment /i/ after the underlying nasal, prohibits the environment necessary for Nasalization. This explains why there is no case where /ɲ/ causes nasalization of a preceding vowel.

13.6 Why /ɲ/ behaves like a cluster. Section 13.2 shows that /ɲ/ behaves like a cluster of consonants. This conclusion stemmed from the fact that no consonant could be combined with /ɲ/. The schwa of *vigne*, for example, drops when the derivational suffix which follows begins with a vowel, e.g. *vignoble*, *vignon*, but remains when the derivational suffix following it begins with a consonant, e.g. *vigneron* /viɲərɔ̃/ and *vigneture* /vinətyʀ/. This behavior seems to allow the avoidance of clusters of the type /ɲC/. But the fact that a single key opens two locks does not necessarily imply that the two locks are identical. The key may be a master key. Schwa is also a master. The fact that it provides a solution to two phenomena does not necessarily imply that these phenomena are alike or identical. This situation illustrates clearly the remarkable usefulness of schwa. It serves in breaking up true clusters and in separating /ɲ/ and a consonant (or a consonant and *h*-aspiré). The breaking up of clusters is a structural function. It reflects a structural property. The breaking up of sequence /ɲC/ or /Ch/ is not structural. It reflects the aberrant behavior of /ɲ/ and /h/. From this, it follows that the cluster argument was really a nonargument in the sense that it claimed a structural explanation for an idiosyncratic type of behavior.

13.7 The rule. The palatalization of /n/ to yield /ɲ/ is highly similar to that of /l/ to yield /ʎ/. In light of this similarity and given that no rule ordering is required of one case which conflicts with the rule ordering of the other, the two rules are combined into one.

> RULE. /l/-/n/-PALATALIZATION (final version). In stem-final position of native vocabulary, a segment which is [consonantal], [sonorant], [coronal], [anterior], [nonhigh], and [nonfront] and is followed by a [nonconsonantal], [noncoronal], [nonanterior], [high], [front] segment, becomes [noncoronal], [nonanterior], [high], and [front], and the conditioning segment deletes.

In other words, /li/ becomes /ʎ/ and /ni/ becomes /ɲ/.

13.8 The orthographic trap. Under what appears to be the influence of spelling, some phoneticians have attempted to distinguish between the palatal nasal of *magnifique*, *montagne*, *agnelet*, etc. and that of *nielle*, *denier*, *panier*, etc. In all dictionaries which provide a phonetic transcription, the latter are transcribed with /nj/ and the former with /ɲ/. One type of support for this view is that some people (fewer and fewer of them) do claim that they normally produce the two classes with a contrast, i.e. that they distinguish between *la nielle* and *l'agnelle*. But many do not. Speakers who do and phoneticians who agree with them may be influenced by spelling. It is, of course, possible to produce /ɲ/ differently from /nj/. But one needs to know the spelling of the relevant words to do so.

While there is little reason to suspect a well-distributed contrast between palatal nasals spelled differently, there is good reason to distinguish between those cases where /ɲ/ alternates with /nij/ and those where it exhibits no alternation. The word *nier*, for example, can be pronounced /ɲe/ or /nije/. Alternations of this type can be found most commonly across dialects but are also found in one individual's speech. There are other words, like *denier*, *panier*, *montagnard*, where the palatal nasal does not alternate with /nij/. *Panier* must be pronounced /paɲe/, not */panije/, *montagnard* /mɔ̃taɲaʀ/, not */mɔ̃tanijaʀ/. Similarly, one finds *lier* versus *chatelier*, *scier* versus *huissier*, where the first (monosyllabic) word can alternate but the second of the pair cannot. The restrictions on these facts are not clear and need further research. Nevertheless, the fact that the palatal which does not exhibit alternation is spelled *gn* or *ni* suggests that the distinction made on orthographic (or strictly phonetic) grounds has little phonological correlation.

13.9 Conclusion. The palatal nasal /ɲ/ has been shown to differ from other segments in a fundamental way. It is derived from a sequence /ni/ which undergoes Palatalization. Evidence in support of this derivation was found in a number of alternations /$\tilde{V}$d ~ VN/ which can only be accounted for if (1) Homorganic Consonant Insertion and (2) the proposed analysis of /ɲ/ are adopted. A number of distributional facts and constraints are also explained if the proposed analysis is adopted, among them (1) the fact that /ɲ/ occurs only at morpheme boundaries, (2) /ɲ/ is always followed by a vowel (or a boundary where the vowel is deleted), (3) /d/ is the only homorganic consonant inserted. Without this analysis, these facts and constraints remain largely unexplained.

13.10 Questions.
1. State in features the palatalization of /l/ and then that of /n/. Determine whether it is a good idea to combine them into one rule as has been done.
2. It is sometimes claimed that French has a /ŋ/ just like the last sound of English *sing*, *rang*, or *tung*. On the basis of the following data, agree or disagree with this claim.

	Marseilles Speech	Standard French
il est grand	/ilegʀã̃ŋ/	/ilegʀã/
une grande femme	/ynøgʀãndøfamø/	/yngʀãdfam/
un drole de machin	/œ̃ndʀɔlødømaʃẽŋ/	/œ̃dʀɔldəmaʃẽ/
ils manquent de tout	/ilmã̃ŋkødøtu/	/ilmã̃kdətu/
gong	/gõgø/	/gõgə/
smoking	/smokiŋgø/	/smɔkiŋ/

3. /l/ ∼ /n/-Palatalization is actually stated too generally and needs to be constrained. How would you propose to constrain it to avoid its application to words like *nier, lier, lire, plier*?

4. Using the learned/native distinction to constrain /l/ ∼ /n/-Palatalization is supported by some of the following words and not by others. Which is which?

stagnation, lignification, vigneture, ignifugé, magnat, magnanime, signature, indigne, diagnostic, magnétisme.

5. /l/ ∼ /n/-Palatalization collapses two rules: (1) the palatalization proper of /l/ and /n/, and (2) the deletion of the conditioning palatal: /i/. State these two rules in features and suggest how you would determine whether they are best stated separately or collapsed.

Chapter 14
Velum down, nasal out

14.0 Introduction. In Chapters 4 and 7, references were made to nasalization. Four nasalized vowels were identified in Chapter 4. They are the last sounds of *divin, chacun, cochon,* and *éléphant*. In Chapter 7, a rule of nasalization was said to be a special case of the greater process of assimilation. Nasalization is generally a regressive assimilation. Two types of nasalization must be distinguished: (1) a phonetic, noncontrastive assimilation such as that found in most languages which do not have the second type (English is one of them), and (2) a phonological nasalization, as typified by French and Portuguese. This second type often creates oppositions which are different in meaning, e.g. *tas ≠ temps, dais ≠ daim, pot ≠ pont, bru ≠ brun*. In the theoretical context adopted here, the first type is a low level rule, which does not affect subsequent rules, while the second must be ordered earlier. The purpose of this chapter is to place nasalized vowels in the context of the system established so far.

14.1 Alternations

14.1.1 Alternations with /ɛ̃/. There are more alternations with /ɛ̃/ than with all other nasalized vowels combined.

(1) /i/ alternates with /ɛ̃/

/i/	/í/	/ɛ̃/
divinité	divine	divin
câlinerie	câline	câlin
gaminer	gamine	gamin

Words in the first and second columns are derivationally related while words in the second and third columns are inflectionally related. Hence, it can be said that the /i/ ~ /ɛ̃/ alternations rest on inflectional and derivational morphology.

(2) /e/ alternates with /ɛ̃/

/e/	/ɛ/	/ɛ̃/
plénitude	pleine	plein
sérénade	sereine	serein
freiner	freine	frein

As in (1), these columns exhibit relations of derivational and inflectional morphology.

(3) /a/ alternates with /ɛ̃/

/a/ ~ /ə/	/ɛ/	/ɛ̃/
germanique	germaine	germain
puritanisme	puritaine	puritain
santé	saine	sain
grenier	graine	grain

The first column includes either learned vocabulary (if /ã/ or /a/ is used) or native vocabulary (when /ə/ is used). *Graine* is not the feminine equivalent of *grain* but a related word. As for the others, they are clear cases of inflectional morphology.

(4) /ɛ/ alternates with /ɛ̃/

/ɛ/	/ɛ/	/ɛ̃/
craignons	craignent	craint
geignons	geignent	geindre
peignant	peigne (subj.)	peins (*peindre*, indic.)

These examples constitute strong support for the rule of Nasalization. All morphologically related items, which these pairs and triplets constitute, should be entered under one stem, with inflections to be added to the stem. It was demonstrated in Chapter 13 that /ɲ/ is derived from /n/. For that analysis to hold, /n/, not a nasalized vowel, must have occurred in *peins*, *geindre*, and *craint*.

14.1.1 Alternations with /ɛ̃/

Also, the /d/ of *peindre*, *geindre*, and *craindre*, being a homorganic segment, must have been inserted on the basis of point of articulation identity with /n/. But if /n/ was present at some level and is not present now, some process must account for its disappearance. That process is composed of two rules: Nasalization and Nasal Deletion. Hence, any attempt to reject the rule of Nasalization in favor of having nasalized vowels in the underlying representation must also reject relating the singular and plural verb forms shown in (4). The consequences of such a radical decision are not worth consideration.

(5) /jé/ alternates with /jɛ̃/

/ə/	/jɛ/	/jɛ̃/
venons	viennent	viens
tenez	tiennent	tient
chenil	chienne	chien
Algérie	algérienne	algérien

The leftmost column contains three pretonic and one posttonic schwa. The three pretonic schwas also alternate with null, as they can be deleted under certain conditions (cf. Chapter 15). The posttonic schwa in *Algérie* is always deleted in final position. It is a word-final marker of the feminine inflection (like the final schwa in *algérienne*, which also deletes) and it alternates with /jɛ/ and /jɛ̃/, just as the other schwas.

The example in (5) are cases of derivational and inflectional morphology. Regarding the verbs *tenir* and *venir*, it should be noted that they constitute further support of the type discussed in (4). Their forms in the future, namely, *tiendrai* and *viendrai*, are composed of the stem followed by a homorganic stop, followed by the appropriate inflection. Again, it can be said that /n/ is needed to effect the proper consonant insertion and it must also effect the nasalization of the preceding vowel in the first three persons of the present indicative.

(6) /ə/, /i/, and /wa/ alternate with /wɛ̃/

/ə/	/i/	/wa/	/wɛ̃/
fenil			foin
		soigne	soin
	minuscule		moins

The /i/ of *minuscule* is the learned equivalent of /e/ which diphthongizes (cf. épiler ~ poil, Chapter 10). There are no inflectionally related pairs in this group. By itself this group would not constitute sufficient evidence for nasalization. There is more, however.

(7) /u/ and /ɔ/ alternate with /wɛ̃/

/u/	/ɔ/	/wɛ̃/
acupuncture		pointe
	jonction	jointe
	grogner	groin
	longueur	loin

Those alternations were examined in the context of Diphthongization in Chapter 12. There, it was decided to extend the scope of that rule on the basis of evidence that might have been convincing. This evidence is not very strong: it is circumstantial at best. Some of the derivational relations may not be clear to all speakers of French. They are retained in this book to reinforce the concept of word families established in Chapters 8 and 9.

The seven categories just discussed constitute paradigmatic evidence that Nasalization as a rule is needed to derive /ɛ̃/. Some provide stronger evidence than others. Together they provide substantial support for Nasalization.

14.1.2 Alternations with /ã/

(8) /a/ alternates with /ã/

/a/	/ã/
volcanique	volcan
tanne	tan
printanier	printemps

(9) /ə/ alternates with /ã/

/ə/, /e/, /i/	/ɛ/	/ã/
apprenez	apprennent	apprends
cinéraire		cendre
générique		genre

Of these alternations the stronger support comes from the second set, where inflectional and homorganic evidence echoes cases of /ɛ̃/.

14.1.3 Alternations with /œ̃/

(10) /y/ alternates with /œ̃/

/y/	/ý/	/œ/
embrumer	embrume	embrun
communauté	commune	commun
aucunement	aucune	aucun
importuner	importune	importun

(11) /œ/ alternates with /œ̃/

/ø/	/ǿ/	/œ̃/
déjeuner	déjeune	à jeun

The foregoing examples show cases where inflectionally related items must be related by Nasalization. It also shows clearly the [high] ~ [low] relationship of oral and nasal vowels in pairs of related words. In the front rounded system adopted here, the high and the mid vowel both have a low vowel equivalent when Nasalization has operated. In the context of a theory where relations must be stated as rules, this means that a nasalized front vowel must be lowered. In fact, this lowering applies to all nasalized vowels (14.2.3).

14.1.4 Alternations with /ɔ̃/

(12) /ɔ/ alternates with /ɔ̃/

/ɔ/	/ɔ/	/ɔ̃/
donnera	donne	don
tonalité	entonne	ton
bonhommerie	bonne	bon
	lionne	lion
	gasconne	gascon
	patronne	patron

The rule of Nasalization is well supported by the evidence given, where pairs of words are inflectionally related.

14.1.5 Alternations in a prefix.
Paradigmatic evidence considered up to this point has been found exclusively in stems. In this section, evidence from the prefix *in-* is cited.

(13) /ɛ̃/ alternates with /in/

/ɛ̃/	/in/
insouciant	inégalé
incapable	inactif
implacable	inusité
instrumental	inouï

The negative prefix *in-* is subject to the application of Nasalization if it occurs in the proper environment. If /in-/ is preconsonantal, the rule applies. If it is prevocalic, the rule does not apply.

Although the alternation in (13) is highly productive, a formally similar prefix, *en-*, does not exhibit any oral/nasal alternation.

(14) *en-* before vowels and consonants

Prevocalic /ãn/:	Preconsonantal /ã/:
enivré	encaisser
enherber	ennoblir
	enguirlander
	enterrer

The few alternations found here are of highly questionable importance. *En-* is pronounced /ɛn/ in *s'énamourer*, which is now archaic, or in *énurétique*, a recently created medical word.

Although no oral/nasal alternation is available in (14), *en-* constitutes support for nasalization anyway. The /ãn/ ~ /ã/ alternation is dependent indirectly upon nasalization. Both are nasalized but only /ã/, in preconsonantal position, is subject to the deletion of the conditioning nasal (14.2).

14.2 The rules. There are cases (*on, en, quand, brin, emprunt*) where nasalized vowels do not alternate with oral vowels. In the context of the system adopted here, these nasalized vowels are also derived from an oral vowel via Nasalization. That analysis allows for a generalized derivation of all nasalized vowels.

Before stating the rule, it is necessary to determine its scope. It has been established in 14.1 that VNV sequences do not yield nasalized vowels, while VNC sequences do. The same question must be asked about VNG (where *G* stands for 'glide'), VNObst (where *Obst* stands for 'Obstruent'), VNL (where *L* stands for 'liquid'), and VNN.

Table 14.1

VNV	VNG	VNN	VNObst	VNL	VN
inactif	inouï	innombrable	incapable	inlassable	écran
sonne	fanion	innovateur	insensible	enrhumé	son
inexprimé	union	savamment	contente	denrée	lin
VN	VN	VN	$\tilde{V}$	$\tilde{V}$	$\tilde{V}$

Table 14.1 leads to the conclusion that nasalization takes place when VN is followed by a nonnasal consonantal segment or by a word boundary.

> RULE. NASALIZATION (final version): A vowel is nasalized if it is followed by a nasal and either a word boundary or a [nonnasal] consonantal segment.

This rule must be followed by another which deletes the conditioning nasal. This insures a two-step derivation from VN to V, with VN as an intermediate structure. The second derivational step, VN becoming V, is achieved via Nasal Deletion.

> RULE. NASAL DELETION (preliminary version): A nonsyllabic nasal segment is deleted if it is preceded by a nasalized vowel.

14.2.1 Nasalization and borrowing. These two rules do not apply to recently borrowed vocabulary. Compare *wagon* and *Washington*. *Wagon* /vagõ/ has been completely assimilated. It is found in a number of compound words (*wagon-bar, wagon-lit*) and serves as a stem on which affixes are attached (*wagonnet, wagonier*). It has become part of the native vocabulary. Its original initial glide has been gallicized to initial /v/ just as happened from Latin to French *vitam* (/witam/) > *vie*. Its VN sequence is subject to Nasalization and Nasal Deletion. *Washington* /waʃiŋgtòn/, however, has not become a French word. It is clearly identified with the history and language of another nation. No nasalization has taken place. Only the English stress placement has changed, giving way to the French stress assignment on the last syllable.

In the framework of vocabulary classes established in Chapters 8 and 9, it might be thought that Nasalization is limited to native vocabulary, but that is an oversimplification. Nasalization applies to some learned forms like *santé*, *bonté*, *substantif*, *documenter*, *suralimenter*, *alimentation*.

14.2.2 Two rules, not one. It has been claimed that a single rule of nasalization would produce the correct output by nasalizing and deleting the conditioning nasal in one step. That is not a satisfactory analysis of the facts because there are instances where a given structure is an exception to Nasal Deletion but not to Nasalization. Enclitics like *on*, *en*, *la*, etc. are, by their very nature, closely tied to the next word in the sequence. This closeness sets the stage for phonological linking and for elision. In the case of *on* and *en*, which are subject to Nasalization, the conditioning nasal must not be deleted if it is followed by a word-initial vowel, e.g. *on arrive*, *en arrivant*, *j'en ai*, but *on travaille*, *en travaillant*, *j'en possède*. Liaison is merely allowing a final consonant to remain and not be deleted by Final Consonant Deletion nor, in the case of *on* and *en*, by Nasal Deletion. Final Consonant Deletion applies only to obstruents. It does not affect *on* and *en*. This constraint, however, is totally independent of Nasalization, which must take place. The fact that one rule is constrained while the other is not subject to the same constraint suggests that a combined rule would be difficult to state and would have to be subdivided to allow for a statement of the constraint.

Another case, already considered, supports the two-rule analysis. The argument is the same as the foregoing argument but does not involve liaison. *Enivré* and *enherber*, both pronounced with /ãn/, are not subject to Nasal Deletion, but must undergo Nasalization. Liaison is not involved here because the phenomenon in question is word-internal. The only way to allow the application of Nasalization to these words is to treat the prefix *en-* exceptionally, marking it as subject to Nasalization. Once *enivré* and *enherber* are nasalized, Nasal Deletion must be prevented from applying to them, whereas it must apply to *encaisser*, *enguirlander* etc. This can be achieved by altering Nasal Deletion very slightly.

> RULE. NASAL DELETION (final version): A nonsyllabic nasal segment followed by a nonsyllabic segment (including a word boundary) is deleted if it is preceded by a nasalized vowel.

With this slight modification the grammar can handle the data of 14.1.5. This analysis is strongly dependent on the two-step solution and constitutes support for it.

The modification brought to Nasal Deletion has no consequence for the grammar except that it allows for a smooth handling of these exceptional cases. Since Nasalization applies to these exceptionally, no other cases of nasalization in a VNV string exist and Nasal Deletion in its revised form does not affect the rest of the grammar.

14.2.3 Nasalized Vowel Lowering. French is characterized by a rule which lowers all nasalized vowels. This lowering is substantiated by the existence of alternations between *fine* and *fin*, and between *brune* and *brun*. In these forms oral vowels are [high], whereas nasalized vowels are [low]. While this alternation in height is clear with respect to the front vowels, it is less obvious in the [nonfront] nasalized vowels. The low rounded nasalized vowel /ɔ̃/ alternates with low /ɔ/ only, not with any other vowel. The unrounded /ã/ alternates mainly with /a/, but see also 14.1.2, for an alternation with /e/ and /i/. The best way to account for the low nature of nasals is to have a rule, Nasalized Vowel Lowering, effect this shift.

RULE. NASALIZED VOWEL LOWERING (final version): All nasalized vowels become [low].

In connection with this rule, it might be instructive to address the problem posed in Question 3, in 14.5.

14.2.4 *en*-Adjustment. An alternation between front unrounded vowels and /ã/ was discussed in example (9), Section 14.1.2. This alternation, found in *prendre* and all its compounds (*surprenez*, *comprennent*, *méprends*), is also found in derivational morphology, as in *cinéraire*/*cendre*, *génération*/*gendre*. In addition to the rules of Nasalization, Nasal Deletion, and Nasalized Vowel Lowering, another rule is needed to insure the proper results. It is a minor rule applying to the small class of words just mentioned.

RULE. *en*-ADJUSTMENT (final version): In certain stems, the nasalized vowel /ɛ̃/ is made [nonfront].

14.3 Ordering. Nasalized Vowel Lowering and Nasal Deletion are not ordered with respect to each other but both are dependent on the prior application of Nasalization. Therefore the order of application is (1) Nasalization and (2) Nasalized Vowel Lowering and Nasal Deletion.

Nasalization is not ordered with respect to Diphthongization and the two fronting rules. These rules apply to vowels whether they are nasalized or not. Furthermore, the environment of these rules is restricted to Class D stem vowels whereas Nasalization is only phonologically conditioned.

In contrast to these nonorderings, Nasalization is ordered before /wa/-Adjustment, as shown in Chapter 9. An order of application must also be imposed between Nasalization and what for now is being called Final Schwa Deletion, a rule which can alter the environment of Nasalization. This is shown in the derivations in Table 14.2.

Table 14.2 clearly shows that the deletion of final schwa modifies the feminine form in such a way that it becomes subject to Nasalization when in fact it should not be. Therefore, Final Schwa Deletion must follow Nasalization.

14.4 The conditioning nasal. In Chapter 13 it was determined that the palatal nasal does not figure in the underlying inventory of French but rather

Table 14.2

	fine	*fin*
Underlying representation	fin-a	fin
Posttonic Vowel Reduction	fin-ə	...
Final Schwa Deletion	fin	...
Nasltn., N-Del., Nas-V-Low.	*fɛ̃	fɛ̃
Underlying representation	fin-a	fin
Posttonic Vowel Reduction	fin-ə	...
Nasltn., N-Del., Nas-V-Low.	...	fɛ̃
Final Schwa Deletion	fin	...

is derived by a palatalization rule labeled /l/-/n/-Palatalization. An order of application is imposed here between /l/-/n/-Palatalization and Nasalization: Nasalization is ordered before /l/-/n/-Palatalization to underscore the fact that the palatal /ɲ/ plays no role as the conditioning nasal in Nasalization.

The role played by /m/ in conditioning Nasalization is at best marginal. The only alternations of the type /Vm/ ~ /Ṽ/ are those of *parfumer*/*parfum*, *nommer*/*nom*, *sommes*/*sont*, and *essaime*/*essaim*, which constitute scant evidence in contrast to thousands of cases of nasalization with /n/ as the conditioning nasal.

It should be noted in passing that French no longer has a rule on Nasal Assimilation. As the orthography of *combien*, *compter*, *emblème*, *ampleur* suggest, French had a rule of Nasal Assimilation, a rule which causes a nasal to assimilate in point of articulation to a segment that follows it, but that rule became inoperative because of the Nasal Deletion rule, which tends to delete those nasals likely to enter into the environment of Nasal Assimilation.

While the palatal nasal does not figure in the underlying inventory of French phonemes, the status of phoneme must be granted to both /m/ and /n/. The bilabial nasal occurs word- (or syllable-) initially and in a few cases word- (or syllable-) finally; but there is little evidence that would suggest that /m/ occurs before consonantal segments either in the underlying representation or later, as a result of assimilation. The few cases of Homorganic Consonant Insertion of a /b/ between an /m/ and an /R/ would constitute cases where /m/ is the conditioning nasal.

It is therefore fair to conclude that /n/ is the nasal par excellence and that it is at work as a conditioning nasal in Nasalization more frequently than orthography might suggest.

14.5 Questions

1. The sound /ɛ̃/ has many different graphic representations. Find a word which corresponds to each of those listed here.

   (a) *yn* .... (b) *ym* .... (c) *ein* .... (d) *ain* ....
   (e) *aim* .... (f) *en* .... (g) *in* .... (h) *im* ....

2. Write the derivation of each of the following words, i.e. *embrun*, *moine*, *fond*.

3. In Chapter 4, it was pointed out that for many speakers the last sound of *flocon* is not a low but a mid vowel. This suggests that Nasalized Vowel Lowering is too general. Write an alternate rule to account for these facts. Should that rule be a revision of Nasalized Vowel Lowering, or should it be a rule that alters its effect on all nasalized vowels?

4. In answering the previous question, you may have proposed a rule which excludes back segments in your modified Nasalized Vowel Lowering. Note, however, that there are some nasalized mid vowels which alternate with low vowels, e.g. *bourgeon/bourgeonner*. How are these nasalized mid vowels derived in the context of the modified Nasalized Vowel Lowering? Make a list of ten alternations such as *bourgeon/bourgeonner* and propose a solution which is both economical and general to account for the height of /õ/.

5. The sibilants in *résister* and *persister* are treated differently in the phonology of French. In the former, the sibilant is voiced while in the latter it remains voiceless. In the verb *insister* voicing does not take place either. What do these facts suggest?

6. The preceding question assumes that forms in *-sist* are necessarily related. It also assumes that the voicing rule solves the problem. The scope of the information given in question 5, however, is quite limited. There are, in fact, some counterexamples. Show how *assister*, *subsistance*, and *exister* are exceptions to that putative rule.

7. The prefix *in-* has several allomorphs e.g. /i-/, /in-/, /im-/, /il-/, /iʀ-/, /ɛ̃-/, as in /imɔral/, /inublijabl/, /immɔral/, /illegal/, /iʀʀɛspõsabl/, and /ɛ̃kʀœvabl/, respectively. Propose a solution to account for these facts.

8. What does the spelling of *bonbonne* (borrowed from Provençal *boumbuono* in the mid 1800s) suggest about nasal assimilation in French? Support your answer with *bonbon*, a word created in the early 1600s.

9. Write the rule of Nasalization with the syllable as environment rather than in terms of what segments follow the conditioning nasal. What are some consequences of this change?

Chapter 15
Schwa, the chameleon

15.0 Introduction. No segment of French has been more studied and more misunderstood than schwa. This elusive segment has several derivational sources. Its phonetic make-up is unclear. Its very existence has been questioned. Researchers have been baffled by its behavior, especially in strings where some elements may drop while others do not. In this chapter a fairly novel approach is taken to the description of schwa. It may lead, it is hoped, to a more cohesive analysis of this complex phenomenon.

The chapter is divided into three sections. In the first section, I consider reduction, a process examined in Chapters 6, 8, 9, and 10. Thus, Section 15.1 constitutes a summary of the findings from earlier chapters. In Section 15.2, centered around the concept of syllabicity, the basis of my claim about the phenomenon studied here is set forth. Section 15.3 deals with demotion.

15.1 Reduction

15.1.1 Posttonic Vowel Reduction.

The historical source of schwa is well known. In posttonic position Latin /a/ became /ə/ in French. It has remained /a/ in Spanish and Italian. Other vowels in posttonic position were deleted by Apocope. In many instances /a/ was a feminine gender marker. The only vestiges of /a/ as a marker of the feminine gender are those of *ma*, *ta*, *sa*, and *la*, all monosyllabic. Otherwise, the change is complete and no alternations are available that illustrate this reduction.

RULE. POSTTONIC VOWEL REDUCTION (final version): A posttonic /a/ is reduced to /ə/.

By ensuring that there is such a rule, we are able to show that /a/ is the feminine marker in French as in other Romance languages. Monosyllabic forms like *ma*, *ta*, *sa*, and *la* are not subject to Posttonic Vowel Reduction and retain their /a/, while all other feminine words end in schwa. The rule applies also to learned words borrowed from Greek via Latin, accounting for the final schwa of *problème*, *poète*, *axiome*, etc.

15.1.2 Reduction of pretonic /a/.

(1) /a/, /ə/, /ɛ/ alternations

porta	portera	portèrent
chanta	chanterions	chantèrent
grange	grenier	grain
fragile	freluquet	frèle

The /a/ of the leftmost column can be reduced to the schwa of the middle column or can be fronted as shown in the rightmost column. The /a/ of *chanta* (third person singular in the simple past) is the theme (or thematic) vowel of the first conjugation (the so-called -*er* verbs). A thematic vowel is one which serves as marker of a particular inflectional class. This means that so-called -*er* verbs are in fact /-aR/ verbs in their underlying representation. With /a/ as a theme vowel for first conjugation, it is easy to see that Low Vowel Fronting can derive the forms in /ɛ/ in tonic position while /a/ remains in some forms of the simple past (marked as exception to Low

Vowel Fronting). Low Vowel Reduction changes pretonic /a/ into /ə/ in such paradigms as the future and the conditional. The schwa of the present indicative, which contrasts with the /a/ of the simple past, is derived from the theme vowel by Posttonic Reduction (15.1.1).

15.1.3 /ɛ/ reduced to schwa.

(2) /ɛ/, /ə/ alternations

chandelle	chandelier
mène	menons
sème	semons
appelle	appeliez

The /ɛ/ of words in the left column does not alternate with /a/, as does the /ɛ/ in 15.1.2. It reduces to schwa in pretonic position, however. Hence, two /ɛ/ must be distinguished, as indicated in 11.4.

15.1.4 Alternations of schwa with diphthongs.

(3) /jɛ/ alternates with schwa

pied	peton
palmier	palmeraie
tiens	tenions

(4) /wa/ alternates with schwa

poil	pelage
doivent	devions
poids	pesage

The diphthongs of (3) and (4) were discussed in 9.2 and 9.3. They were shown to be derived from low and nonlow vowels, respectively.

15.1.5 Low Vowel Reduction.
This review of pretonic reduction reveals that schwa can have /a/, /ɛ/, and /e/ as underlying segments. In 8.3.2, a rule of Pretonic Vowel Reduction was proposed, which changed /a, ɛ, e/ into schwa. However, when, in 10.3.3, Pretonic Vowel Adjustment was stated more generally (as a unitary process replacing two unrelated rules), it was found to overlap with Pretonic Vowel Reduction (to the extent that both rules lowered /e/ to /ɛ/). Consequently, the reduction rule did not need to be stated in such a way as to apply to /e/. It must simply apply after Pretonic Vowel Adjustment and refer only to low vowels, i.e. the /e/ lowered to /ɛ/ by the adjustment is therefore subject to the reduction rule. Pretonic Vowel Reduction was therefore replaced by a reduction rule, Low Vowel Reduction, applying exclusively to low vowels marked weak.

Low Vowel Reduction does not apply to fronted or diphthongized vowels (which are marked strong). It cannot apply to weak /ɔ/ because no such vowel remains after Pretonic Vowel Adjustment has applied, raising low back vowels to [nonlow]. It cannot apply to unmarked /a/ (*captif, han-*

neton), to unmarked /ɔ/ (*portail, portique*), to unmarked /ɛ/ (*rêverie, rêvasser*), or to weak vowels in initial position. It is also inapplicable to word-final (posttonic) /a/, which was accounted for in 15.1.1. These restrictions on Low Vowel Reduction are all accounted for in Chapter 10, except one: the phonetic constraint which prevents word-initial schwa and which accounts for such words as *amour* and *amant*, with an initial /a/, instead of */əmuʀ/ and */əmã/. In short, considering the constraints on rule ordering and the restrictions placed on it, Low Vowel Reduction can simply be said to apply to weak /a/ and weak /ɛ/ (in stems of Class C (Figure 8.1)) in word-medial open syllables.

RULE. LOW VOWEL REDUCTION (final version): In open syllable and word-medial position a weak low vowel becomes [central] and [lax].

15.2 Syllabicity. In Chapter 6, rules that insert and delete segments were outlined. The interrelationship of these rules with syllable structure was also examined. In connection with the word *people*, used in Section 6.2.3 as an illustration of epenthesis (the insertion of a supporting schwa), no clear-cut differences were shown between epenthesis and the operation which makes a segment syllabic. That question is discussed here.

15.2.1 The phonetic stuff of schwa. Schwa has been traditionally classified as a vowel in spite of a number of traits which would suggest otherwise. For example, schwa can be deleted in a large number of circumstances while the real vowels cannot. Schwa is never stressed in word-final position while vowels are (but see 15.2.5). Schwa is not found in initial position whereas vowels are. The phonetic nature of schwa is in part responsible for these discrepancies in the distribution of schwa. French phoneticians and phonologists disagree as to whether schwa is a phonetic entity. Some see schwa as a phonetic segment in its own right. Others say that it is a phonological unit realized as a real vowel at the phonetic level. And a third group says that the schwa can be realized either as phonetic schwa or as another vowel.

The position taken here is that what is called schwa is either realized as /œ/ (or as /ø/, depending on the dialect) or it triggers a rule which makes the preceding segment syllabic. The bundle of features identifying schwa in Figure 5.8 is necessary for some intermediate step in derivations; but, at the phonetic level, schwa is nonexistent, having been fronted to /œ/, or having caused the syllabicization of a preceding segment.

When the reflex of schwa is /œ/ or /ø/, then schwa is, of course, not distinguishable phonetically from the /œ/ of *seul* or the /ø/ of *deux*, respectively. Under some special circumstances, schwa can take group stress, though not contrastive stress. Examples in (5a) are acceptable; those in (5b) are not.

(5a) Sur c*e*, nous sommes rentrés.
Arrêtez-le!
Rends-l*e*!

(5b) *Sur c*é*, et pas çá, nous sommes rentrés.
*Arrêtez-l*é*, plutôt qu'elle.
*Rends-l*é* moi!

When the reflex of schwa is a syllabic segment, its phonetic nature is different from that of other vowels. These differences suggest why phoneticians and phonologists have been unable to agree on the nature of that segment.

The structure of the French syllable is, or tends to become, CV. In English, it is VC. That this is so can be shown in several ways. Take the words *il* and *eel* from French and English, respectively, and ask speakers of these languages to pronounce them with clear enunciation. The result is an exaggerated syllabicization of the final liquid in both cases. But there is also a striking difference. In English, the supportive schwa-like element precedes the liquid. In French, it follows.

Another fact that supports my claim about the syllable structure of French and English relates to syllables in abbreviated words. Compare *labo*, *prépa*, and *récré* to *lab*, *prep*, and *rec*, for *laboratory*, *preparatory*, and *recreation*. This is not to deny the existence of such words as *prof* and *bac* for *professeur* and *bachalauréat*, but the evidence on abbreviations is not limited to the foregoing. Kinship terms like *maman* and *papa* abbreviate to /mmã/ and /ppa/, ending clearly with a vowel. Their equivalents in English are *mom* and *dad* or *pop*, all of which end in a consonantal segment. The childish word for *aunt* in English is *aunty*, but the French equivalent goes even further, as it drops the final consonants of *tante* to make the word *tata*.

A careful study of onomatopeic formation also supports my claim that French syllables are CV in nature while English syllables are VC. In passing, compare *cocorico*, *ouaoua*, *cuicui*, *glouglou*, and *vlan* with their equivalents: *cock-a-doodle-do*, *arf-arf*, *chirp-chirp*, *glug-glug*, and *wham*.

When words end in a consonantal segment in French, that segment is often supported by some phonetic swelling which occurs after the segment in question has been produced. In other words, epenthetic support in French results in a CV-like syllable. The opposite order is true of English, where the supportive syllabic swelling takes place before the segment to be supported is released, thereby creating a VC-like syllable. A case in point involves the suffix *-ism* in English and its equivalent in French. Compare French *cubisme*, which ends in /izm̩/ or /ism̩/, where /m̩/ stands for /mœ/ (or for /mø/), with English *cubism*, which ends in /izm̩/, where /m̩/ stands for /əm/.

It appears therefore quite clear that the syllable structure of French is CV, whereas that of English is VC. The rest of this chapter depends crucially on this conclusion.

15.2.2 Syllabic liquids.

(6) Alternation of /yl/ with /l̩/

musculature	muscle	/myskl̩/
circulaire	cercle	/sɛrkl̩/
angularité	angle	/ãgl̩/
populisme	peuple	/pœpl̩/
séculaire	siècle	/sjɛkl̩/

That the pairs of words in (6) are related is supported by the fact that the stressed vowels of the words in the right column can be traced to the stem vowel of the corresponding words in the left column by way of such rules as High Vowel Lowering (*circul-/cercl-*), Low Vowel Fronting (*popul-/peupl-*), Diphthongization (*sécul-/siècle*). While different rules relate their stem vowels, one fact is common to all these forms. The words in the right column end with an obstruent followed by a syllabic liquid, while their left column equivalents feature a liquid flanked by two vowels, one on each side. As was seen in 6.3.2, the vowels which precede the liquid in learned vocabulary are deleted by Syncope in the derivation of the native forms, yielding the obstruent-liquid cluster in word-final position.

There are two ways in which the word-final liquid can be made syllabic: (1) phrase-finally, by Phrase Final Syllabicization, and (2) before another word, if that word begins with a consonant, via Word Boundary Syllabicization. The specification of these two rules is discussed here in 15.2.2. For now, an examination of how *cercle, peuple, siècle,* and *séculaire* are derived is in order (see Table 15.1).

Table 15.1 Derivation of *cercle, peuple, siècle,* and *séculaire.*

	cercle	*peuple*	*siècle*	*séculaire*
Underlying representation	sírkul	pópul	sékul	sɛkul-ár
High Vowel Lowering	sérkul	...	...	...
Apocope	sérkl	pópl	sékl	...
Phrase-Final Syllabicization	sérkl̩	pópl̩	sékl̩	...
Diphthongization	...	...	sjɛkl̩	...
Low Vowel Fronting	...	pœpl̩	...	sɛkul-ér
High Vowel Fronting	...	...	...	sɛkyl-ér
Closed Syllable Adjustment	sérkl̩	...	...	...
Vowel Harmony	...	...	...	sɛkyl-ér

128 / 15 Schwa, the chameleon

When a syllabic liquid occurs word-finally, it can be affected by speech speed. In careful speech, words with syllabic liquids are generally pronounced as shown in the left column of (7). In fast speech, the syllabic quality of the liquid may be lost in phrase-final position and, at word boundaries, /l̩/ and /ʀ̩/ are even deleted. This is shown in the right column of (7).

(7) Liquid deletion

	Careful speech:	Fast speech:
cercle fermé	/sɛʀkl̩fɛʀme/	/sɛʀkfɛʀme/
cable d'acier	/kabl̩dasje/	/kabdasje/
quatre coups	/katʀ̩ku/	/katku/
cadre léger	/kadʀ̩leʒe/	/kadleʒe/

The deletion just illustrated applies only at word boundary. Therefore, *entretien*, *simplement*, *autrefois*, *repeuplement* retain the syllabic liquid even in fast speech.

> RULE. SYLLABIC LIQUID DELETION (final version): In fast speech, a syllabic liquid after an obstruent is deleted if it immediately precedes a word boundary followed by a consonantal segment.

(8) Alternation of /ili/ with /l/

affabilité	affable
possibilité	possible
susceptibilité	susceptible
mobilité	meuble
solubilité	soluble

Suffixes in *-ité* and *-té* are noun-forming devices which are added to the underlying forms of the adjectives in the right column: /afabili/, /posibili/, etc. As in the case of the alternation in (6), posttonic vowels are deleted. Here, this is accomplished by both Syncope and Apocope. The deletion of the two underlying /i/ segments brings about the obstruent-liquid cluster which needs to be supported in phrase-final position. For that purpose Phrase-Final Syllabicization makes the liquid syllabic. Table 15.2 illustrates this.

Table 15.2 Derivation of *affable*, *meuble*, *mobilité*.

	affable	*meuble*	*mobilité*
Underlying representation	afabili	mɔbili	mɔbili-te
Syncope	afabli	mɔbli	...
Apocope	afabl	mɔbl	...
Low Vowel Fronting	...	mœbl	...
Phrase-Final Syllabicization	afabl̩	mœbl̩	...

15.2.2 Syllabic liquids

Whereas the clusters of (6) and (8) are created by the application of vowel deletion rules, those of (9) are inherent in the underlying representation of the words listed.

(9) Syllabic liquids in inherent clusters
    amplitude   ample
    aptitude   apte
    marbrier   marbre
    lévrier   lièvre
    ouvrir   ouvre

A cluster-final liquid, whether it is in an inherent cluster or in a derived one, may or may not be syllabicized, depending on its environment. If it is followed by a vowel, at word boundary or word-internally, then it cannot be syllabicized. If, by contrast, a cluster-final liquid is not supported by a vowel, then it must be made syllabic. This syllabicization is accomplished phrase-finally, between words, and word-internally as indicated in the following rules.

> RULE. PHRASE-FINAL SYLLABICIZATION (final version): In phrase-final position, a nonsyllabic segment preceded by one or more obstruents becomes [syllabic].

> RULE. WORD BOUNDARY SYLLABICIZATION (final version): A nonsyllabic segment preceded by a consonantal segment and followed by a word boundary and one or more consonantal segments becomes [syllabic].

Beyond the syllabicization of liquids, these two rules also make some true consonants syllabic. As stated here, Phrase-Final Syllabicization can cause the syllabicization of liquids as in *Elle est célèbre* or *Elle est souple*, but also that of obstruents, as in *Il joue de la harpe, Elle est peu orthodoxe*, or *Il s'écarte*. Word Boundary Syllabicization, as stated here, is designed to break up clusters created by the adjacency of words, some of which end and others begin with one or more nonsyllabic segments. In other words, the syllabicized segments may be liquids as in *sucre d'orge, nombre décimal, simple soldat*, or obstruents as in *ours blanc, acte premier, aphte contagieux*, or *herse roulante*.

In the correct ordering of rules, after Word Boundary Syllabicization and Phrase-Final Syllabicization have applied, no unsupported cluster remains.

Some schwas, however, do remain. The next rule is intended to eliminate all such phonological entities. It uses schwa as a catalyst for creating other syllabic segments.

> RULE. SYLLABIC ABSORPTION (final version): In atonic position schwa is absorbed into the immediately preceding segment which it makes [syllabic].

Segments which have undergone any of the foregoing three rules are referred to, henceforth, as 'syllabicized segments'. This term is to be regarded as a shortcut for any lengthy circumlocution that would make reference to prior application of either of these three rules.

Not all schwas have in fact been eliminated from the grammar. Only those which act as schwa have been so eliminated. The tonic schwas, found in Section 15.2.1, are not made syllabic. They are excluded by the restriction placed on Syllabic Absorption, namely, that it applies only to nontonic schwas. Instances of tonic schwa, e.g. *Prends-le*, *Sur-ce*, etc. are discussed in 15.2.5.

While it has been suggested here that Syllabic Absorption should apply word-internally, no such restriction was stated in the rule itself. A word of explanation is needed here to account for that apparent omission. The reason for not mentioning this domain is simply that there are no word-initial schwas in the language. Consequently, even if the rule is stated so broadly as to apply both word-internally and at word boundary, it applies only word-internally.

15.2.3 In postvocalic position. The analysis of schwa as a catalyst for Syllabic Absorption has several advantages. One such advantage is that it obviates the need for a rule of schwa deletion in postvocalic position.

(10) oublier   oublia   oubliera   /ubliʀa/
      clouer   cloua   cloue   /klu/
      jouer   joua   jouerions   /ʒuʀjɔ̃/
      tuer   tua   tuerie   /tuʀi/
      remercier   remercia   remerciement   /ʀəmɛʀsimɑ̃/

The examples of (10) show that /a/, the thematic vowel of the first verb group, weakens to /ə/ and must be deleted if it follows a vowel. The same is true of /a/ which marks feminine forms.

(11) né   / née   mort   / morte
      joli / jolie   pris   / prise
      plié / pliée   heureux / heureuse
      loué / louée   gros   / grosse

When a schwa follows a nonsyllabic segment, that segment is protected from deletion. This is the case in the second member of each pair in the right column. The final members of these pairs are subject to Final Consonant Deletion. The result is a phonetic difference between the members of these pairs. No such difference is evident in the pairs in the left column. The schwa which stands for the feminine leaves no phonetic mark. A way of accounting for this fact is to have a schwa deletion in postvocalic position. No such rule is needed in this analysis, however, because Syllabic Absorption applies vacuously to words with vowel + schwa sequences. It makes all segments syllabic, whether those segments were or were not syllabic in the first place.

In other words, one rule does both tasks: it deletes schwa after consonants and after vowels.

15.2.4 After a glide. Other than the cases where /a/ reduces to /ə/ after the sequence /li/ (/li/ → /ʎ/ → /j/), there are no cases of a schwa after a glide. To insure that no high vowel is glided before a schwa, the rule of Syllabic Absorption is ordered to precede Gliding. Consider the following order.

Table 15.3 Derivation of *une ouïe, la pluie*.

	une ouïe	la pluie
Underlying representation	uia	pluia
High Vowel Lowering	oia	...
High Vowel Fronting	...	plyia
Back Vowel Raising	uia	...
Gliding	uja	plyja
Posttonic Vowel Reduction	ujə	plyjə
Syllabic Absorption	*uj̣	*plyj̣

Now, consider instead the derivations of *ouie* and *pluie* in Table 15.4.

Table 15.4 Derivation of *ouie, pluie*.

	ouie	pluie
Underlying representation	uia	pluia
High Vowel Lowering	oia	...
High Vowel Fronting	...	plyia
Back Vowel Raising	uia	...
Posttonic Vowel Reduction	uiə	plyiə
Syllabic Absorption	ui	plyi
Gliding	wi	plɥi

15.2.5 Tonic schwa. The very mention of tonic schwa should be a contradiction. Schwa is a reduced vowel. By definition it is weak. How can it be stressed? A partial answer to the question lies not in phonology but in syntax. French, like other Romance languages, has syntactic elements such as articles, possessive adjectives, and some personal pronouns which are weakened. Syntax, like phonology, has weak and strong forms. These weak elements, known as clitics, behave like inflections in their dependence on the stronger classes. The words in which 'stressed schwa' is found are of those weak elements. Not all such elements retain their schwa in stressed position. *Me* as in *je me rase* is weak but it becomes diphthongized in tonic position: *Rasez-moi!* The same is true of *te/toi, se/soi*. When a weak element like *le* or *ce* is thrust into tonic position by a syntactic permutation (*il le prend/prend-*

le!) or deletion (as *sur ce* implies, from a string like *sur ce fait*), then there appears to be no choice but to have a stressed vowel. In such cases schwa, which cannot be stressed, changes to /œ/ and stress can fall on /œ/, which is not a weakened vowel. So, tonic schwa is not an appropriate term although it constitutes an easy reference for the phenomenon just described.

Support for this syntactic explanation can be noted in the fact that tonic schwa is never found as a lone syllabic peak, i.e. never in an utterance composed of a single syllable. To a question like *Qui a bu tout le vin?* one cannot answer, **Je*, but *Moi*: schwa is put in tonic position only by some syntactic accident. It is not capable of standing as the peak of a one-syllable utterance.

There appears to be a sort of cooperation between syntax and phonology. Some syntactic elements are made weak (cliticized) and concurrently phonology sees to it that their vowels are reduced. When syntax places some clitics in tonic position, phonology is then forced to modify the reduced vowel. Here, it makes the vowel tense, front, and rounded; it makes it /œ/.

> RULE. TONIC SCHWA (final version): In tonic position schwa becomes /œ/.

This rule applies after En-Haut for the dialect described here and before En-Haut for the dialects in which *ce* in stressed position rhymes with *ceux*. In the first case, En-Haut raises round vowels before schwa can be made round via Tonic Schwa and consequently subject to En-Haut. No further movement takes place in this instance. In the second case, schwa becomes /œ/ via Tonic Schwa and then /ø/ by the application of En-Haut.

15.3 Demotion. A number of clitics (*je, te, me, se, le, ne*), the article *le*, the demonstrative adjective *ce*, the prefix *re-* (as in *recommencer*), and even *de-*, a formerly productive prefix now fused in words like *dehors, demander, demain, dessus*, are all instances of Syllabic Absorption. Some of these have alternations, suggesting that their schwa is derived, while others have no alternations. In the latter, it might be best to assume that schwa occurs in the underlying representation. Whatever their sources, all schwas occur in all the items mentioned at some point in the derivation. All are subject to Syllabic Absorption. Beyond that, at the phonetic level, under some conditions, some of these syllabicized segments may lose their syllabicity. This is accomplished by a rule known as Syllabic Demotion. The environments in which Syllabic Demotion operates constitute the topic of the present section (15.3). First, demotion will be examined in prevocalic position (15.3.1), then in phrase-initial position (15.3.2), and finally in strings of contiguous syllabicized segments (15.3.3).

In the following discussion, orthography is used with some diacritics to help the reader understand readily whether a given segment is to be syllabic or not. A diagraph in italics (such as in *Le*clerc) indicates that the consonant must be pronounced as syllabic. Parentheses (e) indicate that the preceding segment may be pronounced as syllabic, e.g. *on l(e) voit* can be pronounced as either /ɔ̃lvwa/ or /ɔ̃lvwa/. An italic *e* with a slanted line (*e̸*), means that the segment is not pronounced as syllabic. For example, in *J(e) caress̸e ma chatt̸e*, the final *e* of both polysyllabic words must not be pronounced. This system is used to show both the 'correct' and the 'incorrect' pronunciation of the sequences of words examined.

15.3.1 Prevocalic demotion. This type of demotion is known traditionally as elision, a rule which deletes the orthographic *e* of monosyllabic words before a vowel.

(12a) l'ami   but not   *le* ami
(12b) l'oiseau   but not   *le* oiseau
(12c) il m'entend but not   *il *me* entend
(12d) c'est lui   but not   *ce* est lui
(12e) il s'essuie but not   *il *se* essuie

Elision is also believed to delete *a* in the article and the pronoun *la* in prevocalic position. Evidence to that effect is found in (13).

(13) Preconsonantal: Prevocalic: Violation:
     je la vois   je l'entends   *je la entends
     la nouvelle   l'ancienne   *la ancienne
     la margarine   l'huile   *la huile
     la dinde   l'oie   *la oie

It should be noted, however, that Elision is a sweeping process with respect to schwa but not at all general with respect to /a/. In fact, it applies only to *la* as a pronoun or article. It does not apply to *là* or to *ça*.

(14) ça ouvre à six heures
     *ç'ouvre à six heures
     il est là-haut / là-en-bas.
     *il est l'haut / *l'en-bas.

The behavior of /a/ in atonic position suggests that the deletion of /a/ is a minor rule applying to the article or the pronoun, whereas the deletion of schwa is general. A rule which attempts to make both statements would be complicated and unbalanced, and would be ad hoc. If, instead of complicating Elision unnecessarily, it were said that Elision applies only to schwa and another rule converts /a/ to make it conform with the input of Elision, two objectives would be accomplished. First, Elision would be stated generally, simply, and without exceptions. Second, the exceptional behavior of /a/ would be accounted for by an exceptional rule. That is the solution adopted here. A rule, /la/-Syllabe, changes /la/ into a syllabicized segment, /l̩/, which is itself subject to the Elision rule.

RULE. /la/-SYLLABE (final version): The article or pronoun /la/ becomes /l/ if followed by a nonconsonantal segment (a vowel or a glide).

Subsequently, the Elision rule can apply to any monosyllabic syllabicized segment, the foregoing included, if that segment is followed by a vowel or a glide.

RULE. ELISION (final version): A syllabicized segment becomes [nonsyllabic] if followed by a nonconsonantal segment.

There are some cases where Elision and other rules applying at word boundaries fail to apply. The cause for these is unclear, as is seen later; but it is certain that these exceptions are not due to anything in the behavior of schwa.

Some words, many beginning with an *h* in spelling, some foreign borrowings, and yet others, like *onze*, do not allow Elision to apply.

(15) Elision:
    l'outre
    l'âge
    l'omoplate
    l'héroïne
    l'un et l'autre
    l'homme
    l'ouïe des électeurs
    l'ouest

No Elision:
    la housse
    la hâche
    la hanche
    le héros
    le onzième
    le home
    le oui des électeurs
    le western

The fact that a pair like *héro/héroine* is split strongly suggests that the list of words must be treated as exceptional. One ad hoc solution is to have an /h/ before each of the words in question to enable them to avoid elision and to delete the /h/ after Elision has applied. However, the problem is compounded when one considers further cases of no Elision.

(16) Elision:
    l'un et l'autre
    Il prétend qu'on ne
      badine pas avec
      l'amour.

No Elision:
    le un place du marché
    La première scene *de* 'On
      ne badine pas avec
      l'amour'.

It appears that any word otherwise subject to Elision can be made an exception if somehow removed, if somehow quoted. The exact nature of this exception to transitional rules like Elision and Liaison is still not clear. Current grammar simply fails to account for these facts.

15.3.2 Phrase-Initial Demotion. Speakers of French seem to disagree considerably over the demotion of phrase-initial syllabicized segments. In this analysis, Phrase-Initial Demotion is rather conservative, reflecting, for better or for worse, my own habits.

(17a)   J(e) n'en sais rien.
(17b)   J(e) vous en prie.
(17c)   J(e) donnerai ça à Paul.
(17d)   J(e) porte un gilet.
(17e)   C(e) courrier est en retard.
(17f)   C(e) tableau est affreux.
(17g)   *Je* cherche un livre.
(17h)   *Ce* savon mousse bien.
(17i)   *Ce* zèle me dépasse.
(17j)   *Ne* sors pas sans moi.
(17k)   *Te* rappelles-tu?
(17l)   *Re*tirez-vous!
(17m)   *Le*vez-vous!

Only strident segments are subject to Phrase-Initial Demotion, as illustrated by (17a) to (17f), contrasted with (17j) to (17m). Examples (17g), (17h), and (17i) further show that a strident segment in the next word prevents the application of the rule.

RULE. PHRASE-INITIAL DEMOTION (final version): A phrase-initial syllabicized strident segment may become [nonsyllabic] if it is followed by a word boundary and a nonstrident segment.

15.3.3 Contiguous syllable segments. Best known among the studies of this phenomenon is the work of M. Grammont, immortalized as his 'loi des trois consonnes'.

(18) Loi des trois consonnes
   'La règle générale est qu'il [schwa, *J.C.*] se prononce seulement lorsqu'il est nécessaire pour éviter la rencontre de trois consonnes.'

No critique of the 'loi' is developed here. It is mentioned for the purpose of reference only. The reader is invited to read the pertinent pages in Grammont (1948: 116-28). Like Dell (1973), I am convinced that any rule, the purpose of which is to describe this phenomenon, must distinguish consonants which used to be followed by a schwa from those which were never followed by a schwa in the derivational history of strings of segments. Grammont's 'loi' does not make that distinction. Dell's rules refer to schwa in their statement of these facts. My analysis does not refer to schwa. It accounts for the distinction just mentioned in terms of syllabicity.

In 15.2 it was established that certain consonants become [syllabic] if they occur in an unsupported cluster (*possible*, *apte*, *célèbre*) or if they are followed by a schwa, irrespective of schwa's origin. Consider the contrasts in (19) and (20).

(19) la p(e)tit¢
    tout l(e) mond¢
    j(e) vous r(e)merci¢
    il a ach(e)té ça

(20) un os *de* poulet
    exac*te*ment
    un por*te*feuill¢
    au*tre*ment

The syllabic segments /p, l, R/ and /ʃ/ in (19) are all preceded by a vowel (another syllabic segment), and may be demoted to nonsyllabic status. The italicized syllabic segments in (20) are preceded by a consonantal segment. They could be demoted only if they were followed by a vowel (Elision). But the syllabic segments of both (19) and (20) are followed by consonantal segments. The only difference between both sets is that the forms of (19) allow the segments under consideration to demote, thereby creating a coda for the preceding syllable, while the forms of (20) do not allow Demotion. In (20), the consonant which blocks demotion already serves as coda of the preceding syllable.

The number of consonants (obstruents and liquids) occurring after a segment considered for Demotion is not a factor in preventing Demotion, even if the resulting string includes three or more consonants in succession.

(21a)   on s(e) tracass¢
(21b)   Je m(e) bross¢ les dents
(21c)   plus d(e) splendeur
(21d)   sans l(e) sculpteur

Some of the *e*'s in (21) must not be pronounced. They are crossed out with a slanted line, according to the established convention. The ones in parentheses precede clusters of two or three consonants. They are usually subject to Demotion, especially in fast speech.

While the number of nonsyllabic segments is not as crucial as Grammont's Law suggests, the number of desyllabicized segments is in fact crucial. Consider (22), which illustrates this point with a striking contrast.

(22a)   Il dit qu*e* j(e) trembl¢.
(22b)   Il dit qu*e* j(e) t*e* rendrai ton livre.
(22c)   *Il dit qu*e* j¢ t¢ rendrai ton livre.

These examples show that the demotion of *je* is possible before a segment not previously syllabicized (e.g. the /t/ in *je tremble*), but not possible before a desyllabicized segment (e.g. the t¢ of (22c)).

Beside the strings in (22), those in (23) are also possible, where the status of *que* is changed from (22).

(23) Il dit qu¢ je t¢ rendrai ton livre.

These facts suggest that, depending on whether a given segment has been desyllabicized, preceding adjacent segments are or are not subject to Demotion. In a series of syllabicized segments, a number of things can happen. It is possible that all remain syllabicized, as is the case in a number of Midi

15.3.3 Contiguous syllable segments / 137

dialects. Even in Standard French, cases of no demotion are found, but their frequency is in inverse proportion to the number of stringed syllabicized segments.

(24a)   Vous le revoyez.
(24b)   Il me le redonne.
(24c)   Je te le redonne.
(24d)   Je ne te le redonne pas.

The more consecutive syllabic segments there are, the less likely it is that all of them will remain syllabic. However, they are not all desyllabicized in one fell swoop.

(25a)   *Il m¢ l¢ r¢donne.
(25b)   *J¢ t¢ l¢ r¢donne.
(25c)   *J¢ n¢ t¢ l¢ r¢donne pas.

The examples in (22)-(25) suggest that Syllabic Demotion must apply to syllabicized segments in succession. That type of rule application is termed iterative. Syllabic Demotion is an iterative rule. It applies from right to left.

When a syllabicized segment S_1 is followed by another syllabicized segment S_2, then S_1 may become nonsyllabic provided that it is preceded by a syllabic segment.

(26a)   On le reconnait. /ɔ̃lʀ̩kɔnɛ/
(26b)   Je me le paye. /ʒml̩pɛj/
(26c)   Il ne me le redemande pas. /iln̩ml̩ʀd̩mɑ̃dpa/

In (26a), le is demoted because /ɔ̃/ is syllabic and /ʀ/ is syllabicized. In (26b), /ʒ/ is syllabicized, hence syllabic, so me can be demoted. In (26c), Syllabic Demotion applies twice. In both instances, the conditions are met. Syllabic Demotion is optional in this environment. Therefore it allows the following versions of (24b) and disallows the starred sequences.

(27)   Logically possible strings of (24b)
(27a)   /ilm̩ʀdɔn/   but not   (27d)   */ilm̩ʀ̩dɔn/
(27b)   /ilml̩ʀdɔn/   (27e)   */ilml̩ʀ̩dɔn/
(27c)   /ilml̩ʀ̩dɔn/   (27f)   */ilmlʀdɔn/
                                    (27g)   */ilml̩ʀdɔn/
                                    (27h)   */ilm̩lʀdɔn/

Examples (27d) to (27g) are ungrammatical because they are cases of Demotion of me after a nonsyllabic segment. Example (27h) is not grammatical because of restrictions discussed in connection with the examples in (22). It is easy to see that, given a longer string of syllabicized segments, every second one drops. The following rule has just that effect.

RULE. SYLLABIC DEMOTION (final version): A syllabicized segment may become [nonsyllabic] if preceded by a syllabic segment and followed by either (1) a syllabicized segment, or (2) one and only one desyllabicized segment, if the next segment is [nonconsonantal], or (3) one or more never syllabicized segments. (This rule applies from right to left, iteratively.)

15.3.4 In word-final position. In Chapter 6, the rule of Final Schwa Deletion was discussed and its role in derivation was illustrated. No specific formulation for that rule was given, and until the present discussion on syllabicity, it was assumed to exist as suggested in Chapter 6. It must now be evident, however, that no schwa can undergo any rule in the present system since all schwa segments are erased by the application of Syllabic Absorption. In place of Final Schwa Deletion, this analysis calls for a demotion rule, Word-Final Demotion.

RULE. WORD-FINAL DEMOTION (final version): In posttonic position, a syllabic segment is generally demoted if it is word-final or followed by inflectional markings.

Word-Final Demotion need not refer to syllabicized segments, although syllabicized segments are indeed those segments to which it is intended to apply. The reason for not mentioning syllabicized segments is metatheoretic. It is more costly in the overall evaluation metric to state a rule that refers to the application of other rules than to state one that does not. Consequently, one avoids unnecessary complication of the grammar whenever possible. In this case, the term 'syllabicized' does not refer simply to a feature of a given segment but to the fact that the segment in question has undergone the application of either Syllabic Liquid Deletion or Syllabic Absorption. The term 'syllabicized' contrasts with the term [syllabic], which refers simply to a feature. Word-Final Demotion need not refer to syllabicized segments because, given the order of application of rules, all other syllabic segments are excluded from occurring in the stated domain of the rule.

Word-Final Demotion, however, is stated so as to apply to syllabicized segments, in word-final position as well as before inflections. This is to ensure that demotion takes place before plural markers, before the second person singular marker in the present indicative of verbs of the first conjugation, and before the third person plural marker in a number of verbs.

Word-Final Demotion does not apply to the so-called tonic schwa, because by rule (Tonic Schwa) such segments have been made vowels (/œ/) and vowels are not subject to Word-Final Demotion. That vowels are not subject to Word-Final Demotion follows from the fact that they are always stressed in word-final position; Word-Final Demotion is restricted to segments in posttonic position. Word-Final Demotion also fails to apply to another set of desyllabicized segments, namely, those which occur word-finally but are

15.3.4 In word-final position / 139

followed by words beginning with a [nonconsonantal] segment. These are demoted by Elision which, of course, precedes Word-Final Demotion.

Word-Final Demotion applies in phrase-final position, whether or not the segment affected figures in a consonant cluster. Its application accounts for the phrase-final segments in *elle est allemande*, *sa robe est ample*, *il est habile de la dextre*, which do not end phonetically with a syllabic segment. When the last segment is the liquid /R/, it devoices, as was discussed in Chapter 7. When the last segment is the liquid /l/, it devoices if and only if it is phrase-final and if it is in a cluster with a voiceless obstruent.

> RULE. /l/-DEVOICING (final version): In phrase-final position in clusters with a voiceless obstruent, /l/ devoices.

It is helpful now to turn to some sample derivations to illustrate the role and scope of the rules discussed in this chapter. The first derivation (see Table 15.5) illustrates liaison in contrast to a case of Final Consonant Deletion. In this and other derivations, the segments shown in a given line are those which the given rule has affected. In other words, a blank means that no change has taken place. Note also the difference between the symbols ø and ∅ (a zero with a slash through it). The former is a phonetic symbol for front rounded mid vowels (it is not used in the derivations). The latter represents a null set, i.e. a segment deletion.

Table 15.5 Derivation of *des petites bêtes*, *des petites olives*.

	des petites bêtes	*des petites olives*
Underlying representation	dez pətítaz bétaz	dez pətítaz ɔlívaz
Posttonic Vowel Reduction	ə ə	ə ə
Final Consonant Deletion	∅ ∅ ∅	∅ ∅
Syllabic Absorption	p∅ t∅ t∅	p∅ t∅ v∅
Syllabic Demotion	p t	p t
Word-Final Demotion	t	v
	/de p tit bɛt/	/de p tit z ɔliv/

The next derivation (Table 15.6) illustrates Elision and ties in with Chapter 14 in that it shows the derivation of the word *enfant*, alternant of *infantile*.

Table 15.6 Derivation of *C'est l'enfant de choeur*.

	C'est l'enfant de choeur
Underlying representation	sə ɛt lə infant də koʀ
Low Vowel Fronting	œ
Nasalization	˜ ˜
Nasal Deletion	∅ ∅
Nasal Vowel Lowering	ɛ̃
en-Adjustment	ã
Final Consonant Deletion	∅ ∅
Syllabic Absorption	s̩∅ l̩∅ d̩∅
Elision	s l
Syllabic Demotion	d
Voicing Assimilation	t
	/s ɛ l ã f ã t kœʀ/

The next derivation (Table 15.7) illustrates the interplay between /la/-Syllable and Elision.

Table 15.7 Derivation of *Ils l'attendent* (where *l'* is feminine).

	Ils l'attendent
Underlying representation	ilz la atandət
Nasalization	˜
Nasal Deletion	∅
Final Consonant Deletion	∅ ∅
Syllabic Absorption	d̩∅
/la/-Syllabe	l̩∅
Elision	l
Word-Final Demotion	d
	/il l atã d/

The next derivation (Table 15.8) illustrates Syllabic Absorption in its relationship to the rules of demotion, particularly with the iterative application of Syllabic Demotion.

Table 15.8 Derivation of *Je te le redemande*.

	Je te le redemande			
Underlying representation	ʒə tə lə ʀədəmandə			
Nasalization	̃			
Nasal Deletion	∅			
Syllabic Absorption	ʒ∅ t̪∅ l∅ ʀ∅d∅		d∅	
Phrase-Initial Demotion	ʒ̩			
Syllabic Demotion	l		d	
Word-Final Demotion			d	
Voicing Assimilation	ʃ			
	/ʃ t̪ l ʀ̩ d mã d/			

The last derivation (Table 15.9) illustrates the application of Word Boundary Syllabicization.

Table 15.9 Derivation of *la simple vérité, un ours splendide*.

	la simple vérité		*un ours splendide*	
Underlying representation	la símplə veʀite		yn uʀs splandídə	
Posttonic Vowel Reduction	ə			
Nasalization	̃		̃	̃
Nasal Deletion	∅			∅
Nasalized Vowel Lowering	ɛ̃		œ̃	
Word Boundary Syllabicization			s̩	
Syllabic Absorption	l∅			d∅
Word-Final Demotion				d
	/la sɛ̃ pl̩ veʀite/		/œ̃n uʀs̩ splã did/	

15.4 Questions

1. What is the difference between English and French syllabicization? Both rules apply to break up clusters but their outputs are different. Explain how they are different.

2. State which rules have applied in the derivation of the following strings of words.
   (a) encre de Chine   /ãgd̩ʃin/
   (b) un seul secret   /œ̃sœls̩kʀɛ/
   (c) il devra répondre   /ild̩vʀaʀepɔ̃dʀ/

If a particular order of application is required, state that order. Then, propose the rule(s) needed to account for the following alternative to (c).
   (c′) il devra répondre   /idvʀaʀepɔ̃dʀ/

3. Consider the following sentence which has potentially five consecutive syllabicized segments.

Il faut que je te le refasse.

List all possible sequences, separating them into two classes: acceptable and not acceptable. Then check your answer by applying the appropriate rules.

4. Demonstrate the appropriate ordering between Syllabic Demotion and the two rules of assimilation needed to account for the following data.

(a) Je te retrouve dans ce compartiment. /ʃt̥ʀtRuvdãskɔ̃partimã/
(b) Je les regarde. /ʒleʀgaʀd/
(c) Ce garçon court vite. /zgaʀ̥sɔ̃kuʀvit/

Note. The small circle /₀/ placed below a liquid (ʀ̥) indicates that liquid is voiceless.

5. Consider the following utterances that involve demotion. Then state why the starred sequence is ungrammatical. How does the grammar developed here insure that such strings are not generated?

ellè oublié   ellè me lè demande
ellè sort   *elle mè le dèmande
ellè pleure
ellè scrutine

6. You have no doubt heard utterances like /uvlapɔRt/ for *ouvre la porte*. Now consider the following, where *rouvre* means 'open again'.

(a) Il veut que je te rouvre la porte.
(b) Il veut que je trouve la porte.

In fast speech, the second /R/ of *rouvre* is dropped, as it was in *ouvre*. This is done by Syllabic Liquid Deletion. One might expect then that strings like (a) and (b) would be pronounced identically in fast speech. Yet native speakers of French do not produce (a) and (b) identically. How do they distinguish between (a) and (b)? How is this distinction accounted for in our grammar?

7. If the underlying representation of *ânerie* were said to be /anRi/, our grammar would produce the incorrect output */ãdRi/. Why? What must be done to prevent this incorrect output and to insure that /anRi/ is derived. What does the solution you proposed suggest about French orthography?

8. If it is true that only the /a/ of articles and pronouns with the form /la/ and the /ə/ of clitics (satellites) are elided, then how do you explain that we write (a) but not (b)?

(a) S'il venait, je sortirais.
(b) *Si il venait, je sortirais.

Make sure that your explanation takes into account the fact that no elision occurs in (c).

(c) Si elle venait, je sortirais.

Part Four.
Some practical observations, eclectic remarks, and drill-oriented applications.

Part Four is composed of nine practical lessons which constitute the practical counterpart to the more systematic Parts One, Two, and Three. In this fourth part of the book you are given possible applications of principles and facts studied earlier. These lessons are eclectic in their contents and in coverage, but each contains sample drills intended to improve pronunciation. This, however, is not a drillbook; it is a book for drillmasters, with suggestions on how to compose drills. It is felt that drills should be devised as specifically as possible for the students who use them. There are numerous regional and idiosyncratic reasons for tailoring drills to the individual's needs rather than using a monolithic workbook.

Whenever possible, the sample drills reflect the rules and principles discussed in the earlier parts of the book, but they are not limited to these rules and principles. I believe that an eclectic approach blending phonetic manipulations with phonological alternations is best in that it adds breadth to the learner's experience.

Additionally, the lessons in Part Four contain remarks on the descriptions presented in Parts One-Four, some quantitative data such as frequency of occurrence of individual sounds, and some sound-to-letter correspondences.

Chapter 16
Sound production

16.1 The buckshot effect. In Chapter 3, the action of the heart, on which we have no control, was contrasted with that of the breathing apparatus. I pointed out that inspiration and expiration could be altered and that the production of speech sounds involves the infinite number of ways in which we can modify the process of expiration. Actually, in speaking a language we take advantage of only a very small number of such modifications. First, we group as the 'same' sound a set of sounds which fit criteria of similarity. These criteria are language-dependent. For example, French speakers do not distinguish between the last sounds in *mouse* and *mouth*: they interpret both as belonging in the category of the first sound of *sac*. It would be wrong to say that they cannot hear it for they do! Proof of this is found in the phenomenon of 'zaizaiement' or lisping. French children who lisp are corrected by their parents, just as are English-speaking children. Hence, the French do hear the difference between *mouse* and *mouth*, between *think* and *sink*, but to them it is mere phonetic difference, to which they attach no semantic significance. For another example of how speakers classify as belonging together sounds which can be quite different to other speakers, consider the vowel system of Arabic. Speakers of Arabic use only three vowels: *a*, *i*, and *u*, as in French *pas*, *pie*, *pou*. Any sound resembling, say, *i*, they subconsciously interpret as *i*. So, the difference between *seat* and *sit* or *fit* and *fée*, which is significant to speakers of English and French, respectively, is well within the margin of acceptability when producing the Arabic *i*. On the other hand, there are some sounds in Arabic which nonnatives do not perceive as significant but must learn to keep apart if they are to speak Arabic correctly, for example /k/ and /q/, which the French hear as /k/ only.

Each language establishes arbitrary targets for the production of sounds. Children (or adults) learning a given language must learn to hit within an area of the target for each sound. No one is required to hit the bull's eye. In fact, there may be no bull's eye, or if there is, it is quite large.

The other way by which we fail to use the enormous variety of sounds potentially afforded us by our vocal apparatus is the principle of which the foregoing is the logical result. Chapter 2 showed how speech sounds are the products of combinations of sounds. To the production of any speech sound there corresponds a set of numbers relating to its frequency, amplitudes, harmonics, etc. Highly sensitive machines can record as different (and almost always do) what may appear identical to us. Put another way, we can repeat the same sound, say *a*, 20 times and not give the exact same sound twice, as recorded by these machines. In short, there is an infinity of possibilities available to us. Clearly, man cannot use an infinity of sounds: for one thing, he would not be able to learn an infinite number of sounds. So languages use only a portion of what is available, generally about three dozen sounds. The logical consequence of this is that the infinite sound spectrum is split into the target areas mentioned previously. The metaphor of the target and the idea that qualitative precision is not necessary seem to be summed up in the name I like to give to this phenomenon: the buckshot effect.

16.2 Glottal aperture. You may have located your glottis by taking a deep breath and holding it with your mouth open. The glottis serves as a valve when we want to trap air in our lungs. We can also retain air in our lungs by keeping our diaphragm contracted but that demands more energy and is an unreliable method of keeping air in.

The glottis, as a valve containing our vocal cords, can produce sounds which are not part of our verbal communication. It can, for example, fail to remain closed while we make a sudden effort, as in lifting, causing us to emit an inarticulate grunting sound. You might say that this sound has meaning, but note that its meaning is not linked to its appearance in a word (like the meaning difference between *sink* and *think*). It conveys (technically, connotates) meaning in somewhat the way of *pst!* or *tsk tsk*.

16.2.1 Aspiration. The glottis has three general positions: (1) open, for voiceless sounds and breathing; (2) slightly open, for voicing; and (3) closed, for protection when swallowing, for trapping air, etc. One more position can be identified, in fact, between the slightly open, voicing position and the breathing position, the one used for whispering and for producing the first sound of *hero*. Air escapes more rapidly through this opening than through the one used for voicing. Recite a French poem while whispering and then in a normal speaking voice. You go further on one full breath of air when speaking normally than when whispering. Why? Because the glottal opening is larger for whispering. It's like blowing air out of any air-tight chamber: the smaller the valve opening, the longer it takes. This additional position of the glottis causes what is known as aspiration (a misnomer, since the air flows out). Certain languages make great use of aspiration, others little use. French is of the second type. It used to have an *h* sound but lost it. It is left with some minimal aspiration in words ending with *p*, *t*, or *k*. On the other hand, some languages use aspiration extensively, even in producing vowels. These vowels are known as voiceless vowels. English has no voiceless vowels (except, as with all languages, when whispered) but it makes more use of aspiration than does French. In particular, English has an aspirated *h*.

What, you may ask, is the meaning of '*h-aspiré*'? French grammars indeed refer to this term in the context of 'liaison' and 'elision'. One must pronounce as *z* the *s* of *les* in *les hommes, les enfants* but not pronounce it in *les femmes, les héros, les hollandais*. This is liaison. Similarly, one must drop the last vowel of the article before another vowel, as in *l'âme, l'homme, l'humilité*, but not in *le croissant, le héro, le hollandais*. That is elision. The French *h* used to be pronounced with aspiration, just as in English. Progressively, it was lost in different words. When it was pronounced, it acted just like a consonant, preventing liaison and elision. The orthographic *h* in words which lost the phonetic *h* early, was called '*h-muet*'. This '*h*' does not prevent liaison and elision. It is a mere orthographic archaism. The formerly pronounced *h* was called '*h-aspiré*'. Its name and its function have remained, even though it is no longer pronounced.

16.2.2 Closure. Another way we use the glottis is by completely blocking the air and releasing sharply. Some speakers of English, especially in the northeast of the USA, use this sound, known as the glottal stop, in some words like *bottle*. Most English speakers do not. The glottal stop is not used in French either, but some languages use this consonant just as naturally as we use *p* or *k*. Hold your breath with your mouth open, blocking air at the glottis. Release sharply as you produce the word *are*. Now without blocking the air at the glottis produce the word *are*. There is no difference in meaning in the sentence *Are you producing a glottal stop?*, whether or not you blocked air at the glottis. If you block air at the velum, producing *k*, the sentence becomes meaningless: **Car you producing a glottal stop*. The same drastic meaning changes occur between occurrence or nonoccurrence of a glottal stop in those languages where the glottal stop is used. Yet, to a speaker of French or English, it is a meaningless and insignificant little noise.

Glottal aperture, the relative opening of the glottis, is an important factor in speech production. Its greatest importance, discussed in Section 5.6, lies in the production of voicing, a characteristic shared by all 5,000 or so languages spoken on our planet.

16.3 Articulatory habits. In addition to differing from one another in terms of the sounds they employ, languages are different in the way they produce sounds, each language developing its own articulatory characteristics. French and English have quite different articulatory habits.

The lips of an English speaker rarely pucker. They do not retain any position steadily. Instead, they are constantly shifting and remain stationary only in the so-called neutral position, just before speech. The tension of the whole articulatory apparatus is low, almost nonexistent. The velum is not clearly lowered or raised, yielding a seminasalization in some speakers. The whole effect of this muscular relaxation is that vowels are not clear; they become preceded and followed by glides; consonants are fully released before the articulation of the following vowel begins. In short, the articulatory effort is low and expiration is wasteful.

The lips of the francophòne are extremely mobile: they jut forth, pucker, spread wide, and retract frequently in speech. When they assume a position, they briefly retain it before rapidly switching to the next stationary position. The tension of the articulatory muscles is very high. The velum is always clearly up or down, yielding a clear oral or nasal segment. The whole apparatus anticipates vowels, which begin their vibrations and resonances with or briefly after the onset of the preceding consonant. An impression of phonetic clarity and distinctness results. The articulatory effort is great, expiration minimal.

16.4 Posture and breathing. Language drills are not mental exercises (what an understatement!). They are habit-forming physical exercises. To do them correctly, whether in class or in the language laboratory, the learner must not be given to sleep or relaxation. Drills are work!

Before drill sessions, students should do stretching exercises to awaken their bodies and breathing exercises to awaken their speech apparatus. During drills, they should sit up, preferably with no support, and they should breathe with deep diaphragm-drawn breaths. Since most people have forgotten how to breathe from the diaphragm since their baby-crying days, they need to be taught to do what they did naturally in infancy.

Breathing Exercise 1

(1) Take hold of your chair with your arms straight down your sides. Hold securely to prevent movement in your shoulders.

(2) Relax your stomach muscles so as to allow your belly to protrude.

(3) Breathe in slowly but as deeply as possible. Hold your breath for a few seconds.

(4) Without moving from this position, slowly let the air out.

(5) Repeat this procedure three times.

Breathing Exercise 2

(1) Repeat steps (1) and (2) of the previous exercise, then

(3) Breathe in slowly, making sure not to use your glottis to hold your breath. As you do, you will notice that your stomach muscles are tight. What you have done is equalize the pressure of the diaphragm and that of your stomach muscles on your abdominal cavity. Control of these muscles to allow air to enter the lungs and to leave them at will is known as control breathing. Singers use it, and so should speakers.

(4) Without moving from this position and without using your glottis, let the air out.

An alternative to (4) is to let the air out by producing one vowel or more, even all vowels.

(5) Repeat this procedure before you do any drills.

16.5 Keep up interest. Discourage slouching; send the yawner to splash water on his face. Inject humour between drills. Make the drills crisp and fast moving. If one must be repeated, punctuate the repetition with another drill, an explanation, an encouragement, or a joke. Above all, you must honestly care about the progress of your students, and make them feel that your satisfaction depends heavily on their progress. Therefore, praise the students' progress and always encourage them.

With so much emotion and physical effort going into a drill session, it should be a surprise to no one if students and teacher are drained of their energy in a half-hour of intensive drilling. Do not drill for any more than one half-hour. If your assigned class sessions are longer, stop after 30 minutes and take a well-deserved break. (If you did the job right, it is deserved.)

16.6 Assessment. There is no magic way to improve pronunciation. Even an active and intensive drilling will have little or no immediate effect on how the spoken French of a given person is perceived. This is because our perception of someone's speech is not quantitative but largely subjective. We sometimes think we hear an accent because we are looking for one. If instead of an overall subjective judgment, a systematic assessment is carried out, then a dramatic improvement can be found in the speech of students who have drilled segment by segment—as, for example, with Valdman, Salazar, and Charbonneau's Drillbook (1971).

In drill courses aimed exclusively at improving students' pronunciation, this contrast between subjective and quantitative assessment has consistently proven to hold. In a course called Corrective Phonetics, I usually give a diagnostic test at the beginning of the course and the same test at the end. It is so constructed as to test one segment per utterance (each utterance having between 10 and 30 segments) and contains 25 utterances, 15 as repetitions of recorded speech, and 10 in a reading passage. The students do not know that they will take the same test, nor do they see or hear it during the term, as I keep the cassettes on which they recorded themselves. In both evaluations of their performance, the only errors recorded are those made on the segment determined beforehand as the one to be tested. In theory, therefore, the students could massacre the rest of the utterance and still be given credit, provided that the segment in question is pronounced correctly.

In the initial administration, students make in general between 6 and 12 errors. Rarely does anyone have a perfect score (it happened once over some 200 cases) or more than 20 wrong. The rate of improvement on these errors is remarkable. As a rule, students make half as many mistakes at the end as they made at the beginning of the course, but I have had classes where a particularly assiduous student began with some 16 errors and ended with 3 or 4 errors.

Now to the point of all this. I grade the test on 30 points, leaving 5 points for my subjective opinion (fluency, general impression). Almost invariably, my judgment on these 5 points differs by no more than one point between the two administrations. My subjective judgment remains virtually unchanged while my 'forced' objective assessment is drastically modified.

Admittedly, a person's fluency and good pronunciation are generally judged subjectively. Such is the nature of life in society. To improve one's oral French and to acquire real fluency, nothing can replace residence in a francophone environment. Drilling, however, can create the awareness needed to set in motion this unknown mechanism within us which will slowly reshape our articulatory habits.

Chapter 17
Segment production

17.1 Preeminence of the vowel. French is a vocalic language. Vowels are distinguished from nonvowels in a number of ways, not the least of which is that only vowels can be syllabic peaks. This is not true of English, which bestows this distinction upon its liquids and nasals as well. The segments /r, l, m, n/ are syllabic in *speaker*, *cattle*, *consonantalism*, and *common*, respectively. French speakers learning English must be made aware of this fact. If not, they will gallicize these and similar words, as was done with the borrowing of *speaker* (meaning *announcer*), which is pronounced /spikœR/. Syllabic segments other than vowels never carry the word stress in English. The fact that the word stress is on the sound /œ/ is further proof that French replaced a syllabic /ɹ/ by /œR/.

Because vowels are given such importance and because they are always clearly produced, spelling problems rarely involve vowels. The French have no difficulty distinguishing between *capitale* and *capitole* whereas English speakers have problems learning which spelling corresponds to which meaning. Similarly, *Abel* and *able* rhyme in English but *fable* and *Abel* do not rhyme in French. Some spelling problems arise in French from the fact that final consonants are generally not pronounced. Although the English speaker may find this problem with final consonants odd, he should keep in mind that his difficulty in spelling vowels is equally surprising to a Frenchman.

17.2 Even-stressed rhythm. French and English differ in the relative importance they give to vowel segments. The stress system of English weakens neighboring vowels in ways which do not occur in Modern French. French syllables receive the same amount of stress except for the last one, which is slightly stronger. This differs from English, which has a stress pattern similar to a syncopated piece of music. Keeping the 'musical' metaphor, French contrasts with English in that it is more like Gregorian chant. An easy way of imitating the stress pattern of French is to say each syllable as if counting.

Exercise 1
(1) Repeat and fill in the number of syllables.
(1a) un, deux, trois   Couvre-toi!   ...3....
(1b) un, deux, trois, quatre Il est entré.   ....

(1c) un, deux, trois, quatre, cinq   Téléphonez-lui! ....
(1d) un, deux; un, deux, trois   Bonjour, Mademoiselle. ..2-3..
(1e) un, deux, trois; un, deux, trois   Je lui donne un coup de main. ....

(2) How many syllables are there in the following? Answer in first column.
(2a) L'amiral se frottait les mains. ....
(2b) A toutes heures du jour, il dort. ....
(2c) Jusqu'ici tout va bien. ....
(2d) Elle s'intéresse aux moindres détails. ....
(2e) Il jouait de la contrebasse. ....

(3) Note that in some sentences there is a break just as in (1d), which is shown as *un, deux; un, deux, trois*. In the second column in (2) indicate the make-up of the line with the break, as was done in (1d). Answer in the second column.

(4). Now transcribe the vowel sounds of the sentences (1a-1e) and (2a-2e).
(1a) / .... / (2a) / .... /
(1b) / .... / (2b) / .... /
(1c) / .... / (2c) / .... /
(1d) / .... / (2d) / .... /
(1e) / .... / (2e) / .... /

(5) Keeping in mind the actual sentences, repeat only the vowels. Say them as if you were enumerating them, making a break where necessary.

(6) Say the sentences again.

Exercises of this type are quite important for developing a good French stress pattern. They are easy to make and they take up little class time. Another way of enumerating is with the alphabet, e.g. *ABCDEF... Il nous a endormi*. Poetry can also be used successfully.

Model: ABCDEF/ABABCD
Quand tu seras bien vieille au soir à la chandelle.

The important thing is to make sure you have the right count. In alexandrine verse there must be a total of 12 syllables. There can be 2 groups of 6 syllables or 3 groups of 4. Each group of 6 can be split up as 4-2, 2-4, 1-5, 5-1, or 3-3. Exercise 2 is an example.

Exercise 2
Le ciel, le juste ciel, par le meurtre honoré,
   2 — 4   /   3 — 3
Du sang de l'innocence est-il donc altéré?
   2 — 4   /   3 — 3
Si du crime d'Hélène on punit sa famille,
   3 — 3   /   3 — 3

Faîtes chercher à Sparte Hermionne et sa fille
4 — 2 / 3 — 3
Laissez à Menelas racheter d'un tel prix
2 — 4 / 3 — 3
Sa coupable moitié dont il est trop épris.
3 — 3 / 3 — 3
Mais vous, quelles fureur vous rendent sa victime?
2 — 4 / 2 — 4
Pourquoi vous imposer la peine de son crime?
2 — 4 / 2 — 4

(Racine, *Iphigénie*)

For advice on scansion, see Champigny (1963: 55-70).

17.3 Vowel distinctness. Ask an English-speaking seven- or eight-year-old to read the letter *o*. In all likelihood, the child will begin phonation before his articulators have assumed the proper position. His lips will open more widely than needed for /o/ (depending on his regional dialect, they may open to /ɔ/); they will then progressively close, never stopping at any specific aperture until the obstruction is equal to that of /w/ and phonation stops. This shift from open /ɔ/ to /w/ is recognizable by English speakers as /o/. It is differentiated from /u/ by the starting point: open /ɔ/ begins /o/, closed /o/ begins /u/. Otherwise these two English vowels share the same articulatory 'slur'. Although in principle /o/ is rounded, the child will round his lips only slightly and this rounding will begin and end during phonation.

Ask a French child to produce the letter *o*. He will round his lips to the exact position for /o/. His tongue will be appropriately retracted and stationary. Then, he will begin phonation, allowing exhaled air to cause the vocal folds to vibrate. Next, he will end phonation. Finally, once phonation has stopped, he will relax his articulators.

The difference is striking. Each language is set in its way. A second language student must learn to meet the demands of his target. The English speaker's target includes, among others, even-stressed rhythm and vowel distinctness. There are other situations where English speakers are called upon to strive for sound distinctness. Music and singing are cases in point. For example, when learning to play the violin one must learn to identify the right spot on the string for each note. Beginners characteristically miss the correct frequency and work into it. The effect is not at all pleasing to the ear. They must learn to avoid such 'slurs'. The same is true of voice training. An apprentice singer may have a tendency to imitate popular singers, who often break the rule of vowel distinctness. It is quite common among English-speaking popular vocalists to hold a syllabic liquid or even a voiceless fricative as if it were a vowel. Voice instructors speak against that practice and require vowel distinctness in singing. A term they often use is 'pure' as in 'Make your vowels pure!' French teachers must also insure that vowel distinctness and even-stress rhythm are respected.

To work on vowel distinctness, a student needs only a mirror and the willingness to sing. The mirror is used to keep close watch over one's lips, to make sure that they remain stationary throughout the phonation of each vowel. Singing, actually chanting, is needed to work more easily into vowel distinctness.

Exercise 1

(1) Anticipate all vowels before producing the consonants which precede them.

  (a) Round your lips and keep them rounded and slightly apart.
     toujours
     murmure
     soudure

  (b) Open to /o/. Keep lips rounded.
     peu d'eau
     deux creux
     deux boeufs
     yeux bleus

  (c) Open to /ɔ/.
     jeune homme
     leur coeur
     voleur

In all these cases the lips should not move except to produce labial nonsyllabic sounds. The tongue should not move during phonation of each vowel.

  (d) Spread your lips for /i/.
     iris
     il y lit
     dix civils
     six cyclistes

  (e) Open lips to /e/.
     dé
     des prés
     zézayer
     désespéré

  (f) Open to /ɛ/.
     père fier
     l'ère terciaire
     cinq insectes frèles

(2) Repeat (a)-(f), deleting the consonants. Chant the vowels, making sure to lengthen them and to keep your lips in the same position.

(3) Chant (a)-(f) with the consonants inserted.

(4) Repeat step (3) without lengthening the vowels.
(5) Repeat (a)-(f) without chanting, making sure to keep each vowel crisp and unchanged.

17.4 Consonants. French has fewer nonsyllabic sounds than English. The difficulty in acquiring consonants is therefore more a problem for the French speaker learning English than it is for the English speaker learning French. Nevertheless, there are a few characteristics in the consonantal system of French to which English speakers must give some attention.

17.4.1 Unaspirated initial stops. English voiceless stops are aspirated in word-initial position; French stops are not. In word-final position, English stops may be unreleased or aspirated. French stops may only be aspirated. English intervocalic stops /t/ and /d/ may become a single flap of the tongue against the alveolar ridge. No such phenomenon exists in French.

Avoiding English interference in the production of French voiceless stops requires practice and a vigilant ear. Listen to students on magnetic tape.

One way to avoid aspirating initial stops is to anticipate the articulation of the following vowel: in other words, the following exercise. Note that in English words where the stop is not initial, namely, English words beginning with *s*, the stop is not aspirated. Hence, one can try pronouncing initial stops of French words with an *s* preceding, to get the feel of what an unaspirated stop is like.

Holding a loose sheet of paper vertically in front of your mouth (or a lit match, if you prefer 'striking' illustrations), produce the following words: *span*, *stan*, *scan*, followed by *pan*, *tan*, *can*. You should have used up three matches by now, one for each initial stop. If you held a paper in front of your mouth, the aspiration of the initial stops should have displaced the paper more than that of the stops following /s/. These are graphic illustrations of aspiration and nonaspiration in English. Now try producing *peint*, *tas*, *qui*. The puff of air created by the release of the initial stops of these French words should not affect the paper or the lit match. Students attempting to acquire a good French pronunciation are advised to do this test at intervals to verify that they have not reverted back to old habits.

Like all exercises, the following are intended to enable the student to achieve the desired behavior. Whether the student will continue to produce voiceless stops without aspiration is, of course, dependent on motivation, practice, etc.

Exercise 1
(1) Produce the following, making sure that the *p*, *t*, or *k* of the French words sound like the ones in the second column.

English:	English:	French:
pot	spot	pate
tock	stock	toque
car	scar	car
care	scare	Caire
pool	spool	poule

When a student seems unable to do this exercise, it is generally because he or she is unaware of the difference between aspiration and nonaspiration. The best way to enable the student to discriminate is to make him or her produce the desired segment. This is achieved by using a bit of trickery, an unexpected change in the syllable order.

(2) Repeat the following, making sure to give each syllable the same value.
(2a) /Rɛs-pa-Rɛs-pa-Rɛs-pa-Rɛs-pa-Rɛs/ *paresse*
(2b) /tɛs-kõ-tɛs-kõ-tɛs-kõ-tɛs-kõ-tɛs/ *comtesse*
(2c) /mãs-kɔ-mãs-kɔ-mãs-kɔ-mãs-kɔ-mãs/ *commence*
(2d) /gRɛs-ti-gRɛs-ti-gRɛs-ti-gRɛs-ti-gRɛs/ *tigresse*

This exercise is aimed at making the student treat the initial consonant as if it were preceded by an /s/. After practicing with similar phonetic manipulations (with *coulisse, culasse, police, potasse, terrace*, etc.), the slower learner is ready to return to (1).

An alternative to (1) is an exercise like (3), which is, in fact, closer to what the French actually do.

(3) Anticipation exercise. Get ready to say the vowel, then incidentally produce the consonant which precedes it in the word. Make sure to say the vowel at the same time.
(3a) Get set for /i/, now say *qui*
(3b) Get set for /i/, now say *tigre*
(3c) Get set for /e/, now say *tes*
(3d) Get set for /ɛ/, now say *caisse*
(3e) Get set for /ɛ̃/, now say *pain*
(3f) Get set for /ɔ/, now say *port*
(3g) Get set for /u/, now say *pou*

17.4.2 Word-final stops. In English, stops in word-final position can be unreleased whereas in French, final stops are always aspirated. Hence, the English speaker learning French should be careful to release all final stops. The French interpret an unreleased stop as no segment. For example, an unreleased /t/ in *chatte* is interpreted as *chat*.

17.4.3 Word-medial stops. Most American speakers use a flap where the British counterparts use an alveolar stop. In some American dialects, the flap is glottal. French /t/ and /d/ are not flapped. This difference in articulation does not create grave problems. Once they are aware of these differences, most American speakers have little difficulty avoiding the flapped /t/ and /d/.

In both French and English, all stops are unreleased when they are immediately followed by a consonantal segment, e.g. French *captif* and English *captive* are transcribed /kap⁻tif/ and /k'æp⁻tɪv/, respectively. The /⁻/ indicates that the preceding segment is unreleased.

17.4.4 Point of articulation. Most so-called equivalent consonants have the same point of articulation in English and French. The exceptions are /t/, /d/, which are alveolar in English and dental in French. This contrast is minimal and generally audible only to trained phoneticians, linguists, or diction instructors.

17.5 Liquids. The liquids represent some of the greatest sources of difficulty between English and French. More than vowel distinctness and even-stressed rhythm, the liquids betray the speaker of one language attempting to speak the other. Having uvular /R/ in English does not identify one as a speaker of French because other languages have uvular segments, but such a speaker can hardly pass for a Midwesterner.

17.5.1 Uvular consonant vs. retroflex vocoid. Liquids are segments which share features of vowels and consonants. If a line XY were drawn with the X extreme representing 'vowelness' and the Y extreme representing 'consonantalness,' /R/ and /r/ would be far apart. The segment /r/ is produced with lip rounding, with the jaws apart as for a mid vowel, the body of the tongue lying low, retracted, and the blade of the tongue raised so as to allow the tip to curve up and back. The sound /r/ can serve as a syllable peak. In contrast, /R/ is produced by a trill or flap of the uvula against the root of the tongue. It involves no rounding, no retraction of the tongue, no specific aperture of the rest of the mouth. It is not a syllable peak.

As liquids, /r/ and /R/ have in common their ability to assimilate in voice with adjacent consonants. French *trente*, *prise*, *crème* have voiceless /R/'s, while the /R/'s of French *dragé*, *brise*, *graine* are voiced. Similarly, English *prom*, *train*, *crank* have voiceless /r/, whereas English *broom*, *drain*, *granny* have a voiced /r/.

Probably the greatest problem regarding /R/ and /r/ is that they are spelled alike. If the French /R/ is learned from the beginning as a consonant, the English speaker encounters less difficulty. The converse is also true for French speakers. The carryover of the features of one's familiar segment into the equivalent in the target language is quite natural. Because this approach requires that students learn to speak long before learning to read, it is not practical. Whether this is attempted or not, students must be carefully advised on how to produce these sounds.

A speaker of French learning English should be told to produce the glide /ɥ/. First show the student, by a drawing, the tongue's position when it is retroflexed; then with the tongue flat in his mouth, have the student curl the tip of the tongue up and back from the lower front teeth past the upper front teeth, and slightly past the alveolar ridge. As the tongue curls up and backward, the back of the tongue will become concave. Impressionalistically, he will go from /ɥ/ to /ʃ/ to /r/. Then have him practice this /r/ with adjacent voiceless stops.

/tɥiː/   /tʃiː/   /triː/ tree
/pɥuv/   /pʃuːv/ /pruːv/ prove

After the student has learned to produce the voiceless clusters, switch to practicing clusters with voice stops and eventually to practicing the initial /r/ alone.

A speaker of English learning French encounters a great deal of difficulty with /ʀ/. The most important point to keep in mind is to avoid anything produced with the blade of the tongue. Teachers should be adamant on this point.

The teacher should produce a sequence with a /g/ followed by a back vowel and have the student repeat. Then he is to repeat but without allowing a complete closure of the /g/ at the velum. The result is /γ/, a fricative. Call it the French /ʀ/! Repeat with front vowels. Finally, attempt voiced and voiceless clusters with /ʀ/. (See Exercise 1.)

Exercise 1
(1) /ga/ → /γa/   gars, rat
(2) /gi, ge, ga/ → /γi, γe, γa/   gui, gai, gant → riz, raie, rang
(3) /dγoːl/, /gγɛ/, /bγiz/   drôle, grain, brise
(4) /txiãgl/, /kxyel/, /pxiz/   triangle, cruel, prise

The velar fricatives in Exercise 1 are not the Standard French /ʀ/. To achieve the uvular /ʀ/, students will have to practice production progressively farther back until the uvula, or pendulous tip of the velum, vibrates. One way of achieving a uvular articulation is to open the mouth as wide as possible. This will enable the student to get 'the feel' of the uvular articulation. Frequent conscious practice of /ʀ/ is the key to successful articulation. One must keep in mind that the orthographic sign *r* is realized very differently in English and French.

17.5.2 Nonvelarized /l/ and its environment. The difference between the English and the French /l/ is not as striking as that between /ʀ/ and /r/. The French /l/ is produced by allowing the air to flow laterally while the blade of the tongue presses against the alveopalatal region. It is so produced in all environments. In English, only prevocalic /l/ is so produced. In all other environments English /l/ is a strikingly different sound. In postvocalic, syllable-final, or preconsonantal position in English, e.g. *hell, help, helping*, the tongue is less fronted than in French. In contrast to French, the tip of the tongue may be slightly retroflexed but the principal contrast is that in English the back or root of the tongue is retracted backwards and upwards toward the velum to produce what is frequently referred to as the 'dark *l*' or 'postvocalic *l*' of English in contrast to the 'light *l*' which occurs in French and in prevocalic position in English.

The pedagogical consequences are obvious: French speakers learning English must learn an altogether new sound. English speakers learning French must develop a new set of habits in all nonprevocalic environments.

To produce the retroflex /l/, a speaker of French should begin with a low front unrounded vowel, namely, /ɛ/, and make the tongue curl up and back until it is concave with its tip pressed against the alveopalatal region.

Initially, the speaker of English should add a lax vowel after every nonprevocalic /l/. This results in what might appear to be a French regional dialect, that of the Midi. Subsequently, the vowel is reduced to null while retaining the convex shape of the tongue.

Exercise 1

bɛlə → bɛl	bel, belle
sɛlə → sɛl	sel, celle
palə → pal	pâle
malə → mal	mal, malle
kɔlə → kɔl	col
fɔlə → fɔl	fol, folle
silə → sil	cil
pilə → pil	pile
kulə → kul	coule, coulent
fulə → ful	foule
sœlə → sœl	seule, seul
mœlə → mœl	meule

Chapter 18
Transcription

18.0 Introduction. The virtues of the feature analysis are twofold. On the one hand, features identify classes of sounds: the class characterized by syllabic, or by stress, or even by tense. On the other hand, features enable us to distinguish between sounds: tense versus nontense, low versus nonlow, nasal versus nonnasal. In this chapter, we are concerned with this second property. More specifically, we are concerned with the notion of contrast.

18.1 Memorizing French sounds. Before discussing the notion of contrast and practicing with the contrastive segments, it might be well to memorize all the segments of French. There is no right or wrong way to list the segments in order to memorize them but a systematic arrangement of all

158 / 18 Transcription

segments might prove useful since it would enable you to reconstruct the 'system' from the memorized list. For this reason, the following order is suggested. Segments should be listed in groups beginning with the least aperture (i.e. closure) progressively to the greatest aperture. Each group will list the anteriormost segment first, progressively regressing to the farthest back segment. This order corresponds to Figure 5.3. It is reproduced here without reference to the classes or points and manners of articulation.

Figure 18.1 The sounds of French.

p	t		k
b	d		g
m	n		ɲ
f	s		ʃ
v	z		ʒ
l	R		
j	ɥ		w
i	y		u
e	ø		o
ɛ	œ	ə/a	ɔ
ɛ̃	œ̃	ã	ɔ̃

From this list, once it is memorized, one can reconstruct easily such complex tables as Figure 5.4. From the same list one can easily retrieve all members of a given class.

18.2 Consonantal contrasts

18.2.1 Voiced vs. voiceless stops. Both English and French discriminate between voiced and voiceless consonants. In voiced consonants, the vocal cords vibrate during production, while in voiceless consonants they do not. Furthermore, in the case of stops English uses another feature to distinguish between voiced and voiceless segments: voiceless stops are aspirated in word-initial position, while voiced stops are not. With the possibility of two distinct ways for discriminating between these two sets, English speakers tend to take aspiration as the distinctive feature just as much as voicing. This choice presents no problem within English but it leads to confusion when, as in the case of French, the speaker of English must discriminate between voiced and voiceless stops solely on the presence or absence of voicing. Often, the absence of aspiration in French voiceless stops leads the English speaker into believing that the stops in question are voiced.

The state of affairs just outlined constitutes a typical example of what has come to be known under the general term of interference. In short, the internal structure of language L_1 is different from that of language L_2. As a result of this difference, it is predicted that speakers of L_1 will have difficulty with L_2 and vice versa. Although perhaps a bit simplistic, this view is by and large true and can serve as a rule of thumb for inexperienced teachers unfamiliar with actual difficulties encountered by students.

The only solution for interference is keen awareness of a given structural difference and practice in making the new sound or pattern seem more natural to the learner in the hope that the point will be learned.

Exercise 1
Cover the words below and answer the questions (on the tape). You will hear two words. Repeat them and identify the one beginning with a voiceless stop (by writing *1* or *2* in the right-hand column to indicate the first or second segment).

	1	2	
(a)	port	bord	.....
(b)	quai	gai	.....
(c)	doux	tout	.....
(d)	gueux	queue	.....
(e)	bain	pain	.....
(f)	grue	cru	.....
(g)	poire	boire	.....
(h)	thé	dé	.....
(i)	gare	car	.....
(j)	teint	daim	.....

Exercise 2
Context can be helpful in identifying sounds but context is not always sufficient. In the next exercise the stops occur in full sentences, in word-medial, word-initial, or word-final position. Repeat and identify the word or phrase where the voiced stop occurs (by writing *1* or *2* in the column at the right). Cover the contrasting pairs.

(a) J'aime les ports / bords de mer. .....
(b) Elle veut du thym / daim. .....
(c) Prends ton thé / dé. .....
(d) Il arrive en gare / car. .....
(e) Les poissons / boissons lui plaîsent. .....
(f) C'est un gars / cas unique. .....
(g) C'est un bec / bègue. .....
(h) Ils l'ont tanné / damné. .....
(i) Voici l'auteur / odeur. .....
(j) Voilà la tortue / tordue. .....

18.2.2 Voiced vs. voiceless fricatives

Exercise 1
Repeat the pairs and identify the word with the voiced segment.

(a) cache / cage .....

(b) chouchou / joujou ....
(c) scène / zen ....
(d) fil / ville ....
(e) champs / gens ....
(f) fente / vente ....
(g) actif / active ....
(h) onze / once ....
(i) cause / Causse ....

Exercise 2
In this exercise you will hear pairs of sentences. Repeat them and identify the sequence with the voiceless segment (by writing the number corresponding to its order in the pairs).
(a) Il est sorti de sa cache / cage. ....
(b) C'est mon petit chouchou / joujou. ....
(c) Les gens / champs de la ville sont encombrants. ....
(d) Elle oublie les fils / villes. ....
(e) En vaut-il / faut-il autant? ....
(f) On court après les chausses / choses des autres. ....
(g) Ils craignent les roses / rosses. ....

18.2.3 Voiced vs. voiceless segments

Exercise 1
Find the final voiced segment and transcribe it.
(a) cache, cap, cave / /
(b) fric, frise, glisse / /
(c) place, glace, glaise / /
(d) fiche, fil, figue / /
(e) hâtif, hâtive, attique / /
(f) rif, rite, ride / /
(g) bec, baisse, bègue / /

Exercise 2
Repeat each of the following and write the symbol for each word-initial segment.
(a) cas, tas, sac   /   /,/   /,/   /
(b) gare, pare, jupe   /   /,/   /,/   /
(c) chasse, tasse, face /   /,/   /,/   /
(d) peu, deux, feu   /   /,/   /,/   /
(e) voeu, zoo, jamais   /   /,/   /,/   /
(f) boeufs, deux, gueux /   /,/   /,/   /

18.2.4 Nasal vs. oral segments

18.2.4.1 Nasal consonantal segments. The only feature differentiating between /b/ and /m/ is nasal. Segments /p/ and /m/ are kept distinct by two

18.2.5 Vowels vs. glides / 161

features: nasal and voice. The bilabial and dental nasals of French present little difficulty to speakers of English. The palatal nasal, /ɲ/, is distinct from the English velar /ŋ/.

Exercise 1
Identify the palatal nasal and indicate its number in the series of words.
(a) fille, mine, signe ....
(b) line, ligne, bille ....
(c) haillon, oignon, fanon ....
(d) fanion, fanon, canon ....
(e) billot, anneau, agneau ....
(f) canote, cantonne, cañon ....

Exercise 2
Repeat the words and transcribe the word-initial segments.
(a) benne, peine, Maine   /   /, /   /, /   /
(b) poule, moule, boule   /   /, /   /, /   /
(c) basse, passe, masse   /   /, /   /, /   /
(d) main, bain, pain   /   /, /   /, /   /
(e) pâle, balle, malle   /   /, /   /, /   /
(f) millet, billet, pillard /   /, /   /, /   /
(g) père, mère, berbère   /   /, /   /, /   /

18.2.4.2 Nasal oral segments

Exercise 1
Repeat and transcribe the word-final vowel of each word below.
(a) l'atout   /   /   (h) du sang   /   /
(b) l'athée   /   /   (i) du thym   /   /
(c) l'ennui   /   /   (j) dix nains   /   /
(d) les sons   /   /   (k) des champs   /   /
(e) les ans   /   /   (l) aucun   /   /
(f) vingt ans   /   /   (m) le daim   /   /
(g) l'auto   /   /   (n) les sons   /   /

18.2.5 Vowels vs. glides.

The three high vowels /i/, /y/, and /u/ are identical in every way to the glides /j/, /ɥ/, and /w/, respectively, except that vowels are syllabic and glides are not. In the following exercise, both members of each pair are acceptable. Some regions of France tend to prefer the vowel, others the glide in each of these words. Standard French calls for the glide.

Exercise 1
Repeat each word and indicate whether the glide is in the first or the second member of each pair (by writing *1* or *2*).
(a) /tɥe/   /tye/   (tuer)   ....
(b) /bue/   /bwe/   (bouée)   ....

(c) /lwa/ /lua/ (loua) ....
(d) /nɥaʒ/ /nyaʒ/ (nuage) ....
(e) /mɥet/ /myɛt/ (muette) ....
(f) /muet/ /mwet/ (mouette) ....

Exercise 2
Repeat and write down the number of glides in each utterance.
(a) le piano de Louis ....
(b) Le diable emporte le portier. ....
(c) Souvenez-vous des mois les plus froids. ....
(d) La mouette disparaissait dans les nuages. ....
(e) Ça tuera les truites du ruisseau. ....
(f) Demande lui trois fruits. ....
(g) La soeur du roi est folle. ....

18.3 Vowels in contrast. The aperture continuum goes from the stops to the most open vowels. The three degrees of aperture of vowels are greater than the apertures of other segments. The contrasts practiced here are between high, mid, and low vowels.

18.3.1 Front vowels: /i/, /e/, /ɛ/

Exercise 1
Repeat each sequence and count the number of front unrounded high vowels. Enter the number in the left column.
(a) Arrêtez à mi-chemin. ....
(b) Les préparatifs étaient fort avancés. ....
(c) Il y avait de dangereux repris de justice. ....
(d) L'incinérateur est détraqué. ....
(e) La planification y est établie. ....
(f) Les rives du Mississippi sont belles. ....
(g) Compléter la fiche signalétique. ....

Exercise 2
Replay the preceding exercises and count the front unrounded mid vowels. Enter the number in the right column.

Exercise 3
Repeat each sequence and transcribe the vowels between the slanted lines.
(a) Elles étaient hébétées. / /
(b) Ses idées les hantaient. / /
(c) Imitez les caissiers. / /
(d) Delayez les cachets. / /
(e) Nous l'avons échappé belle. / /
(f) Sa timidité lui est nuisible. / /

18.3.2 Front rounded vowels: /y/, /ø/, /œ/

Exercise 1
Repeat each sequence and count the number of front rounded high vowels. Enter number in the left column.
(a) Eustache est un hurluberlu.
(b) Il eut fallu que vous fussiez arrivé.
(c) Les obus tombaient par dessus.
(d) dans une odeur de géranium
(e) C'est l'attribut de la tribu.
(f) Les trompeurs trompés sont stupéfaits.
(g) Heureux qui comme Ulysse sera aventureux.

Exercise 2
Replay the preceding exercise and count the front rounded low vowels. Enter the number in the right column.

Exercise 3
Repeat each sequence and transcribe the vowels between the slanted lines
(a) deux heures précieuses perdues / /
(b) Eugène a le coeur sur la main. / /
(c) des yeux bleu ciel et des cheveux d'ébène / /
(d) la fureur de l'empereur / /
(e) Leurs deux filleules s'émeuvent. / /
(f) L'abus est dangereux et onéreux. / /
(g) Les aveux de mon neveu sont scabreux. / /

18.3.3 Back vowels: /u/, /o/, /ɔ/.
There are no unrounded back vowels in French.

Exercise 1
Repeat each sequence and count the number of mid back vowels. Then enter the number in the left column.
(a) Paul posait les pots dans l'eau.
(b) Ton auto est souillée de mégots.
(c) Vos veaux ne feront pas de vieux os sans vous.
(d) Nos poteaux sont à gauche de vos saules.
(e) C'est faux! Vos poteaux sont sous l'eau.
(f) Vous osez réchauffer le couscous!

Exercise 2
Replay the preceding and count the high back vowels in each sequence. Enter the number in the right column.

18 Transcription

Exercise 3
Repeat each sentence and transcribe the vowels between the slanted lines.
(a) Les pôles sont couverts de glace. / /
(b) Les votes de la gauche nous consolent. / /
(c) L'école du môme est encore sans réchaud. / /
(d) L'eau dormait autour du radeau de roseaux. / /
(e) Les gros mots font des maux trop proches. / /
(f) Les nôtres rehaussent les vôtres. / /

18.4 Transcription

Exercise 1
Transcribe the following monosyllabic words.
(a) pou / / (f) temps / /
(b) fais / / (g) rond / /
(c) jus / / (h) lin / /
(d) soeur / / (i) seau / /
(e) corps / / (j) char / /

Exercise 2
Transcribe the following two-syllable words.
(a) envie / / (f) tamis / /
(b) poussin / / (g) croupier / /
(c) écho / / (h) silence / /
(d) rayé / / (i) jovial / /
(e) ennui / / (j) amphi / /

Exercise 3
Transcribe the following three-syllable utterances.
(a) une envie / / (f) tamiser / /
(b) le poussin / / (g) deux croupiers / /
(c) un écho / / (h) en silence / /
(d) c'est rayé / / (i) lui! jovial? / /
(e) pas d'ennuis / / (j) à l'amphi / /

Exercise 4
Transcribe the following three-syllable utterances.
(a) peu d'ennuis / / (f) littéraire / /
(b) six poussins / / (g) arrondi / /
(c) Quelle envie! / / (h) dictionnaire / /
(d) Ratissez! / / (i) mes lunettes / /
(e) balnéaire / / (j) montre en main / /

Exercise 5
Repeat and transcribe the following sentences.
(a) Nous voulons des oeufs frais. / /
(b) Les gens des villes sont encombrants. / /

(c) Le diable emporte le portier. / /
(d) Arrêtez à mi-chemin. / /
(e) Deux heures précieuses de perdues. / /
(f) Vos poteaux sont à gauche de nos saules. / /
(g) Les aveux de mes neveux sont scabreux. / /
(h) Paul posait les pots de fleur dans l'eau. / /
(i) Eugène a le coeur sur la main. / /
(j) Les trompeurs trompés sont stupéfaits. / /

18.5 The importance of transcription. It is useful to students to learn the phonetic symbols and the sounds that they represent because, as they increase their vocabulary, they can learn to pronounce the new words acquired. Good dictionaries like that of Robert (1968) transcribe all entries. For those interested in researching pronunciation in greater detail, two entries from references listed at the back of this book are recommended: Juilland (1965) and Warnant (1968).

Knowing how to transcribe phonetically is even more important for teachers whose responsibility, among other things, is to teach students how to pronounce the language and to correct their pronunciation errors. A teacher capable of transcribing can discreetly jot down errors made by students as they answer a question or make an oral presentation, without interrupting them, and can then make the appropriate corrections later.

Chapter 19
Liaison and elision

19.1 Enchainment and liaison

19.1.1 Their nature. French tends to form syllables made up of consonant and vowel (CV). One very obvious case where this takes place is in 'liaison', in which a consonant is, as it were, revived to create a CV syllable. Such a syllable is formed of the last segment in a word (a consonant) and the first segment of the following word (a vowel), e.g. *plusieurs amis*. When the consonant thus used to create this CV syllable is not otherwise pronounced, e.g. *plusieurs copains*, the process is called 'liaison' (from the French *liaison*). When the consonant is pronounced under all circumstances, e.g. *avec Antoine/avec Toinou*, those cases which have a created CV syllable, e.g. *avec Antoine*, are known as 'enchainment' (from the French *enchaînement*).

19.1.2 Practical steps. Enchainment requires no drilling since the deletion or lack of deletion of the final segment is not dependent on the segment following. Students simply have to know when to retain the consonant. They must learn that in monosyllabic words and in recently borrowed foreign words, final consonants are not deleted (words in small caps are borrowed), e.g. *sec, sac, lac, bec, mat, frac, cinq, zinc, net,* JOB, CLUB, SNOB, *cep, coq,* VOLT, *cap,* SCALP, RAID, OUED, *donc,* GROUP, CROUP. A few polysyllabic words also have final consonants which are pronounced, e.g. INTROIT, EXEAT, FELDSPATH, JULEP, HANDICAP, THALWEG, ICEBERG, POUDING, SMOKING, ALMANACH, KODAK, VARECH, BIFTECK, *avec, ressac, échec, médoc,* etc. Some drilling may be done which mixes words which have pronounced final consonants with words subject to Final Consonant Deletion in order to help the learner remember those words which retain their final consonant.

It may also prove helpful to the learner to be told that the letters *c, f, b, g, k, g* are always pronounced in word-final position, except for: (1) *c* in *estomac, tabac, escroc, croc, accroc,* and *caoutchouc*; (2) *f* in *clef* (also spelled *clé*); (3) *b* in *radoub* 'refinish the hull of a ship'; and (4) the *c* of French *zinc,* which is always voiced. The letter *v,* found in words of Slavic origin such as *Kiev, Kroustchev, Rimsky-Korsakov,* is generally never voiced but instead is pronounced /f/. The letter *l* is always pronounced in final position except in *coutil, outil, fusil, saoul, cul* (*cul-de-sac*), and in those cases where *l* serves as a marker for the palatal segment /j/ (cf. Chapter 12).

Other letters have a less systematic relationship to sounds. A good rule of thumb is to assume that foreign words are not subject to nasalization and therefore retain final *m* and *n*: *Birmingham* rhymes with *gamme,* not with *gant*; *gentleman* with *manne* (or *mènent*), but not with *ment*. Finally, the *f* of *neuf* is pronounced before any consonant and before vowels when the word is not commonly bound with *neuf*. Hence, *neuf antériorités différentes, neuf excellentes occasions* are pronounced with /f/; but *neuf heures* and *neuf ans* require a /v/.

19.1.3 Voicing and devoicing in liaison. Liaison, we have seen, is a process which saves a final consonant from deletion by allowing it to form a syllable with the following nonconsonantal segment (vowel or glide). One consonant, /s/, clearly changes its voicing when it occurs in liaison. *Gros* /gʀo/ becomes *grosse* /gʀɔs/ and *grosseur* /gʀɔsœʀ/ when suffixes are added; but it becomes /gʀoz/ in liaison, as in *gros homme* /gʀozɔm/. This behavior indicates that the latent final consonant in *gros* is an /s/ and that the following things happen to that /s/: (1) if it is followed by a suffix, it remains; (2) if it is followed by a word which begins with a vowel and which is in a certain syntactic relationship with it, it is voiced; (3) under all other conditions, it is deleted.

The /s/ which marks the plural is subject to the same voicing and deletion. Cases where it would remain voiceless cannot be attested, however, as suffixes are not added after the plural marker.

In addition to /s/, other consonants such as /g/ are altered at word boundaries. For example, /g/ becomes /k/ (*sanguin* but *sang humain*/ sãkymɛ̃/), *grand* /gʀã/ becomes *grande* /gʀãd/ and *grandeur* /gʀãdœʀ/

when suffixes are added; but it becomes /gʀɑ̃t/ in liaison, as *grand homme* /gʀɑ̃tɔm/ demonstrates. But these cases are far less frequent than the /s/ ~ /z/ cases. They should be learned in conjunction with the few words in which they are found.

19.1.4 Practice

Exercise 1

You will hear a sequence of words. Repeat. Then, given another word as a replacement, say the new sequence, making the appropriate adjustment. Cover the first two columns as you do the exercise.

(1) très *content*	heureux	....
(2) les *rejetons*	enfants	....
(3) Quand *je* sors . . .	il	....
(4) Il n'y a rien *là*.	ici	....
(5) nos *femmes*	enfants	....
(6) gros *livre*	ours	....
(7) trop *fort*	aimable	....
(8) que dis-*je*	on	....
(9) chez *nous*	eux	....
(10) beaucoup *travaillé*	étudié	....
(11) il faut *lire*	écrire	....
(12) deux *soldats*	hommes	....

Exercise 2

This drill is organized like the preceding one except that the left column has the word beginning with a vowel, and the word intended as a replacement begins with a consonant. This drill contains cases of both liaison and enchainment.

(1) très *habile*	capable	....
(2) ces *enfants*	bébés	....
(3) avec *Annie*	Marie	....
(4) un fils *obéissant*	prodigue	....
(5) un os *énorme*	cassé	....
(6) rien *à faire*	de bon	....
(7) un chef *ingénieux*	de gare	....
(8) de gros *hommes*	messieurs	....
(9) un petit *oiseau*	moineau	....
(10) le dernier *acte*	chapitre	....
(11) sept *heures*	mesures	....
(12) tout *entier*	plein	....

19.2 Elision. Schwa is never pronounced before a vowel or glide. It is dropped. This dropping of schwa is the most frequent case of elision. For example, the schwa of *le* is dropped before *algérien* but retained before *nord africain*: *l'algérien, le nord africain*. This type of alternation is not difficult to learn for those studying the written language. A strictly oral approach to French as a second language does present problems for learners. A piece of evidence from the history of French supports this contention. The possessives *ma*, *ta*, *sa* used to behave like *la*: the segment *a* was deleted before a vowel. Hence, the words *ma amie* were pronounced /mami/. The two words were eventually reanalyzed as *ma mie*, which constitute the Modern French forms. In learning situations, such as the ones which occur nowadays, the student encounters no difficulty with elision because spelling reinforces the rule.

There are three types of deletions generally known as elision: (1) the dropping of schwa in monosyllabic words like *le*, *me*, *te*, *se*, *ce*, *ne*, *je*; (2) the dropping of /a/ in *la* (article or pronoun); and (3) the dropping of schwa in posttonic position (hence in polysyllabic words). The first two are cases of elision; the third results from applying Final Schwa Deletion. (The details of the present analysis can be examined in Chapter 15.) On a practical level, all three involve a deletion. They can be drilled together.

Exercise 1

You will hear a sequence of words. Repeat it. Then, given another word as a replacement, say the new sequence, making the appropriate adjustment. Cover the first two columns as you do the exercise.

Model: le *camarade*	ami	.........l'ami.........
(1) le sont *des fous*	un fou	....
(2) il me *parlait*	appelait	....
(3) on se *félicite*	admire	....
(4) une petite *voiture*	auto	....
(5) un admirable *flic*	agent	....
(6) tu la *connais*	aime	....
(7) je *pars*	arrive	....
(8) *nous* le sommes	vous	....

19.3 Syntactic conditioning

19.3.1 *Liaison obligatoire.* The words of the sentence you are reading are separated on the printed page by the same amount of spacing. Not so in the equivalent spoken utterance. For example, in the first sentence of this paragraph, the pause between *reading* and the following *are* is greater than that between *are* and *separated*. The pause between *page* and *by* is greater than that between *by* and *the*. This can be perceived by creating a longer pause after *are* and *by*. The resulting sentence is unacceptable and possibly incomprehensible.

Some groups of words fit together more closely than others. Some of these groups are called phrases. There are noun phrases, composed of a noun (as nucleus) and satellite words, and verb phrases, composed of a verb as nucleus and satellite words. In French, satellite words which occur before such nuclei are very closely linked to the nuclei and to one another. This linking is evidenced by contractions, e.g. *au, aux, du, des*, by elision, and by enchainement and liaison. In prenominal and preverbal position, linking is compulsory: '*liaison obligatoire*'.

Some groups of words which fit together very closely and require liaison are frozen expressions, e.g. *tant et plus, pieds et points liés, quant à (moi), à tout instant, rien à faire, vas-y, de plus en plus, comment allez-vous?, par monts et par vaux, tout à l'heure, de mieux en mieux, pot au feu, de fond en comble.*

In the following drill, the learner hears a word sequence and must decide whether there is a *liaison obligatoire* (or more than one) and between what word types it occurs. The examples are entered in column 1, the answers in column 2. A third column can be used by the student to enter his answer. The first two columns must be covered when doing the exercise.

Exercise 1

(1) tes amis	adj‿noun	....
(2) un grand homme	adj‿noun	....
(3) Je les entends.	pr‿verb	....
(4) Nous y sommes.	pr‿pr	....
(5) Elles en ont.	pr‿pr‿verb	....
(6) ses énormes orielles	adj‿adj‿noun	....
(7) deux yeux	numeral‿noun	....
(8) les autres enfants	art‿adj‿noun	....
(9) ces enfants-ci	adj‿noun	....
(10) un appel téléphonique	art‿noun	....
(11) Vous en écoutez.	pr‿pr‿verb	....
(12) nos premiers efforts	adj‿noun	....
(13) Quelles études faites-vous?	adj‿noun	....
(14) Quels imbéciles!	adj‿noun	....

Exercise 2

Same directions as for Exercise 1.

(1) J'en attends.	pr‿verb	....
(2) d'autres illustrations	adj‿noun	....
(3) Habituons nous-y!	pr‿pr	....
(4) Vous écoutez.	pr‿verb	....
(5) plusieurs arbres	adj‿noun	....
(6) deux énormes arbres	adj‿adj‿noun	....
(7) nos premières amours	adj‿noun	....
(8) Quelles horreurs!	adj‿noun	....
(9) un assez ingénieux ingénieur	adj‿adv‿adj‿noun	....
(10) vingt et un éléphants	adj‿noun	....
(11) cent arbres émondés	adj‿noun‿adj	....
(12) On nous y en achetera.	pr‿pr‿pr‿verb	....

(13) Peut-on en avoir.   verb‿pr/ pr‿verb*   ....
(14) Tout y est.   pr‿pr   ....
(15) aucun homme   adj‿noun   ....

*There is no liaison between *on* and *en* in (13) because *on* is closely linked to one verb, *peut*, while *en* is closely linked to another, *avoir*. These two pronouns are brought together by the question inversion but they are not closely linked.

When giving the foregoing drills to beginners, it is suggested that columns 2 and 3 be in the reverse order and that column 1 not be covered. This facilitates the exercise while still enabling the student to discover the scope of the rule.

There are other cases of obligatory liaison: (1) between adverbs and the word they modify, e.g. *très habile, assez illustre, trop aimable, bien élevé, fort habile*, (2) after the relative pronoun *dont*, e.g. *le sujet dont il parle*, and (3) between conjoined nouns. In this third instance the nouns conjoined by *et* must be plural, e.g. *parents et alliés, garcons et filles, hommes et femmes, bêtes et gens*, but not **chefs ou soldats, *parent et ami*. Of these cases only the first is of sufficient frequency to be included in drills. The others can be learned as frozen units.

19.3.2 *Liaison interdite.*

It is inappropriate to link in a number of circumstances. One must not link: (1) when there is a pause between the words, e.g. *vieillards,/ enfants,/ hommes et femmes*; (2) when the second word begins with *h-aspiré*, e.g. *les hollandais, ces hallebardes, un héro, des haricots*; (3) when the second word is a foreign word beginning with a yod, e.g. *des/yaourts, les/yens japonais, ces/yachts, vos/yards, en/yod*; (4) when the second word is a numeral, e.g. *cent/un, vers les/une heure, un/huitième, ils sont/onze*.

A sequence noun + adjective where the noun is singular forbids liaison, e.g. *un savant/oranais, un vent/impétueux, un soldat/intrépide*. The rule does not hold in the plural, where liaison is optional, e.g. *des savants oranais, des vents impétueux, des soldats intrépides*.

No liaison is allowed after *et*, e.g. *Paul et/un ami, simple et/intelligent*, nor is one generally allowed before *et* when *et* conjoins adjectives, e.g. *un homme grand/et fort, un roi méchant/et cruel*.

Even though an *s* is added for the plural of compound nouns which have liaison or enchainment in the singular, no liaison with the *s* is allowed and the consonant required in the singular is retained in the plural, e.g. *un fer-à-repasser* vs. *des fers à repasser, un guet-apens* vs. *des guets-apens, le pot-au-feu* vs. *les pots-au-feu*.

Traditionally, a third group of liaisons is recognized. These are optional, known in French as '*liaisons facultatives*'. Generally, optional linking is made or not made depending on the degree of formality associated with a communicative utterance. The more liaisons, the more elevated the register of the speaker at a given time. That is, however, an oversimplification. There are degrees of linking; some syntactic configurations constitute easier linking grounds than others; some sounds are more likely to cause linking than others. In fact, we are far from knowing exactly what the whole linking hierarchy is between the two extremes, obligatory and forbidden, of the linking continuum. Pedagogically, the extremes should be learned first; leave to extensive exposure to spoken French the task of providing a further role model for what links and when.

Exercise 1

You will hear some word sequences corresponding to what is written in the left column. In the right column enter the name of the phenomenon: *L* for liaison, *NL* for no liaison, *E* for elision, *NE* for no elision, *EN* for enchainment. Optional cases (i.e. where liaison is neither obligatory nor forbidden) can be entered as *O*. More than one of these phenomena may occur in a given utterance. Enter them all in the right column. (In doing this drill, students should cover the left and center columns.)

Model: On habitait Nice.		........L........
(1) en Espagne	L	....
(2) l'oiseau	E	....
(3) le premier homme	L	....
(4) le meilleur alcool	EN	....
(5) Donnez leur-en deux.	EN	....
(6) Il était aveugle.	EN/L	....
(7) On en avait apporté.	L/L/O	....
(8) les uns et les autres	L/O/L	....
(9) Ecrivez le un à droite.	NL/NL	....
(10) les héros de la Hollande	NL/NE	....

Exercise 2

Same directions as for Exercise 1.

(1) deux ancêtres	L	....
(2) Mangez-en.	L	....
(3) les langues étrangères	L	....
(4) Il fallait y penser.	O	....
(5) un savant/allemand	NL	....
(6) le huit Avril	NE/L	....
(7) les haricots égoutés	NL/O	....
(8) Lui et vous avez bien travaillé.	NL	....
(9) Vingt-deux arriveront demain.	NL	....
(10) un chat aux yeux émeraudes	NL/L/O	....

Chapter 20
The front rounded vowels

20.0 Introduction. As seen in Chapters 8 and 10, there is a strong tendency to front vowels in French. That tendency is quite old. Consequently, the fronted vowels are the result of shifts which took place at different times in the history of the language. Speakers of the language are, by and large, unaware of fronting shifts. Speakers of other languages hearing French are often struck by the degree of fronting. Also, actors in the English-speaking world, for example, use the front rounded vowels and the word-final stress to mimic the French language. In this book, a distinction has been made between fronting cases which are manifested by alternations and those which are not. In this lesson we deal with both groups.

20.1 Phonologically derived front segments

20.1.1 Low front rounded /œ/. As seen in Chapter 8, there are alternations between /ɔ/ and /œ/: *professoral ~ professeur, éditorial ~ éditeur, solitude ~ seul, mort ~ meurt, favori ~ faveur, horaire ~ heure, odorant ~ odeur, honorifique ~ honneur, floraison ~ fleur,* etc. Fronting changes the /ɔ/ of underlying forms to make it /œ/. While English speakers have /ɔ/, as in *bought, fought, wrought,* they do not have /œ/. The segment /œ/'s nearest equivalent in English is /ʌ/, as in *but, nut, luck.* Several strategies are available which enable us to help the student to articulate /œ/. One such is an exercise which fronts /ɔ/.

Exercise 1
You will hear words with the sound /ɔ/. Repeat the word; then say it again with the tip of your tongue pushing slightly against your lower front teeth. Wait for the confirmation, then repeat again.

Model: bord
Student: bord . . . beurre
Model: beurre
Student: beurre

(1) sort	soeur
(2) port	peur
(3) mort	meurt
(4) corps	coeur
(5) sol	seul
(6) l'or	l'heure
(7) molle	meule
(8) déplore	des pleurs
(9) lors	leur

20.1.1 Low front rounded /œ/

Note that the point of contact between the tongue and the upper part of the oral cavity may differ according to the degree of fronting of the vowel. This is shown clearly in the case of final /1/, as in *sol/seule* and *molle/meule*.

Another drill is one which makes use of the alternation, e.g. *professoral~professeur*. Here the student simply repeats.

Exercise 2
(1) professoral .... professeur ....
(2) éditorial .... éditeur ....
(3) solitude .... seul ....
(4) favori .... faveur ....
(5) horaire .... heure ....
(6) odorant .... odeur ....
(7) honorifique .... honneur ....
(8) foliation .... feuille ....

The /ʌ/ of English approximates the /œ/ sufficiently to constitute a good point of departure from English. The segments /ʌ/ and /œ/ differ in that /ʌ/ is unrounded and central, while /œ/ is rounded and more front than /ʌ/.

Exercise 3
Repeat the English word, then the French word.

(1) buff .... bœuf ....
(2) cut .... cœur ....
(3) enough .... un œuf ....
(4) muck .... meule ....
(5) gull .... gueule ....
(6) putt .... peur ....

Once the student has learned to discriminate the sound and can produce it accurately in isolated words, strings of such words in increasing lengths can then be brought together and eventually entire sentences with these words may be introduced.

Exercise 4
Repeat.
(1) heure, beurre, croqueur, moqueur, fondeur
(2) rigueur, extérieure, un meilleur beurre
(3) un promeneur seul, un camionneur rieur
(4) la meule de mon filleul rieur
(5) L'heure de la peur a heurté l'aïeul.
(6) Seuls leurs coeurs peuvent leur rendre leur honneur.

English speakers tend not to round their lips to the degree that French speakers do. English speakers rely on both rounding and partial fronting to distinguish /i/ from /u/, /ɪ/ from /ʊ/, etc. Some speakers make use of one of these two features more than they do of the other. Other speakers of

American English make greater use of the feature round to distinguish between front and back vowels. When the degree of fronting is not utilized as a distinguishing factor, as is the case with many speakers in the southeast United States, the task of teaching a contrast between front and back rounded vowels in French requires another step. The student must be made aware of front/back contrasts. This problem applies to all front rounded vowels in French but it seems more acute in the contrast /y/ ~ /u/, as in *la rue/la roue* (cf. Section 20.1.3).

20.1.2 Mid front rounded /ø/. The sound /œ/ must be kept distinct from /ø/. This is a problem for speakers of English who often tend to close /œ/ too much, especially when /œ/ is followed by *r* if they still haven't mastered /R/.

There are very few cases within French where /œ/ and /ø/ contrast (*jeune* 'young'/*jeûne* 'fast') because /œ/ and /ø/ generally occur in different environments. Most commonly, /œ/ occurs before a coda (i.e. in closed syllables) while /ø/ is found in syllable-final position or before /z/. Consequently, drills must be constructed that will play on this distribution.

Exercise 1

The student will be given a masculine word. He should repeat it and change it to the feminine form. The model provides the masculine form, then leaves time for the student to repeat and say the feminine form; then the model says the feminine form again for the student to repeat.

Model: charmeur .... charmeuse ....
(1) rieur .... rieuse ....
(2) moqueur .... moqueuse ....
(3) joueur .... joueuse ....
(4) baveur .... baveuse ....
(5) buveur .... buveuse ....
(6) rageur .... rageuse ....
(7) logeur .... logeuse ....
(8) plongeur .... plongeuse ....

In another drill, the student is given the feminine form and changes it to the masculine form, which ends in /ø/.

Exercise 2

Change to the masculine form (/øz/ becomes /ø/).
(1) neigeuse .... neigeux ....
(2) monstrueuse .... monstrueux ....
(3) luxueuse .... luxueux ....
(4) présomptueuse .... présomptueux ....
(5) paroles oiseuses .... propos oiseux ....
(6) une boisson gazeuse .... un 'coca' gazeux ....

20.1.2 Mid front rounded /ø/

The front /ø/ must be heard and produced as distinct from /o/, its back equivalent.

Exercise 3
Contrast the following. Listen and repeat.
(1) beau .... boeufs ....
(2) dos .... deux ....
(3) peau .... peu ....
(4) faux .... feu ....
(5) veau .... voeu ....
(6) chevaux .... cheveux ....
(7) oiseaux .... oiseux ....

The mid /ø/ must be heard and produced as distinct from the /y/, which is another fronted vowel. A drill similar to that of Exercise 3 can be used occasionally to retain this contrast.

Exercise 4
Contrast the following. Listen and repeat.
(1) boeufs .... bu ....
(2) noeud .... nu ....
(3) peut .... pu ....
(4) jeu .... jus ....
(5) ceux .... su ....
(6) voeu .... vu ....
(7) pleut .... plu ....
(8) deux .... du ....

Once the student has learned to discriminate the sound /ø/ and can produce it accurately in isolated words, strings of such words in increasing lengths can be brought together and eventually entire sentences with these words may be introduced.

Exercise 5
Repeat.
(1) malheureux ....
(2) valeureux ....
(3) peu valeureux ....
(4) peu valeureux et malheureux ....
(5) Veuillez creuser deux trous. ....
(6) Les yeux du gueux étaient en feu. ....
(7) Plantez deux pieux au milieu. ....
(8) Ce peureux peut pleurer deux heures. ....
(9) L'aveu de ce malheureux m'émeut très peu. ....

The drill can be cast in the more natural context of conversation.

Exercise 6
Respond to the statement with an imperative.

Model: - Je voudrais acheter ce chapeau.
- Achetez-le!
(1) -Nous voulons élire ce candidat.
 -Elisez-le!
(2) -Je tiens à lancer ce libélé.
 -Lancez-le!
(3) -Il faut mener cet aveugle.
 -Menez-le!
(4) -Je dois semer le grain.
 -Semez-le!
(5) -Ils voudraient que je vole le feu.
 -Volez-le!

20.1.3 Front rounded /y/. Drilling /y/ can require different approaches depending on the speech characteristics of the English speakers learning French. In all cases it is important to establish first the correct articulation of other similar vowels. Once the student can identify and produce /ø/, he can turn his attention to /y/. In the case of speakers from the Southeastern United States, it may be best to start out within the front rounded vowels because these speakers tend to front back rounded vowels. They can be taught the front rounded vowels more easily than the back rounded vowels. They should be taught to discriminate /y/ from /ø/ first. When the /y/ is acquired, then the contrast between /y/ and /u/ can be attacked. In the case of speakers whose /u/ is back (most speakers in the United States), the drill to distinguish between /y/ and /u/ should focus on /y/.

The way to find out whether a given speaker has fronted back round vowels in his English is simply to listen carefully. To find out whether this tendency carries over into French, have the speaker utter a syllable with /i/—*si*, for example—and then make him round his lips to say *su*. Then ask, 'Did you say *sou*?' If he answers in the affirmative, he is likely to be a speaker who tends to front back vowels. If he hears the difference, then he is not likely to be a member of this group.

The preceding strongly suggests that the very best way to make someone produce the French /y/ is to draw it from /i/ via rounding. However, note that for speakers who front their back vowels, /y/ may be interpreted as /u/. It is therefore imperative that the student having difficulty with /y/ be drilled not only to distinguish /y/ from /i/, which will be easy (perhaps even unnecessary), but also to contrast /y/ with /ø/ and /u/, which will be a different exercise and should not be passed over lightly.

20.1.3 Front rounded /y/

Exercise 1
Listen and repeat.

(1) si	su ....
(2) dis	du ....
(3) vie	vu ....
(4) Gilles	Jules ....
(5) pile	pull ....
(6) rit	rue ....
(7) confit	confus ....
(8) l'habit	l'abus ....
(9) promis	promu ....
(10) sali	salut ....

This, as any other drill, can be amplified in a broader syntactic context.

Exercise 2
Listen and repeat.

(1) J'ai acheté dix pains.	J'ai acheté du pain. ....
(2) On la vit au marché.	On l'a vue au marché. ....
(3) Demandez à Gilles.	Demandez à Jules. ....
(4) Elle achète des piles.	Elle achète des pulls. ....
(5) C'est un nid.	C'est un nu. ....

Exercise 4 of Section 20.1.2 can also be used effectively. While it may not be needed (or even advisable, depending on the student) in Section 20.1.2, this drill is required when drilling /y/.

When the contrasts between /y/ and /i/ and /y/ and /ø/ have been established, then it is imperative that the contrast with /u/ be drilled. This is the most likely case of confusion, because of phonetic as well as orthographic resemblance between these two segments.

Exercise 3
Repeat after the speaker.

(1) loup	lu ....
(2) roue	rue ....
(3) joue	jus ....
(4) noue	nue ....
(5) vous	vue ....
(6) tout	tu ....

The number of syllables can now be increased.

Exercise 4
Repeat after the speaker.

(1) la fougue	la fugue ....
(2) dix pouces	dix puces ....
(3) une grosse bouche	une grosse bûche ....

(4) une énorme boule .... une énorme bulle ....
(5) Ces gens sont pour .... Ces gens sont purs ....
(6) Ne restez pas dessous .... Ne restez pas dessus ....

These two columns may be reversed, depending on which of the two high round vowels a student needs to learn, and the exercise may be modified so as to have the second column produced by the student. The following drill does just that.

Exercise 5
Listen to the speaker. He will say one or more words. Change the vowel of the last syllable from /y/ to /u/. (With advanced students one can make the task more complex by asking for lexical recognition and requiring that the student write down the word emerging from the change in vowel.) All students should cover the right column as they do the drill.

(1) rue .... roue
(2) jus .... joue
(3) la fugue .... la fougue
(4) dix puces .... dix pouces
(5) C'est un fût. .... C'est un fou
(6) Ne restez pas dessus. .... Ne restez pas dessous

These replacement exercises can be combined with meaning and syntax frames to produce more interesting and possibly more useful drills.

Exercise 6
State the operation indicated and the result. The student should uncover each answer for confirmation only.

Example: six souris - (moins) cinq souris   = une souris
(1) six bouches - cinq bouches   = une bouche
(2) sept choucroutes - six choucroutes   = une choucroute
(3) deux sœurs ÷ deux   = une sœur
(4) trois laitues ÷ trois   = une laitue
(5) quatre russes + quatre russes   = huit russes
(6) six ruses + six ruses   = douze ruses
(7) douze brunes - onze brunes   = une brune
(8) deux brunes + six brunes   = huit brunes
(9) neuf hurluberlus - sept hurluberlus   = deux hurluberlus

Exercise 7
Change the sentence to the compound past tense. Cover the right column.
(1) Vous pouvez .... Vous avez pu ....
(2) Nous entendons .... Nous avons entendu ....
(3) Vous mordez .... Vous avez mordu ....
(4) Nous lisons .... Nous avons lu ....

(5) Vous rompez .... Vous avez rompu ....
(6) Il pleut .... Il a plu ....

Exercise 8
Answer in the negative with *plus*, utilizing the verb in parentheses. Cover the right column.

Example: Allons faire une promenade (sortir) ...... Je ne sors plus
(1) Prends un verre au moins (boire) .... Je ne bois plus
(2) Tu as l'air si triste (rire) .... Je ne ris plus
(3) Occupe-toi! Lis un livre (lire) .... Je ne lis plus
(4) Couche-toi et dort. Ça ira mieux (dormir) .... Je ne dors plus
Tu m'énerves! Je m'en vais (partir) .... Enfin! Il ne partait plus!

This last example may be omitted. It is suggested only because it can give life to the drill and increase the student's motivation.

20.2 Generalized fronting. French is heavily influenced by a fronting tendency not only in terms of the rules discussed in Chapters 8 and 10 but also, in a more subtle way, in the realization of the low back vowel /ɔ/. Gaining ground among French speakers is a shift of the segment /ɔ/ toward the front. The end result of this shift is a segment sometimes very close to /a/, sometimes very close to /œ/. This fronting tendency appears to be a continuation of that discussed in Chapters 8 and 10, but it is not dependent on environment. All nonhigh back rounded segments are fronted.

Speakers of languages which do have a segment /ɔ/ (such as English, e.g. *Paul*, *balk*, *hawk*, etc.) expect French *Paul*, *fort*, *loque*, to occur with a vowel which rhymes with their /ɔ/. They are surprised to discover that the segment /ɔ/ is not produced as they expected but is fronted by many speakers of French. The largest geographic exception to this fronting tendency is found in southern France.

Pedagogically, it behooves the teacher of French to prepare students for this shift. This shift, however, is of less significance than the fronting resulting from alternation. Failure to produce /y/ or /œ/ as fronted vowels can create enormous communication problems, e.g. *roue* ≠ *rue*, *cou* ≠ *cul*, *corps* ≠ *cœur*, *il mord* ≠ *il meurt*. Failure to front /ɔ/ suggests a southern French accent but is perfectly understandable to speakers of French. Warning about this tendency should therefore concentrate on comprehension rather than production.

Exercise 1
Listen to the contrasts between English /ɔ/ and French /ɔ/. The latter is fronted while the former is back.

(1) bought .... botte ....
(2) tell a fawn .... téléphone ....
(3) halt .... récolte ....

(4) wrought .... il rote ....
(5) hawk .... croque ....

Some unstressed vowels are also affected by this phonetic fronting. They are the nonhigh rounded /ɔ/ and /o/. This tendency can be shown by contrasting English and French or by placing the given vowels in contrastive environments (i.e. stressed versus unstressed).

Exercise 2
Listen to the contrasts between the English and the French vowels in the first syllable of each word.
(1) mobile .... mobile ....
(2) Joanie .... joli ....
(3) Sophy .... Sophie ....
(4) roper .... Robert ....
(5) folded .... folie ....
(6) coding .... codifier ....
(7) sole .... soluble ....

Repeat the exercise, making the student repeat after each model word is given.

Chapter 21
Nonhigh oral vowels

21.0 Introduction. The pronunciation of most segments in this chapter is determined by syllabic conditioning. Open syllables—that is, syllables with no coda—have as their peak one kind of vowel, while closed syllables—that is, syllables with a coda—have as their peak a different kind of vowel. For example, the syllable peak of *fée* is /e/ and is not followed by a coda; the vowel is mid. The syllable peak of *fête* is /ɛ/ and is followed by the coda /t/; its vowel is low. This type of distribution of segments in complementary environments is called 'complementary' distribution (in contrast to 'parallel' distribution where the same segment occurs in both environments). Where complementary distribution does occur it is not always absolute, that is to say, there may be exception to that type of distribution.

The sounds of English /i/ and /ɪ/ are for the most part in complementary distribution. Compare *sea* /siː/ and *sit* /sɪt/. In general, it is true to say that the /ɪ/ of *sit* does not occur in stressed open syllables. In other words, there are no words in English like /fɪ/, /tɪ/, /mɪ/, or /glɪ/, although words like *fee* /fiː/, *tea* /tiː/, *me* /miː/, and *glee* /gliː/ do occur in English. The fact that /ɪ/ does not occur in open stressed syllables (but only in closed syllables) and that /i/ does occur in open and closed syllables makes their distribution complementary with regard to open stressed syllables. But these two sounds are not in absolutely complementary distribution because both /i/ and /ɪ/ can occur in closed syllables as is shown by the occurrence of the minimal pair *seat* vs. *sit* where the vowels /i/ and /ɪ/ both occur in a type of 'parallel' distribution which is both functional and contrastive. Such instances of contrastive minimal pairs should be carefully distinguished from instances of 'parallel' distribution where the difference of sound between the two forms is not functional and hence 'noncontrastive', e.g. the word *root* pronounced either /rut/ or /rʊt/ where the difference between the /u/ and the /ʊ/ is not functional and hence noncontrastive, namely, it is merely an alternative pronunciation of the word versus the difference between the sounds /u/ and /ʊ/ in *pool* /pul/ and *pull* /pʊl/ where the difference between the /u/ and the /ʊ/ is functional and contrastive.

Thus complementary is opposed to parallel distribution, and contrastive is opposed to noncontrastive distribution, as described in the previous paragraph. These explanations make it easier to understand what is meant when it is said that although /e/ and /ɛ/ generally occur more frequently in contrastive distribution, they also sometimes occur in complementary distribution, whereas /ɔ/ and /o/ and /œ/ and /ø/, although sometimes in contrastive distribution, tend to occur in complementary distribution more frequently.

21.1 Front unrounded nonhigh vowels: /e/, /ɛ/. There is a tendency for complementary distribution between /ɛ/ in /CVC/ and /e/ in /CV/ position; but this tendency is overshadowed by the more numerous contrasts which occur between these two vowels in open syllables, i.e. in /CV/ position.

21.1.1 Verb forms exhibiting the /ɛ/~/e/ contrast. Depending on whether you wish to drill for one or the other of these two sounds, the two columns can be permuted.

Exercise 1
Change the verb form from the conditional to the future. Repeat after the confirmation.

Model: Je me lèverais.	Je me lèverai. ....
(1) Je mangerais cet abricot.	Je mangerai cet abricot. ....
(2) J'écrirais un livre.	J'écrirai un livre. ....
(3) Je répondrais à sa lettre.	Je répondrai à sa lettre. ....
(4) Je leur demanderais de se taire.	Je leur demanderai de se taire. ....

To make the exercise more lively, one may wish to provide a syntactic context for it.

(1) *Instructor:* —Répondre à sa lettre
　　Student A: —Je répondrais à sa lettre à une condition . . .
　　Student B: —Ah! Vous ne voulez pas vous engager.
　　Student A: —Entendu! J'y répondrai plus vite que vous ne pensez.

(2) *Instructor:* —Ecrire un livre de cuisine
　　Student B: —J'écrirais un livre de cuisine à une condition . . .
　　Student C: —Ah! Vous ne voulez pas vous engager.
　　Student B: —Entendu! Je l'écrirai plus vite que vous ne pensez.

(3) *Instructor:* —S'arrêter de fumer
　　Student C: —Je m'arrêterais de fumer à une condition . . .
　　Student D: —Ah! Vous ne voulez pas vous engager.
　　Student C: —Entendu! Je m'arrêterai plus vite que vous ne pensez.

(4) Rendre la clé à quelqu'un.
(5) Apprendre à taper à la machine.
(6) Acheter un cadeau d'anniversaire à quelqu'un.
(7) Suivre cette voie.

Another possible drill is to give the student a form in a given tense with instructions to change it in the first person form.

Exercise 2

Transform the verb form to the first person, making sure to preserve the tense and mood of the stimulus verb. Repeat after the confirmation.

Model: Nous sortions tous les soirs (Je sortais tous les soirs)　　Je sortais tous les soirs ....

(1) Nous allions au cinéma .... 　　J'allais au cinéma ....
(2) Tu sortiras seul ....　　Je sortirai seul ....
(3) Ils finiront tard ....　　Je finirai tard ....
(4) Si vous les connaissiez tous ...　　Si je les connaissais tous ....
(5) Quand nous entendions sa voix ....　　Quand j'entendais sa voix ....
(6) Elle écoutera sans mot dire ...　　J'écouterai sans mot dire ....

Exercises can be devised which will drill /ɛ/ by requiring the student to change a present form into an imperfect form.

21.1.2 /ɛ/ alternating with /ɛj/ and /ɛje/. A number of verbs in *-ayer* have two possible present indicative forms: one ending with *-aye* /ɛj/ and the other ending in *-aie* /ɛ/. Sometimes there is a related noun form as well, e.g. *balayer/balaye/balaie/balai*. These alternations lend themselves to exercises focusing on /ɛ/.

21.1.3 /ɛ/ in closed syllables

Exercise 1
The infinitive form of a verb and the third person singular form of its present indicative tense are presented. Provide the /ɛ/ form of the verb.

Model: Balayer. Je balaye. ..(Je balaie.)   Je balaie. ....
(1) essayer: J'essaye ....   J'essaie ....
(2) effrayer: Il effraye ....   Il effraie ....
(3) payer: Elle paye ....   Elle paie ....
(4) déblayer: Tu déblayes ....   Tu déblaies ....
(5) délayer: Je délaye ....   Je délaie ....
(6) remblayer: Il remblaye ....   Il remblaie ....

Almost an identical drill can be constructed by using the related noun as a response.

Exercise 2
Provide the appropriate word in the blank.

Model: J'essaye. C'est un ..(essai)..........   essai
(1) Je balaye. J'utilise un ....   balai
(2) On me paye. Je reçois ma ....   paie
(3) On remblaye le talus. C'est un ....   remblai
(4) Etayer, c'est soutenir avec des ....   étais

The *-aie* ending after the name of some fruit designates the type of orchard, e.g. *pomme/pommeraie, mure/muraie, chataigne/chataigneraie,* etc. The following drill can be instructive and interesting because it is cast in the form of definitions.

Exercise 3
Complete the definition.

Model: Un lieu où l'on peut cueillir
des mures est une ....   muraie.
(1) Un lieu où l'on peut cueillir
des pommes est une ....   pommeraie.
(2) . . . des chataignes est une ....   chataigneraie.
(3) . . . des oranges est une ....   orangeraie.
(4) . . . des bananes est une ....   bananeraie.
(5) . . . des noix est une ....   noiseraie.

The drill can be made more challenging by providing the name of the tree instead of the fruit, e.g. *Un lieu planté de noyers est une . . .*

Many more drills can be constructed to emphasize syllable-final /ɛ/ and /e/. Just use your imagination . . . and a good dictionary. For this purpose Warnant's *Dictionnaire de la prononciation* (1968) is recommended.

21.1.3 /ɛ/ in closed syllables. While /e/ and /ɛ/ can contrast in open syllables, they do not do so in closed syllables. Only /ɛ/ occurs in CVC:

Standard French does not allow /e/ in CVC. However, since there are numerous cases where an inflectional change adds a C to a final open syllable, alternations occur. One such alternation, between /e/ and /ɛʀ/, is utilized in the next drill.

Exercise 1
Change the following words to their feminine form. Repeat after the confirmation.

Model: un fermier ..(une fermière) une fermière ..(une fermière)........
(1) un boucher .... une bouchère ....
(2) un meunier .... une meunière ....
(3) un hotelier .... une hotelière ....
(4) un douanier .... une douanière ....
(5) un ouvrier .... une ouvrière ....
(6) un infirmier .... une infirmière ....
(7) un aventurier .... une aventurière ....

The next drill is based on the alternation between words in /ɛ/ and their feminine equivalents in /ɛt/.

Exercise 2
Change the word to the feminine form. Repeat after the confirmation.
(1) seulet .... seulette ....
(2) complet .... complète ....
(3) sujet .... sujette ....
(4) minet .... minette ....
(5) muet .... muette ....
(6) douillet .... douillette ....

Note again that the reverse exercise would drill the final /ɛ/.

Some /ɛ/ in closed syllables alternate with /ɛ̃/ in /CV/, e.g. *sain/saine*, *plein/pleine*, etc. Drills which are the reverse of those presented in Chapter 23 can be used to teach or reinforce /ɛ/ in that environment.

In Chapter 11, we saw that /ɛ/ alternates with schwa /ə/ in a number of verb stems. A drill based on the paradigmatic alternations between the first and the second person plural forms, on the one hand, and the other forms of the present indicative constitutes not only good phonetic practice but also a good review of verb morphology.

Exercise 3
Change the verb form to the singular.
(1) Nous en jetons. .... J'en jette. ....
(2) Nous gelons. .... Je gèle. ....
(3) Vous vous levez. .... Tu te lèves. ....
(4) Vous l'amenez. .... Tu l'amènes. ....
(5) Nous nous promenons. .... Je me promène. ....

21.1.4 Comparison with English. The /ɛ/ of closed syllables in French and English are quite similar. For all practical purposes they are alike: the /ɛ/ of French *sept* 'seven' and the /ɛ/ of English *set* (as in English *set theory*) sound identical. What distinguishes these two words is not the vowel but their consonants. Clearly, no drills are needed to learn /ɛ/ in closed syllables. In open syllables, speakers of English tend to add an off-glide to vowels. This problem was discussed in the context of vowel distinctness in Chapter 17. French /e/ and English /ɪ/ are phonetically very close but they are seldom confused by native speakers of English. English speakers' ability not to confuse these sounds is probably due to the following two reasons: phonologically, /e/ and /ɪ/ occur in different environments, /e/ in open and /ɪ/ in closed syllables. Orthographically, they are represented by different letters (a distinction reflected even in the phonetic alphabet). As in the case of French /ɛ/, the more frequent errors regarding French /e/ in open syllables are due to English speakers' tendency to produce an off-glide in that environment, a problem addressed in Chapter 17.

21.2 Rounded nonhigh oral vowels /ø/, /œ/, /o/, /ɔ/. This section deals with /ø/, /œ/, /o/, and /ɔ/. These sounds are also generally distributed on the basis of syllable structure. Stressed /ɔ/ and /œ/ are always found in closed syllables; there are no French words which end with /ɔ/ or /œ/. The sounds /o/ and /ø/, on the other hand, are generally found in stressed open syllables, although they may occur also in closed syllables. These tendencies combined constitute the so-called 'loi de position', which in fact is less a '*loi*' and more a '*tendance*', as Table 21.1 shows.

Table 21.1 The 'loi de position'.

	/CV/	/CVC/
/o/	/so/ 'saut'	/sot/ 'saute'
/ø/	/pø/ 'peut'	/møz/ 'Meuse'
/ɔ/	.....	/fɔl/ 'folle'
/œ/	.....	/sœʀ/ 'sœur'

21.2.1 Mid vowels before /z/. Syllables ending in a round vowel + /z/ require that the vowel be mid. In other words, Standard French does not allow sequences like /œz/ or /ɔz/. Since the vast majority of words in /øz/ are feminine adjectives, it follows that a drill that changes masculine adjectives into their feminine equivalents would be the most straightforward to construct. Some drills can be devised which change adjectives ending in *-eux*, other drills could change adjectives ending in *-eur*. In either case, the feminine forms would end in *-euse*.

186 / 21 Nonhigh oral vowels

Exercise 1
Make the adjective agree with the noun provided.

Model: un gamin boudeur. (gamine)	(une gamine boudeuse)
(1) un gamin moqueur. (gamine)	une gamine moqueuse.
(2) un visage rieur. (figure)	une figure rieuse.
(3) un homme travailleur. (femme)	une femme travailleuse.
(4) un sourire moqueur. (grimace)	une grimace moqueuse.

Essentially the same drill can also be achieved by using nouns.

Exercise 2
Change the noun to the feminine and make sure the adjectives agree.

(1) un chroniqueur ricaneur	une chroniqueuse ricaneuse.
(2) un pronostiqueur gaffeur	une pronostiqueuse gaffeuse.
(3) un voleur farceur	une voleuse farceuse
(4) un chanteur pleurnicheur	une chanteuse pleurnicheuse.
(5) un masseur baveur	une masseuse baveuse.

Used in reverse, this exercise would drill /œ/ before /R/. The same principle used in Exercise 1 can be used for the alternations between /ø/ and /øz/, as illustrated in Exercise 3.

Exercise 3
Make the adjective agree with the noun in parentheses.

(1) un raisonnement fallacieux. (promesse)	(une promesse fallacieuse)
(2) un zèle religieux. (ferveur)..................	une ferveur religieuse
(3) un garçon envieux (fille)	une fille envieuse
(4) un temps pluvieux (journée)	une journée pluvieuse
(5) un couteau huileux (cuiller)	une cuiller huileuse
6) un age fabuleux (époque)	une époque fabuleuse

Exercise 4
Change the noun to the feminine, making sure that the adjective agrees.

(1) un gueux malchanceux	une gueuse malchanceuse.
(2) un peureux soucieux	une peureuse soucieuse.
(3) un farceur malicieux	une farceuse malicieuse.
(4) un religieux prestigieux	une religieuse prestigieuse.
(5) un voleur supersticieux	une voleuse supersticieuse.
(6) un imprimeur fastidieux	une imprimeuse fastidieuse.

It is a good idea to begin drilling in the direction used in the foregoing exercises, which are easier than their reverse. Once confidence is acquired, you can then reverse the drills and concentrate on final /ø/ and /œR/.

Unlike words ending in /øz/, words ending in /oz/ do not generally alternate with words without /z/. It is therefore comparatively more difficult to construct drills for words in /oz/. Most such words are technical, corresponding to the English words which end in -osis: *métamorphose*, *ecchymose*, *artériosclérose*, etc. The few nontechnical words in /oz/ are *cause*, *pause*, *pose*, *dose*, *rose*, *prose*, and *chose*. One way to drill such words is to use inflectionally related items such as past participles of corresponding verbs (if they exist).

Exercise 5
Change the word to the related noun in /oz/.
(1) causé ....
(2) dosé ....
(3) prosaïque ....
(4) sclérosé ....
(5) posé ....
(6) rosée ....
(7) pausé ....
(8) ankylosé ....

21.2.2 Nonhigh rounded vowels in other checked syllables. Table 21.2, which shows the dictionary occurrences of nonhigh rounded vowels in /CVC/, was drawn from lists provided in Juilland (1965). Two unrounded vowels have also been added to the table for purpose of comparison. The arabic numerals at the intersection of a column and a row indicate the absolute frequency of the column's vowel and the row's consonant in word-final position. Table 21.2 reinforces the statement made repeatedly in this book that there are no /CVC/ syllables where /V/ is /e/. It also shows an absolute preference for /œ/ rather than /ø/ before /R/, and a preference for the mid rather than the low round vowels before /z/.

According to Juilland (1965), in his appendix on word-final 'diphones' (a single segment is a 'monophone', two make a 'diphone', and so on), any absolute frequency below 200 occurrences represents a relative frequency of .5 percent of the total dictionary of French. It is therefore possible to conclude that, for the most part, the contrasts (such as *jeune* and *jeûne*) occurring in the lower absolute frequencies need not imply anything of pedagogical import. Furthermore, it is likely that even bona fide speakers of Standard French may have lived and died without ever realizing some of these contrasts.

On the other hand, the fact that there is no nonhigh rounded vowel contrast before /z/ is indeed of significance. It suggests that it is possible for speakers to produce the low or the nonlow vowels before /z/ without any loss of communicative function. That is, in fact, the case among speakers of the southern regions of France. They tend to produce low vowels in closed syllable (as per the 'loi de position') but they also attempt to emulate media French, where final /z/ requires the nonlow vowel.

Before /d/ in word-final position, Table 21.2 shows almost as many /o/ as /ɔ/. This fairly even distribution seems to be at odds with the tendency suggested in the 'loi', but it does not present a pedagogical problem because it seems to be closely correlated with spelling. All words ending in -*aude* are

Table 21.2 Occurrences of nonhigh rounded vowels and of two unrounded vowels in CVC syllables based on lists provided in Juilland (1965).

	/-eC/	/-εC/	/-øC/	/-œC/	/-oC/	/-ɔC/
/-p/	0	10	0	0	2	57
/-t/	0	511	3	0	10	131
/-k/	0	51	2	0	3	63
/-b/	0	6	0	2	2	22
/-d/	0	30	1	0	29	40
/-g/	0	5	0	0	2	50
/-f/	0	22	0	10	3	12
/-s/	0	155	1	0	32	23
/-ʃ/	0	30	0	0	7	37
/-v/	0	12	0	6	6	1
/-z/	0	94	949	0	77	0
/-ʒ/	0	22	0	0	5	11
/-m/	0	96	2	0	62	155
/-n/	0	570	1	1	19	124
/-ɲ/	0	13	0	0	0	12
/-l/	0	425	0	17	20	190
/-ʀ/	0	1342	0	1303	7	191

pronounced with /od/, whereas those ending in *-ode* are pronounced /ɔd/.

There are more words ending in /os/ than ending in /ɔs/. The orthographic key to the pronunciation of these words is not as simple as that of /od/ and /ɔd/. Words spelled with *au* are pronounced with /o/, unlike words ending in *-osse* and *-oce*, which require /ɔ/. There is disagreement on words ending in *-os*. The word *os* 'bone' is listed as /os/ in Juilland (1965) but as /ɔs/ in Robert (1968) and Warnant (1968). These authors are also split over the transcription of *fosse*: Robert and Warnant use /o/, while Juilland reports /ɔ/.

Because of their low frequency and because of uncertainty in pronunciation due to orthographic and/or dialectal interference, it appears that, at the present stage of the language, drills on final sequences other than /CV/, /Vʀ/, /εC/, /øz/, /εn/, and /ɔn/ are of little pedagogical consequence. Drills for /CV/ and /Vʀ/ sequences have been illustrated in this and previous chapters. It was argued in this chapter that, for English speakers at least, /ε/ in /CVC/ need not be drilled extensively. This chapter also discussed the sequence /øz/ and proposed sample drills. Drills for /Vm/ and /Vn/ are discussed in Chapter 23.

21.3 Low central tense vowel: /a/. The low central vowel /a/ is produced between the front /æ/ of English *that*, *bat*, *gnat* and the back /ɑ/ of English *father, farther*. To give students an idea of what sound they are to produce for /a/ in French *la, sa, sac, parc, plat*, etc., make them isolate the sounds /æ/ and /ɑ/. Then make them go back and forth between these sounds so as to make them experience the front-back movement of the tongue and the degrees of opening of the mouth. Then explain that any sound they produce between these two extremes is an acceptable /a/.

It has been claimed that French has two *a*'s. In this volume it is claimed that there is not enough agreement among speakers to set up two distinct segments. For those readers who, as teachers and students, want to work on these two putative segments, I suggest that they consult the three works already referred to, *Le Petit Robert* (1968), Juilland (1965), and Warnant (1968), to determine which word takes which of these two sounds. Incidentally, the production of the back /a/ should present no difficulty to speakers of English, as it is nearly the same sound as the stressed vowel of English *father*.

Chapter 22
Glides and diphthongs

22.1 Glides. The glides, sometimes also called semivowels, are characteristically vocoids which have lost their syllabicity. This loss is captured by the rule of Gliding. To the high front unrounded vowel /i/ corresponds the high front unrounded glide /j/; to the high back /u/ corresponds the high back glide /w/, and to the high front rounded /y/, the front rounded /ɥ/. These are represented in Figure 22.1, along with some appropriate examples.

Figure 22.1 French glides and vowels.

	Front		Back
	Unrounded	Round	Round
Glides:	/j/ Lyon	/ɥ/ nuit	/w/ Louis
Vowels:	/i/ Lille	/y/ nue	/u/ loue

22.1.1 Phonetic production. To produce the glides, it is best to practice going from two syllables to one, just as in the rule of Gliding. The purpose of this process is to give substance to the vowel to be glided in order for the learner and the instructor to insure that its point of articulation is correct. Glides are so fleeting and devoid of phonetic substance in comparison to vowels that such correction as might be needed may otherwise escape the learner and frustrate both learner and teacher.

It goes without saying that the learner should not attempt drills on /ɥ/ unless /y/ is clearly mastered. To do otherwise would be counterproductive and frustrating, tantamount to building a house without foundations.

Both rounding and degrees of backness distinguish front from back vowels in English. In French, rounding and backness are used independently to distinguish between front and back as well as rounded and unrounded vowels. As a result of the redundancy of these features in English, neither can be said to constitute a distinguishing characteristic on its own within English. Given his native habits, the speaker of English finds it quite difficult to distinguish the contrast which seems so natural to French speakers, that between /y/ and /u/. The problem is compounded when these vowels are glided. While French speakers have no trouble distinguishing between /w/ and /ɥ/, English speakers must be taught first to hear the difference, and then produce it. The difficulty encountered by the beginner is not unlike that which a slow reader would experience at having large chunks of printed material flashed before his eyes. In my experience, this contrast is by far the most difficult task facing the speaker of English learning French sounds.

For a first exercise I prefer to deal with nonsense words composed of the two relevant segments. The student hears a /VV/ sequence and repeats, then its /GV/ equivalent, which he also repeats.

Exercise 1
Repeat each sequence after the speaker.
(1) /yi/ .... /ɥi/ ....
(2) /ui/ .... /wi/ ....
(3) /ye/ .... /ɥe/ ....
(4) /ue/ .... /we/ ....
(5) /ya/ .... /ɥa/ ....
(6) /ua/ .... /wa/ ....
(7) /yø/ .... /ɥø/ ....
(8) /uø/ .... /wø/ ....

If the student cannot reproduce these sound sequences, particularly the one in the right column (which is likely), then recognition exercises are needed. Do Exercise 1 as a recognition drill. Produce the sequences or play a recording of the exercise, asking the student to recognize the glides. If there still is confusion, although the vowels are clearly providing the clues, it must be that the student does not distinguish between the front rounded and back rounded vowels. In this case, no further work with the glides should be attempted until the vowel contrast has been learned.

If the student has no trouble with Exercise 1 as a recognition drill, then, as the next step in the sequence of drills of increasing difficulty, move on to utilizing the right column only. At this point the student no longer will use the equivalent vowel as a crutch for recognition. This is illustrated in the drill in Exercise 2.

Exercise 2
You will hear some glide-vowel sequences. You are to recognize the glide and to write it down.

(1) /wi/ .... (5) /ɥø/ ....
(2) /ɥa/ .... (6) /ɥi/ ....
(3) /we/ .... (7) /wø/ ....
(4) /wa/ .... (8) /ɥe/ ....

You may wish to make up more such drills. If you do, try to incorporate nasalized vowels also. In all cases make sure to use sequences which are indeed used in the language: stay away from /wy, wu, ɥu, wo, ɥo, wœ̃, ɥœ̃, ɥõ, and wõ/ which in French are nonexistent or nearly so.

Once you are satisfied that the auditory discrimination has been mastered, turn to production. Utilizing the articulatory materials studied in Chapter 4, construct a drill to serve as transition from vowel to glide. Since the difference between these segments is simply the loss of syllabicity, Exercise 1 can constitute one such drill. Supplement it with increasingly more complex sequences taken from the language.

Exercise 3
A word will be presented which contains a sequence of two vowel segments. Change the first vowel into a glide. A voice will then be heard (on the tape) to provide confirmation of the correct change. Repeat after the confirmation.

(1) l'ouïe .... Louis ....
(2) nouer .... nouer ....
(3) mouette .... mouette ....
(4) tu es .... tuer ....
(5) remuer .... remuer ....
(6) une muette .... une muette ....
(7) vos rouages .... vos rouages ....
(8) des louanges .... des louanges ....
(9) cette lueur .... cette lueur ....
(10) il s'est rué .... il s'est rué ....

A good exercise to supplement the foregoing is one which bears on the front/back contrast. After learning one /GV/ sequence, the students should learn to produce a contrastive one.

Exercise 4
Change the glide you hear from front to back or vice versa, as the case may be. Repeat after the confirmation.

(1) mɥa .... mwa ....
(2) twa .... tɥa ....
(3) mɥɛt .... mwɛt ....
(4) ãfɥi .... ãfwi ....

(5) bwe .... bɥe ....
(6) nwa .... nɥa ....
(7) sɛlwi .... sɛlɥi ....
(8) la rɥɛl .... la rwɛl ....

Another transformation is to change vowels into glides.

Exercise 5
Change the verb to the first person plural. Repeat after the confirmation.
(1) j'étudie .... nous étudions ....
(2) tu ris .... nous rions ....
(3) elle te remercie .... nous te remercions ....
(4) je t'injurie .... nous t'injurions ....
(5) ils scient .... nous scions ....
(6) tu différencies .... nous différencions ....

This drill becomes more complex if the pronouns in the second column are varied. For if the student is concentrating on the pronoun cue to determine which verb form he should produce, the additional task serves as a distraction and he tends to apply the gliding more subconsciously. This results in a test which reveals how thoroughly the process of gliding has been acquired.

Exercise 6
Change the verb to the plural person given. Repeat after the confirmation.
(1) Je scie. (nous) .... Nous scions. ....
(2) Tu ris. (vous) .... Vous riez. ....
(3) Elle copie. (vous) .... Vous copiez. ....
(4) Je me fie. (nous) .... Nous nous fions. ....
(5) Tu paries. (vous) .... Vous pariez. ....
(6) Elle l'injurie. (nous) .... Nous l'injurions. ....
(7) Elles les renient. (vous) ... Vous les reniez. ....
(8) Tu les purifies. (nous) ..... Nous les purifions. ....

Exercise 7
Provide the infinitive of the verb forms that correspond to the following nouns. Repeat after the confirmation.
(1) vérification .... vérifier ....
(2) identification .... identifier ....
(3) liquéfaction .... liquéfier ....
(4) fortification .... fortifier ....
(5) édification .... édifier ....
(6) glorification .... glorifier ....
(7) pacifiste .... pacifier ....
(8) ossements .... ossifier ....
(9) croix .... crucifier ....
(10) saint .... sanctifier ....

Note: If the last four items prove too difficult, replace them with the French nouns *pacification*, *ossification*, *crucifixion*, and *sanctification*.

These alternations are easy to find, since the process of forming words historically based on the Latin alternation *facere/factum* seems to be still productive in French (cf. Juilland 1965:80-82).

Since there are a number of *-er* verbs that end in /waje/ in the infinitive, it is possible to make up drills like the foregoing which may include added practice of another difficult glide, /w/. Moreover, the student might thus learn some new derived word forms.

Exercise 8
A sequence of two related words will be presented. Provide the infinitive of the corresponding verb. Repeat after the confirmation.

(1) onde, ondoiement .... ondoyer ....
(2) tu, tutoiement .... tutoyer ....
(3) larme, larmoiement .... larmoyer ....
(4) coude, coudoiement .... coudoyer ....
(5) tourne, tournoi .... tournoyer ....
(6) poudre, poudroiement .... poudroyer ....
(7) aboi, aboiement .... aboyer ....
(8) vous, vouvoiement .... vouvoyer ....
(9) vous, voussoiement .... voussoyer ....
(10) fosse, fossoyeur .... fossoyer ....
(11) rouge, rougeoiement .... rougeoyer ....

One sound sequence that gives speakers of English some difficulty is the one in which palatalization tends to apply in English but not in French. Examples that come to mind are the *Bruce Young* and *Lois Yates* of Chapter 7. Similarly, beginners have trouble with words ending in *-ation*, *-otion*, etc. This can be quickly pointed out to students by showing that *ocean* and *notion* rhyme in English but not in French. It is therefore important to underscore these differences by reinforcing them with a drill.

Exercise 9
Change the word given to its nominalized form in *-tion*. Repeat after the confirmation.

(1) actif .... action .... (6) déserter .... désertion .....
(2) négatif .... négation .... (7) dévot .... dévotion ......
(3) concevoir .... conception .... (8) décider .... décision ....
(4) convoquer .. convocation .. (9) suggérer .... suggestion ...
(5) bifurquer .... bifurcation ... (10) combustible .. combustion ..

These drills can be used over again both as a means to achieve correct pronunciation and as occasional review for any English speaker for whom French is a second language. Phonetic production, however, is but one of the aspects of the glides with which students of French need to be familiar.

Glides are formed from vowels according to principles still not well established and around which there is some controversy, as explained in Section 22.1.2.

22.1.2 Constraints on Gliding. In Chapter 12, a constraint on Gliding was discussed which seems to prevent glides from forming if the /VV/ sequence is preceded by a /CC/ cluster. A question at the end of that chapter further suggested that the /CC/ cluster in question must be in the same syllable as the eventual peak (the second V) of the syllable, more specifically, the cluster must be that syllable's onset to prevent Gliding from applying. It was further established that /y/ is an exception to that rule, able as it is to glide, if it is followed by /i/, even when preceded by a cluster. Gliding is therefore constrained in a rather complex way; and it may, in fact, consist of more than one rule. For one, the gliding of /y/ before /i/ is obligatory: there are no /yi/ sequences in the language (but see Section 22.4.2). By contrast, there are alternations between /y/ and /ɥ/, in *muette* for example, which suggest that Gliding is optional. Furthermore, this alternation is not universally distributed. To some speakers only /mɥɛt/ is acceptable, to others only /myɛt/. Here, the position taken is the more encompassing one, allowing either /ɥ/ or /y/, that is, the glide is optional. This optional usage occurs in such drills as Exercise 3, where the left column contains /VV/ variants and the right column shows one of the optional /GV/ variants.

To further complicate matters, the three lexicographers referred to here are not in agreement over how to transcribe words to which both Gliding and Yod-Insertion are to apply. For example, *Le Petit Robert* is in agreement with the way I wrote the rule of Gliding and Yod-Insertion, since it transcribes *semestriel* and *monstrueux* as /səmɛstRijɛl/ and /mɔ̃stRyø/, respectively. But Juilland (1965) transcribes them as /səmɛstRjɛl/ and /mɔ̃stRɥø/, while Warnant (1968) offers /səmɛstRiɛl/ and /mɔ̃stRyø/. It appears, then, that to Juilland the cluster constraint on Gliding is not as powerful as the other works suggest. I personally would not pronounce these and similar words with a /GV/ sequence, although I have heard them said that way. Usage here is not firmly established; and some wavering is taking place. One might expect Juilland to transcribe all the sequences considered here as /GV/; but that is not the case. For example, he lists *confluent*, *tonitruant*, and *congruent* with the /yã/ sequence, a choice which seems to lack consistency when compared to the /GV/ sequence he provides for *monstrueux*. Warnant is consistent in his application of Gliding, e.g. he glides the /y/ in *muet*, the /u/ in *mouette*, and the /i/ in *miette* but not in *truelle*, *clouez*, or *triangle*; but in this last word he does not apply Yod-Insertion, opting for /tRiãgl/ instead of /tRijãgl/. The fact that *triangle* is transcribed without the /j/ by both Warnant and Juilland suggests that they view this rule as, at best, a low level phonetic rule. In my opinion, not providing alternate transcriptions for the words which alternate between the glide and the vowel and not including /j/ in the transcription for the words where it does occur may lead the reader to conclude that certain forms are incorrect, when in fact they are not.

Gliding is also generally obligatory when the /VV/ sequence is word-initial, e.g. *oui, oiseau, huit, huile, ouest, ouate, houer, huitre, iode, ion, ionien, ouailles, oued, ouistiti, iouler, hyoïde, hierarchie*, and *hiatus*. A major exception is *hier*, which may or may not be glided. Depending on individual or dialectal preferences, the words *ouest, iouler*, and *hiatus* are also said with /VV/ sequences.

According to Juilland, the most frequent of final /GV/ sequences are those in /iõ/ with 1677, in /je/ with 1349, in /jẽ/ with 335, in /wa/ with 162 and in /jø/ with 143. Among the /GVC/ or /GVL/ in final position, he reports /jɛʀ/ and /waʀ/ as 477 and 412, respectively, followed by /jɛn/ with 299 and /jøz/ with 164. From these data, one can conclude that the glide /ɥ/ is not as widely distributed in French vocabulary as /j/ and /w/. However, as it occurs in often-used words like *lui, suis, huit, nuit, fruit, cuire*, etc. it is fairly frequent, more so, for example, than /g/, /ø/, or /œ/, as reported in Léon and Léon (1964:42).

22.2 Stem-final /j/. Under the heading of gliding, I have discussed segments derived from vowels before another vowel. The phonetic make-up of the prevocalic glides which English and French share, e.g. /w/ and /j/, is essentially the same. In English, they are often referred to as on-glides, as distinguished from the postvocalic off-glides. This section is concerned with postvocalic glides.

The articulatory movements of the English and French postvocalic glides are strikingly different. While the off-glides of English are generally associated with a movement of closure in the coda of a syllable, the postvocalic glide of French is in fact the onset of the next syllable and it has the same phonetic characteristics as its prevocalic equivalent, although it is often found in word-final position due to the deletion of final schwa.

The only one of the three glides to occur in stem-final position is /j/. Chapter 12 stated that stem-final /j/ is really derived from /-li/ by Palatalization and Yod-Conversion. This two-step process is responsible for such words as *émail, vitrail, portail, travail, abeille, vieil, sommeil, oreille, bouteille, fille, famille, oeil, feuille, houille*, and *fenouil*.

In Chapter 17.3 it was pointed out that the vowels of French must be drilled so as to eliminate from them the off-glides which are so prevalent in the spoken French of native English speakers when they first learn to produce the language of the 'hexagone'. I will not repeat these drills here. The problem at hand is to insure that in learning French, English speakers will not transfer the off-glide of English *buy, essay, pay,* and *obey* into French *bail, essayes, paye,* and *abeille*. The trick is to coax the student into treating postvocalic glides as prevocalic glides. Two approaches are advocated, which can also be combined: (1) use words which place /j/ in prevocalic position for a first approximation, (2) make the students pronounce the forms with an epenthetic schwa after the glide (/j(ə)/).

Exercise 1
Repeat after the speaker.
(1) oreillette .... oreille ....
(2) vous baillez .... il baille ....
(3) vous payez .... il paye ....
(4) nous conseillons .... il conseille ....
(5) réveillez-vous .... réveille-toi ....
(6) une fillette .... une fille ....
(7) c'est un grillon .... c'est une grille ....
(8) voici l'oeillère .... voici l'oeil ....

In this exercise the learner is advised to anticipate the postglide vowel of the left column and to cut off abruptly after /j/ in producing the items in the right column. An alternative method would be to produce a schwa in the words of the right column even if, as in *oeil*, none is allowed. Students are amused when they do this drill because they enjoy imitating the regional accents of southern French speakers.

The stem-final /j/ is found after /a/ in *bail, taille*, after /ɛ/ in *soleil, pareil*, after /i/ in *bille, famille*, after /œ/ in *oeil, orgueil*, and after /u/ in *rouille* and *fenouil*. It is never found after nasalized vowels, schwa, /y/, /ø/, /o/, or /ɔ/. The fact that /j/ does not occur after nasalized vowels is best explained in terms of the derivations given here for nasalized vowels and for /j/ (cf. Chapters 12 and 14): nasalized vowels are derived by assimilation with a following nasal and /j/ is derived from /-li/ preceded by a vowel. These two requirements are incompatible.

22.3 Diphthongs. There is no phonetic feature that distinguishes between glides resulting from Gliding and glides resulting from Diphthongization. But, while these are not distinguished phonetically, they are distinguished phonologically. They enter into alternations, which give the observer clues as to their derivation.

As was seen in Chapter 12, glides that result from Gliding alternate with their homorganic vowel (/ɥ/ with /y/, /w/ with /u/, and /j/ with /i/) if they enter at all into an alternation. Glides that result from Diphthongization are /j/ and /w/. The former is followed by /e/ or /ɛ/ (depending on the syllable structure) and /ɛ̃/, while the latter is followed by /ɛ̃/ or /a/ (depending on whether the syllable peak is nasalized). When an alternation is involved, as is most often the case, the /GV/ sequence alternates with a single vowel /V/, not with two vowels, which is characteristic in alternations involving Gliding.

While the contrast just established has no significance at the level of phonetic representation (i.e. no effect on how to pronounce these three glides), it has great significance in the organization of the storehouse of lexical items known as 'one's vocabulary'. Put another way, these alternations are important for the learner because they show word families in their systematic arrangement.

On the purely practical level, this organization is in no way inferior to one which teaches the glides strictly as phonetic entities unrelated to any vowel by means of Diphthongizing or Gliding. Even at this level, it is best to show glide/vowel alternations because of the high likelihood that the learner will encounter both pronunciations. Our organization is vastly superior at the morphological and lexical levels to any strictly phonetic approach, as has been demonstrated.

The task at hand is therefore to produce drills that will reinforce the phonetic aspect of glides while at the same time reinforcing the relations examined in Chapter 12. Nothing is simpler. We need only utilize the alternations studied. This can be done as follows.

Exercise 1
A learned word will be presented. Give its native equivalent. Repeat after the confirmation.

(1) monacal	moine	(10) crédulité	croire
(2) ponctuel	point	(11) crucifixion	croix
(3) céleste	ciel	(12) mensuel	mois
(4) acupuncture	point	(13) pesant	poids
(5) pédestre	pied	(14) réfrigérer	froid
(6) légal	loi	(15) séricole	soie
(7) fenil	foin	(16) vociférer	voix
(8) épilation	poil	(17) visibilité	voir
(9) lévrier	lièvre	(18) chenil	chien

Exercise 2
The second person plural form of the imperative of the verb will be given. Change it to the singular. Repeat after the confirmation.

(1) Tenez!	Tiens!	(7) Revenez!	Reviens!
(2) Croyez!	Crois!	(8) Retenez!	Retiens!
(3) Venez!	Viens!	(9) Acquerrez!	Acquiers!
(4) Voyez!	Vois!	(10) Buvez!	Bois!
(5) Siégez!	Siège!	(11) Asseyez-vous!	Assieds-toi!
(6) Acquiescez!	Acquiesce!	(12) Accroissez!	Accrois!

22.4 Glides and spelling

22.4.1 The front unrounded glide /j/

22.4.1.1 /V/-*il*. The glide /j/ can be represented by the diagraph (two letters) *il*, if it is preceded by a syllabic segment. Examples of this combination are *ail, bail, pareil, vieil, oeil, deuil,* and *fenouil* (the only *-ouil* word). When preceded by a consonantal segment, *il* is pronounced with a syllable peak, e.g. *cil, fil, vil, mil*.

22.4.1.2 *-ill-*. The glide /j/ can also be represented by the trigraph *-ill* before a syllable peak or a schwa. Examples of *-ille* in word-final position after a consonantal segment are *fille, vrille, grille, bille*, and *quille*. Exceptions to this rule are *ville* (and its composites, e.g. *Trouville, Joinville, Orléansville*), *mille, tranquille, bacille, vaudeville, Achille, Lille*, and *village*.

Examples of words ending in *-ille* preceded by a vowel are *bataille, canaille, fouille, rouille, feuille, acceuille, veillée, vieillard, Cadillac*. Exceptions to this configuration are the composites of *mille*, e.g. *millimètre, milliard, milliampère*.

22.4.1.3 *-i/V/*. The glide /j/ is derived both by Diphthongizing and by Gliding. In all cases of Diphthongization it is represented by the letter *i*. Examples are *assieds-toi, viens, acquiers*, which are pronounced with /je/, /jẽ/ and /jɛ/, respectively. In the cases where Gliding is involved in the derivation, /j/ is derived from /i/ and is represented by *i* as in *niais, lieu, rosier, action, meunière, sciant, mécanicien*, and *miauler*.

22.4.1.4 /j/ as the letter *y*. The letter *y* is often associated with /j/, but under some conditions it is pronounced /i/.

22.4.1.4.1 *y* pronounced as /i/. The letter *y* is pronounced /i/ in pre- or postconsonantal position, e.g.: *Yves, Ysangrin, analyse, Nancy, Annecy, Le Puy*.

22.4.1.4.2 *y* pronounced as /i/ or /j/. The letter *y* is pronounced /i/ when it stands alone, e.g. *il y reste*. If the next word begins with a vowel, Gliding may occur, e.g. *il y a*. In short, *y* is realized as /i/ if the environment forces it to be a syllable peak. Otherwise, *y* is pronounced /j/, subject to the explanations that follow.

22.4.1.4.3 *y* pronounced as /j/ only. The letter *y* before and/or after a vowel is pronounced /j/, as numerous examples to follow will illustrate; but first *abbaye* and *pays* should be pointed out as exceptions. Both end with /ei/. Other cases of pre- and postvocalic *y* result in /j/. They are illustrated in the next section.

22.4.1.4.3.1 Word-initial *y*. The letter *y* in word-initial position is pronounced as /j/, e.g. *Yonne, yatagan, yaourt, Yougoslavie*.

22.4.1.4.3.2 Intervocalic *y*. The spelling system treats *y* in a very interesting way: *y* stands for *ii*. This can be seen in the way that *y* affects the pronunciation of words where it occurs intervocalically. The first of the two *i*'s combines with the preceding letter to represent by coalescence a new segment; the second one is made a glide.

    (i) *oy* = *oii* → /waj/
    (ii) *ay* = *aii* → /ɛj/ or /ej/

Examples of (i) are *loyal, moyenne, foyer, voyou, moyeux, choyant, voyeur, noyau*. Examples of (ii) are *balayeur, essayer, rayonner, payant, pagayons, rayure*, *layette*. When coalescence does not take place, the first of the two *i*'s remains a vowel as in (iii) or is lost as in (iv).

(iii) *uy* → /ɥij/
(iv) *ay* → /aj/

Examples of (iii) are *ennuyeur*, *essuyer*, *bruyant*, *tuyau*, *écuyer*, *appuyez*, all pronounced with /ij/. Illustrations of (iv), which, by the way, constitutes exceptions to (ii), are *Bayonne*, *mayonnaise*, *Lafayette*. The word *gruyère*, which is recorded as /gʀyjɛʀ/, is sometimes regularized to /gʀɥijɛʀ/.

22.4.1.4.3.3 Word-final *y*. Word-final *y* preceded by a vowel is either coalesced, as in *Combray*, which rhymes with *prêt*, or silent, as in *Ney*, *dey*, *Shelley*, which end in /ɛ/.

22.4.1.5 /j/ as the letter *ï*. The diaeresis is used to warn the reader that the segment it dominates does not behave totally as would be expected otherwise. The /j/ in *faïence*, *païen*, *aïeul*, as well as that in foreign words like *Shanghaï*, *Hanoï*, *oïl*, *Haïfa*, is represented with a diaeresis over the *i*. Without this diaeresis, the *i* would coalesce with the preceding vowel to form sounds like /ɛ/ or /wa/, as the case may be. The same principle exists in *maïs*, *naïf*, *typhoïde*, and *sinusoïde*. Note that *ouïe* and *inouï* have a diaeresis when in fact none is needed. The words *oui* and *ouïe* are homonyms.

22.4.2 The front rounded glide /ɥ/. The front rounded glide /ɥ/ is always represented orthographically by *u*. But *u* does not represent /ɥ/ exclusively. It also stands for other sounds, among which are /y/ and /w/. The letter *u* can also be silent.

22.4.2.1 Silent *u*. After *g* and *q*, the letter *u* is generally silent. It occurs as a spelling convention. Examples of *qu* sequences as /k/ are *qui*, *que*, *quoi*, *quel*, *question*, *quitter*, *marquise*, *quinze*, *cinquante*, *quota*, *quatrain*, *quai*, *quand*, *queue*, *quintuplés*. Examples of *gu* as /g/ are *guide*, *guérir*, *sanguinaire*, *fatigué*, *algue*, *Guise* (in *Duc de Guise*), *gueule*, *guet*. The *u* after *g* is intended to prevent confusion between the two realizations of *g*: /g/ and /ʒ/. The latter is illustrated in *gymnastique*, *général*, *gilet*, *gelée*, *gendarme*. The use of the letter *u* is not needed between *g* and the letters *u*, *o*, and *a*. Hence, *gugusse* (nickname for *Auguste* and *Gustave*), *garçon*, *gonfler*, *gourde*, *gant*. Note, however, that *navigua*, *léguant* retain the *u* although it is not needed. The *u* is, of course, needed in a number of other forms in the paradigm of these verbs, e.g. *naviguez*, *naviguera*, *léguer*.

22.4.2.2 *u* as either /w/ or /ɥ/ in *qu* and *gu* sequences. When the letter *u* is not silent, the letter *u* before a vowel is pronounced as a glide. When it precedes /a/ it is realized as /w/ (cf. Chapter 10, Question 1). Examples of this are *equateur*, *Equador*, *loquace* (although /lɔkas/ is also heard), *guano*, *jaguar*, *lingual*. Before other vowels, the letter *u* is pronounced as the front rounded glide /ɥ/, e.g. *aiguille*, *quinquennal*, *équidistant*, *linguiste*. *Quatuor* /kwatɥɔʀ/ illustrates both cases.

22.4.2.3 u as a vowel or a glide. Prevocalic *u* represents a vowel or a glide according to the rule of Gliding. Nothing about orthography adds to the discussion of the problems discussed in Section 22.1.2.

22.4.2.4 u before /j/. As was stated in Section 22.1.2, Gliding applies obligatorily to /y/ when it precedes /i/, yielding /ɥi/. There are, however, instances when *u* precedes the letter *i*; but Gliding does not apply. The reason for this nonapplication is that the letter *i* stands for /j/, not for /i/. More specifically, the letter *i* stands for the glide /j/ which constitutes the marker for the imperfect in the first and second person plural of verbs with an infinitive in *-uer*, as shown in Exercise 1. The facts are presented in the form of a drill, a repetition drill to be exact, but it is obvious that a transformation drill could be devised.

Exercise 1
Repeat after the speaker.

(1) remue	remuer	remuons	remuions
(2) évolue	évoluer	évoluons	évoluions
(3) pollue	polluer	polluons	polluions
(4) sues	suer	suons	suions
(5) tue	tuer	tuons	tuions
(6) puent	puer	puons	puions

It might be instructive to compare the foregoing alternations to those exhibited in the verb *fuir*, where the stem includes the sequence /ɥi/. Here the form for first person plural in the present indicative is *fuyons* /fɥijɔ̃/. The /j/ in *fuyons* is added by Yod-Insertion (the stem is *fui-*, the ending is *-ons*; together they yield /fɥiɔ̃/, to which Yod-Insertion adds /j/ to give /fɥijɔ̃/). Under no circumstances is the letter *u* of *fuir* realized as a vowel, in striking contrast to the letter *u* of *suer* and the other verbs in Exercise 1. Why? Because these letters serve quite different purposes. The *u* of *suer* is the last vowel in the stem, i.e. *su-er*, and as such carries the word stress. The *u* of *fuir* is also in the stem but it does not bear the word stress. Because it is always followed by the stress-bearing /i/ which occurs at the end of the stem, *u* is always glided. How does the insertion of yod, marker of the imperfect in the first and second persons of the plural, affect the derivation of *fuir*? Not at all in the same way as it does the verbs in Exercise 1. This is shown in the derivations displayed in Figure 22.2.

Figure 22.2 The derivation of *suons*, *suions*, *fuyons*, and *fuyions*.

Underlying representation:	su-ɔ̃	su-jɔ̃	fui-ɔ̃	fui-jɔ̃
High Vowel Fronting:	sy-ɔ̃	sy-jɔ̃	fyi-ɔ̃	fyi-jɔ̃
Gliding:	sɥ-ɔ̃	. . .	fɥi-ɔ̃	fɥi-jɔ̃
Yod-Insertion:	. . .	. . .	fɥijɔ̃	. . .
Derived form:	suons	suions	fuyons	fuyions

The imperfect marker /j/ prevents the application of Gliding in *suions*.

22.4.3 The back glide /w/.

22.4.3.1 /w/ spelled *u*. It has already been pointed out that the letter *u* can be pronounced /w/ or /ɥ/, depending on whether /a/ or another vowel follows the *gu* and *qu* diagraph (cf. 22.4.2.2). Further illustrations are *aquarelle*, *quaternaire*, *adequat*, and *Guadeloupe*.

22.4.3.2 /w/ spelled *ou*. This reiterates what was seen in conjunction with the application of Gliding. Examples are *mouette*, *loua*, *zouave*, *ouate*, *couard*, *boueux*. The same diagraph is also found in *couenne* /kwan/, and *pingouin* /pɛ̃gwɛ̃/.

22.4.3.3 /wa/ spelled *oe*. Examples with this diagraph are *moelle*, *moelleux*, *poêle*, *poêlée*.

22.4.3.4 /wa/ and /wɛ̃/ spelled *oi* and *oin*. Examples of these are all the result of Diphthongization. *Soir*, *loi*, *joie*, *noir*, *poil*, *voile* represent *oi* /wa/; *foin*, *loin*, *joint*, *moins* end in /wɛ̃/.

22.4.3.5 *ou* before /j/. The letters *ou* behave just like *u* before the /j/ which marks the imperfect tense of the first and second person plural forms of *-er* verbs that have *ou* in stem-final position. Consequently, the same sort of drill can be devised for *ou* as was employed for *u* by making use of the alternations displayed in Figure 22.3.

Figure 22.3 Drills for *ou* as /u/ vs. /w/.

/u/	/w/	/w/	/u/
joue	jouer	jouons	jouions
loue	louer	louons	louions
échoue	échouer	échouons	échouions
noue	nouer	nouons	nouions

22.4.3.6 *w* pronounced as /w/ or /v/. Borrowed vocabulary tends to retain the flavor of the original language; it tends to, but does not succeed. Here, however, there is a general tendency to pronounce *w* as /w/ in words borrowed from English: *waterproof*, *tramway*, *sandwich* (which rhymes with *fiche*), and as /v/ in words borrowed from German: *wagon*, *Wagram*, *Weimar*, *Weber*.

22.5 Glides in poetry.
The segments of French are generally the same in normal speech and poetry with the notable exception of schwa and the glides. The schwa or mute *e* is discussed in Chapter 24; the glide segments are discussed here.

There is no absolute, but one can say that in poetry the tendency to change a VV sequence into a GV sequence is more conservative than in normal speech. Consequently, there is no case where Gliding occurs in poetry where it does not occur in normal speech. For example, the constraint placed on Gliding regarding CC clusters in the onset of a given syllable is equally applicable in poetry: thus, *tri-age*, *cli-ent*, *tru-ant* are all bisyllabic (the hyphen marks the syllable break).

Sections 22.5.1 and 22.5.2 contain an abbreviated and slightly modified account of a list provided by Martinon (1962) relating to quantity (the number of syllables) in French verse.

22.5.1 Generally bisyllabic sequences in French poetry. The following sequences are generally bisyllabic in French poetry.

22.5.1.1 *ia*. The forms *di-amant*, *confi-a*, *mari-a* are bisyllabic; but *diable*, *diacre*, *liard* are monosyllabic.

22.5.1.2 *ie*. *-ier* verbs in the infinitive (e.g. *étudi-er*, *confi-er*), in the second person plural indicative and imperative (e.g. *appréci-ez*, *confi-ez*), in the past participle (e.g. *mari-é*, *appréci-é*), as well as in *ri-ez*, *inqui-et*, *matéri-el*, *impi-été*.

22.5.1.3 *ian*. *étudi-ant*, *confi-ant*, *fortifi-ant*.

22.5.1.4 *iai* (a variant of *ie*). *confi-ait*, *appréci-ait*, *étudi-ait*.

22.5.1.5 *ion*. In first person plural of verbs in *-ier* (e.g. *appréci-ons*, *confi-ons*). Also a variant of *-ie*. Found as well in nouns in *-tion* and *-sion*: *acti-on*, *passi-on*, *electi-on*, *dicti-on*; but, in the imperfect or conditional of *-er* verbs, *i* is always a glide (see 22.5.2 and 22.4.3.2).

22.5.1.6 *io*. *vi-olon*, *di-ocèse*; but not in *poiche* and *fiole*.

22.5.1.7 *iau*. *mi-auler*, *impéri-aux*.

22.5.1.8 *ieu*. *pi-euse*, *odi-eux*, *furi-eux*; but *pieu*, *mieux*, *vieux* are monosyllabic.

In all the foregoing, Yod-Insertion sometimes applies, yielding /ija/, /ije/, /ijã/, /ijɛ/, /ijõ/, /ijɔ/, /ijo/, and /ijø/.

22.5.1.9 *oe*. *po-ète*, *La Bo-étie*; but see Section 22.5.2.

22.5.1.10 *ue*. *tu-er*, *su-eur*, *effectu-é*, *sensu-el*.

22.5.2 Monosyllabic sequences in poetry. The following sequences are generally monosyllabic in French poetry.

22.5.2.1 *ie*. *Ciel*, *fier*, *fièvre*, *tiers*, and imperfect and conditional forms of verbs (e.g. *saviez*, *aimiez*, *finiriez*). These are all forms that are derived by Diphthongization or that contain an underlying yod.

22.5.2.2 *oi*. Diphthongs *roi*, *loi*, *poil*, *soir*, *boit*.

22.5.2.3 *oe*. *moelle*, *poêle* (which rhyme with *poil*) but see Section 22.5.1.

22.5.2.4 *ui*. Always monosyllabic (e.g. *appui, déduire, fuite, truite*).

22.5.2.5 *ion*. The first person plural in imperfect and conditional forms of verbs (e.g. *aimerions, savions, finissiez*).

22.5.2.6 *oin*. Nasal diphthongs (e.g. *loin, moins, soin, témoin*).

22.5.2.7 *ouin*. *babouin, marsouin*.

Chapter 23
Nasals and nasalized vowels

23.1 Phonetic production. A major problem that faces the speaker of English learning French or the speaker of French learning English is the striking contrast between the two nasalized systems. As a consequence of the rules discussed in Chapter 14, i.e. /VN/ vs. /ṼN/ vs. /Ṽ/, no word-internal /ṼN/ sequence occurs in French (but see Section 23.1.4, where exceptions to this general statement are discussed). Instead of /ṼN/, French allows /Ṽ/ or /VN/, the former when Nasalization and /N/-Deletion have applied, the latter when a vowel following the nasal has prevented the application of Nasalization.

In contrast to the French system, English does not have an /N/-Deletion rule. Furthermore, the lowering of the velum during vowel phonation is less extreme than in French, although in some speakers nasalization is quite pronounced. The degree of nasalization in English, however, is not functional and bears no meaning. All English vowels in the proper environment are nasalized; they are nasalized by some speakers more than by others, but the process is totally predictable phonetically. In other words, while the expected sequence in English is /ṼN/, the expected sequence in French is /VN/ before a vowel and /Ṽ/ elsewhere. This is displayed in Figure 23.1.

Figure 23.1 English /ṼN/ vs. French /Ṽ/ or /VN/.

English: /ṼN/	French: /Ṽ/	/VN/
on	on	donne
can	quand	canne
pen	pain	peine
Sean	Jean	Jeanne

23.1.1 Drilling /VN/. Drills that will enable students to produce /VN/ sequences without a trace of the /ṼN/ tendency of English should begin with a discrimination exercise because in many instances English speakers do not hear what is done in French, just as French speakers do not hear what is done in English. One way of showing them in class what is done in the other language is to speak the students' native language with an accent of the other, transferring the habits of the target language. For example, say *on the rocks* /ɔnzøRɔks/ in such a way that *on* will rhyme with *bonne*. Another way of making your students discriminate is to guide them through drills like the following.

Exercise 1
Listen for the difference between English /ṼN/ and /VC/ sequences.
(1) vim   Vic   vim
(2) song   sock   song
(3) pan   pat   pan
(4) lung   luck   lung

In French the stressed vowels of *vîmes*, *sonne*, *panne*, and *lune* are the same as in *ville*, *sort*, *passe*, and *luge*. To test whether they are indeed avoiding /ṼN/, students should learn the nose-pinch test.

Exercise 2
Pinch your nose so as to close your nasal cavity. Repeat the model /ã/, /õ/, /ɛ̃/. Do you hear the blocked vibrations in your nose? That is fine for nasalized vowels, but you should not feel these vibrations in the stressed vowels of words like *âne*, *donne*, or *tiennent*. Without releasing your pinched nose, repeat the words in the left column. Do that first. Now you need to learn to release your nose just as you begin saying the second syllable. Practice that with the leftmost column again. Do that now. Now turn to the second column. Do the nose-pinch test, releasing the nose as you begin the second syllable. You should hear no vibration in your nasal cavity. For contrast, do the same test with the words in the third column. In this instance, you should hear vibrations in your nose.

(1) papa   panier   pantin
(2) pipette   pinion   pintade
(3) vouté   vannerie   vantard
(4) disette   dîner   dindonneau

Once the students have learned to practice the nose-pinch test, they can be invited to do the foregoing exercise linearly. Make them repeat after the speaker. Some will continue to have nasal resonance in words of the middle column. They need to go through the drills that follow.

A way to produce oral vowels before nasals is to assume, at least at first, that a break separates the vowel from the following nasal.

Exercise 3
Repeat after the speaker.
(1) lai-neux .... lai-ne ....
(2) vei-nard .... vei-ne ....

(3) gê-nant .... gê-ne ....
(4) san-gui-naire .... san-guine ....
(5) mi-neur .... mi-ne ....
(6) rui-neux .... rui-ne ....
(7) bo-nniche .... bo-nne ....
(8) do-nnant .... do-nne ....
(9) co-lo-nnade .... co-lo-nne ....
(10) to-nnerre .... to-nne ....
(11) co-mmu-nal .... co-mmu-ne ....
(12) lu-naire .... lu-ne ....
(13) for-tu-né .... for-tu-ne ....

Another way of placing a break between /V/ and its /N/ coda is to work from a 1-2 sequence to a 2-1 sequence, as in the drill that follows.

Exercise 4
Read the following syllables with an even stressed rhythm.

ne lût	(1)	/nə ly nə ly nə ly nə ly nə/	lune
ne sait	(2)	/nə sɛ nə sɛ nə sɛ nə sɛ nə/	scène
ne ferait	(3)	/nə fʀɛ nə fʀɛ nə fʀɛ nə fʀɛ nə/	frêne
ne va	(4)	/nə va nə va nə va nə va nə/	vanne
ne hais	(5)	/nə ɛ nə ɛ nə ɛ nə ɛ nə/	haine
ne vais	(6)	/nə vɛ nə vɛ nə vɛ nə vɛ nə/	veine

Repeat the exercise, doing the nose-pinch test. You are to pinch your nose on the even syllables.

After the students have acquired the /VN/ sequence by repeating after a model, you can then construct tests that will make them produce the sequence on their own, as a transformation. One such drill requires the student to replace a consonantal segment by a nasal.

Exercise 5
Repeat the word given, then replace the last segment by /n/. Finally, repeat after the confirmation.

(1) sec .... , ... scène ....
(2) jade .... , ... Jeanne ....
(3) luge .... , ... lune ....
(4) miche .... , ... mine ....
(5) dort .... , ... donne ....
(6) figue .... , ... fine ....
(7) digue .... , ... dîne ....
(8) raide .... , ... Rennes ....

A similar drill can be constructed for /m/.

Exercise 6
Repeat the word given, then replace the last segment by /m/. Finally, repeat after the confirmation.

(1) ride .... , ... rime ....
(2) cil .... , ... cime ....
(3) mec .... , ... même ....
(4) poète .... , ... poème ....
(5) os .... , ... homme ....
(6) taule .... , ... tonne ....
(7) daube .... , ... dôme ....
(8) rage .... , ... rame ....
(9) faille .... , ... femme ....

23.1.2 /Ṽ/ not /ṼN/. Another difficulty encountered by English-speaking students of French is the tendency to retain the conditioning nasal in pronunciation. This is particularly noticeable when /Ṽ/ is followed by a bilabial or a dental obstruent. Discrimination in this case is essential because the student does not realize that he or she is not deleting the conditioning nasal. Using vocabulary borrowed from French is extremely useful here because the contrast becomes readily obvious. Words like those in Figure 23.2 should be pointed out to the students.

Figure 23.2 English /ṼN/ vs. French /Ṽ/.

English /ṼN/:	French /Ṽ/:
combat /kãmbæt/	combat /kõba/
grandeur /grændʌɹ/	grandeur /grãdœʀ/
contour /kãntur/	contour /kõtuʀ/

One way to make the students acquire the feel for producing a nasalized vowel without the conditioning nasal (suggested by Francis Gravit) is to point to the *huh huh* answers in colloquial English as examples of /Ṽ/, most probably /ʌ̃/. Ask the students to produce *huh huh* with their mouths slightly open and their lips rounded. This should approximate /õ/. Now correct this articulation to make it properly /õ/ and, from it, make the student modify his or her vocal tract to produce the other nasalized vowels without following it with the conditioning nasal. Those for whom this will not work will need to begin with a discrimination exercise.

Exercise 1
Listen to the difference between the nasal and the oral vowels in the pairs of contrasted words.

(1) émeute .... défunte .... (5) cette .... sainte ....
(2) sec .... cinq .... (6) messe .... mince ....
(3) chatte .... chantes .... (7) bac .... banque ....
(4) rode .... ronde .... (8) côte .... conte ....

Exercise 2
Repeat after the speaker.
(1) plan .... plan-té ....
(2) bon .... bon-té ....
(3) dans .... dan-sé ....
(4) vingt .... vin-gtaine ....
(5) rond .... ron-delle ....
(6) gant .... gan-té ....
(7) mont .... mon-tagne ....
(8) peint .... pein-ture ....

Exercise 3
Read the following syllables with an even-stressed rhythm.

tu repeins	(1)	/ tyʀ pẽ tyʀ pẽ tyʀ pẽ tyʀ/	peinture
t'es bon	(2)	/ te bõ te bõ te bõ te bõ te/	bonté
tes gants	(3)	/ te gã te gã te gã te gã te/	ganté
ses dents	(4)	/ se dã se dã se dã se dã se/	dansez
béton	(5)	/ be tõ be tõ be tõ be tõ be/	tombé
durant	(6)	/ dy ʀã dy ʀã dy ʀã dy ʀã dy/	rendu
c'est lent	(7)	/ sɛ lã sɛ lã sɛ lã sɛ lã sɛ/	lançait
ses reins	(8)	/ se ʀẽ se ʀẽ se ʀẽ se ʀẽ se/	rincé

It is useful, though by no means easy for the learner, to combine the /Ṽ/ and /VN/ sequences.

Exercise 4
Repeat after the speaker.
(1) bon .... bonne .... bonbonne ....
(2) rond .... / Rɔn/ .... ronronne ....
(3) rang .... gaine .... rengaine ....
(4) sans .... Taine .... centaine ....
(5) qu'on .... (tu) bines .... combine ....
(6) on .... dînes .... Ondine ....
(7) tronc .... bonne .... trombone ....
(8) qu'on .... sonne .... consonne ....
(9) rang .... qu'une .... rancune ....

23.1.3 Drills for the nasalized vowels (/Ṽ/). In drilling for nasalized vowels (/Ṽ/), I prefer to use the natural alternations of the language.

23.1.3.1 /œ̃/

Exercise 1
Repeat after the speaker.
(1) l'une .... l'un .... (5) inopportune .... inopportun .....
(2) aucune .... aucun .... (6) peu commune ...... peu commun ..

(3) chacune ...... chacun ..... (7) opportune ....opportun ....
(4) importune .. importun .. (8) si commune ....si commun ......

The alternation /yn/ ~ /œ̃/ is not widely distributed, which accounts for the paucity of words in the previous drill. Such is not the case with the other oral/nasal alternations.

23.1.3.2 /ɛ̃/.

23.1.3.2.1 /ɛ̃/ ~ /in/ alternation.

Exercise 1
Repeat after the speaker.
(1) latine .... latin ....
(2) divine .... divin ....
(3) alpine .... alpin ....
(4) angevine .... angevin ....
(5) poitevine .... poitevin ....
(6) frangine .... frangin ....
(7) libertine .... libertin ....
(8) assassine .... assassin ....

23.1.3.2.2 /ɛ̃/ ~ /ɛn/ alternation.

Exercise 1
Repeat after the speaker.
(1) pleine .... plein ....
(2) sereine .... serein ....
(3) naine .... nain ....
(4) romaine .... romain ....
(5) haïtienne .... haïtien ....
(6) malsaine .... malsain ....
(7) incertaine .... incertain ....
(8) châtelaine .... châtelain ....

23.1.3.2.3 /ɛ̃/ ~ /ɛɲ/ alternation.

Exercise 1
Repeat after the speaker.
(1) elles craignent .... il craint ....
(2) elles peignent .... il peint ....
(3) elles feignent .... il feint ....
(4) elles teignent .... il teint ....
(5) elles étreignent .... il étreint ....
(6) elles contraignent .... il contraint ....
(7) elles éteignent .... il éteint ....
(8) elles empreignent .... il empreint ....

23.1.3.2.4 /an/ ~ /ɛn/ ~ /ɛ̃/ alternation.

Exercise 1

You will hear a learned word whose stem contains the sequence /an/. You are to provide its native equivalents, first the feminine (without nasalization on the vowel), then the masculine form. Listen for the confirmation.

(1) germanique .... germaine .... germain ....
(2) puritanisme .... puritaine .... puritain ....
(3) sanitaire .... saine .... sain ....
(4) romane .... romaine .... romain ....
(5) humanité .... humaine .... humain ....
(6) urbanisme .... urbaine .... urbain ....
(7) républicanisme ...... républicaine .... républicain ....
(8) nanisme .... naine .... nain ....

23.1.3.3 /ã/: The sequence /an/ as alternant of /ã/.

Exercise 1
Repeat after the speaker.

(1) volcanique .... volcan ....
(2) printanier .... printemps ....
(3) planifier .... plan ....
(4) océanique .... ocean ....
(5) anglicanisme .... anglican ....
(6) coranique .... coran ....
(7) paysannat .... paysan ....
(8) artisanat .... artisant ....

The next drill combines the modification of a /VN/ sequence to a /Ṽ/ (as in the foregoing) with the articulatory effort of producing the different sequences in the same word (as in Section 23.1.2, Exercise 4).

Exercise 2
Repeat after the speaker.

(1) fréquence .... fréquent .... fréquemment ....
(2) éloquence .... éloquent .... éloquemment ....
(3) indépendance .... indépendant .... indépendamment .....
(4) confidence .... confident .... confidemment ....
(5) incidence .... incident .... incidemment ....
(6) imprudence .... imprudent .... imprudemment ....
(7) brillance .... brillant .... brillamment ....
(8) insouciance .... insouciant .... insouciamment ....

23.1.3.4 /õ/.

Exercise 1
Repeat after the speaker.

(1) bonne .... bon .... (5) espionne ...... espion ....
(2) patronne .... patron .... (6) wallonne ...... wallon ....

(3) gasconne .... gascon .... (7) bretonne ...... breton ....
(4) bouffonne .. bouffon .... (8) gloutonne .... glouton ....

Exercise 2
Repeat after the speaker.
(1) lancez .... lançons ....
(2) chantez .... chantons ....
(3) sonnez .... sonnons ....
(4) dormez .... dormons ....
(5) ouvrez .... ouvrons ....
(6) compensez .... compensons ....
(7) concurrencez .... concurrençons ....
(8) manigancez .... manigançons ....

Exercise 3
Repeat after the speaker.
(1) porter .... portant .... portons ....
(2) finir .... finissant .... finissons ....
(3) mordre .... mordant .... mordons ....
(4) ouvrir .... ouvrant .... ouvrons ....
(5) offencer .... offençant .... offençons ....
(6) déplacer .... déplaçant .... déplaçons ....
(7) condenser .... condensant .... condensons ....
(8) ensemencer .... ensemençant .... ensemençons ......

All the exercises in this section merely require repetition. They can easily be adapted to transformations in either order, depending on which of the sequences of sounds you wish to emphasize.

Some of the drills just discussed, especially if they are mere repetition drills, can be boring. To allay the feeling of boredom which a long session can generate, punctuate it with exercises like the following.

Exercise 4
You will read the consonant on the left, keeping the rest of the printed words covered. Without uncovering these words, you are to produce them by adding /ɛ̃/, /ã/, and /õ/ to that consonant. The fun part comes in trying to figure out what word you have indeed produced. Check your answers one line at a time.

(1) p .... peint .... paon .... pont
(2) s .... saint .... sang .... son
(3) r .... Rhin .... rang .... rond
(4) l .... lin .... lent .... long
(5) v .... vin(gt) .... vent .... vont
(6) b .... bain .... banc .... bon
(7) f .... fin .... faon .... fond
(8) g .... gain .... gant .... gond

(9) d	daim	dent	don(t)
(10) t	teint	temps	ton(d(s))

23.1.4 Liaison after nasalized vowels. This section deals with the ability of the word-final /n/ to link with an adjacent vowel-initial word. Excluded from consideration as irrelevant here are such cases of liaison after nasalized vowels as *ayant entendu, sang humain, la personne dont il parle*. Rather, we are concerned with whether or not the segment /n/ occurs at the end of each of the words ending with *n*, e.g. *don exceptionnel, un animal féroce, en arrivant, on arrive, en haut, mon ami, faites en arriver, en commun accord, en plein air, moyen âge*, and with whether denasalization occurs, in compliance with the established principle that French words seek /Ṽ/ or /VN/ but not /ṼN/.

23.1.4.1 *Liaison obligatoire.*

23.1.4.1.1 Fixed expressions with a prenominal modifier. In expressions like *en plein air, le bien être, au moyen âge, commun accord, commun effort* where a modifier precedes a noun, the word-final /n/ is not deleted. In a number of these expressions, due to the increased jelling of their components into a single word-like unit, the application of Nasalization is affected. *Plein, bien, moyen* are no longer perceived as ending in /VN#/ but are viewed as a /VN/ sequence before a vowel. Consequently, Nazalisation does not take place. This nonapplication is sometimes referred to as 'denasalization'. That it is not denasalization can be shown by examining the sequence /VN/ in *divin enfant*. Here the nonnasalized vowel is high, just as if it had never been nasalized and never been lowered as a result of Nasalization. To assume that it had been nasalized and subsequently denasalized would also require that the denasalized vowel be raised since *divin enfant* is pronounced /divinãfã/ not */divɛnãfã/.

The so-called denasalization in *en plein air* etc. is optional but the retention of /n/ (i.e. the liaison) is obligatory. There are no appropriate sequences */ãplɛ̃ɛʀ/, */mwajɛ̃az/, or */ləbjɛ̃ɛtʀ/.

The same observations can be made about the possessives, e.g. *mon ami, son elève*, with respect to Nasalization and N-Deletion with the reservation that these sequences are not fixed. Essentially, sequences with the possessive adjective are like the foregoing in that the so-called denasalization takes place but like the following in that the syntactic closeness is not dependent on a fixed sequence as much as it is dependent on a structural configuration.

23.1.4.1.2 Satellites. As already seen in Chapter 19, sequences of words like *un animal, en arrivant, on arrive, mon ami, en avant* contain a nucleus and one or more satellites. These satellites are so closely bound to the nucleus that they cannot be separated from it by any other words and they cannot take contrastive stress. Consequently, although there is a strong tendency in French not to produce /ṼN/ sequences, the even stronger tendency of proximity of satellites to their nuclei overrides it, preventing the deletion of the /n/ and giving phonetic reality to the link between the two words.

Exercise 1
Insert *en* before the present participle. Repeat after the confirmation.
(1) allant	en allant	(5) huilant	en huilant ....
(2) courant	en courant	(6) otant	en otant ....
(3) disant	en disant	(7) induisant	en induisant ....
(4) écoutant	en écoutant ...	(8) ouvrant	en ouvrant ......

Exercise 2
Insert *en*, *un*, or *on* before the following. Repeat after the confirmation.
(1) hôpital	un hôpital	(5) sort	on sort ....
(2) entrant	en entrant	(6) arrive	on arrive ....
(3) enfant	un enfant	(7) arrivant	en arrivant ......
(4) époux	un époux	(8) épouse	on épouse ....

In the next drill the learner is to concentrate on the retention of the final /n/.

Exercise 3
You will hear a sequence like *un ami à toi* and you are to change it to its possessive adjective-noun equivalent, e.g. *ton ami*. Repeat after the confirmation.
(1) un élève à moi	mon élève ....
(2) un enfant à elle	son enfant ....
(3) un ballon à elle	son ballon ....
(4) un objectif à lui	son objectif ....
(5) une idée à toi	ton idée ....
(6) un buvard à moi	mon buvard ....
(7) un album à elle	son album ....
(8) un appareil à toi	ton appareil ....

23.1.4.2 *Liaisons facultatives.* The main reason for considering liaison in the context of nasalized vowels in French is that speakers of English tend to treat the conditioning nasal as a retained consonant, a tendency which, of course, yields to liaison when liaison should not occur. Liaison is, as we have seen, dependent on syntactic closeness. Between the tight closeness of obligatory liaison and the relative distance of 'liaison interdite' there is an area known as 'liaison facultative'. Most liaison facultative cases involve /z/, the liaison consonant par excellence. Since this section deals exclusively with /n/ as a liaison consonant, the potential number of liaison facultative cases is reduced to nil.

23.1.4.3 *Liaisons interdites.* The very title of this section will serve as example. As mentioned in Chapter 19, a liaison is allowed between a plural noun, e.g. *liaisons* and its following adjective, e.g. *interdites*. If the noun phrase is in the singular, however, the final /n/ in *liaison* cannot be a liaison consonant because it is deleted by /N/-Deletion. This deletion is not limited to /n/ but applies to all consonantal segments at the end of nouns, e.g. *un cas/exceptionnel, le paquebot/amarré, ce jardin/ensoleillé, un baudet/entêté*.

23.1.4.3.1 Drills. To ensure that the /ṼN/ tendency of English will not interfere in the French of our students, it is useful to drill them on these sequences.

Exercise 1
You will hear an adjective and a noun. Combine them, making sure not to link the final nasal with the following vowel. Repeat after the confirmation.

(1) obligatoire, une station .... une station obligatoire
(2) attaché, un pelican .... un pelican attaché
(3) amorcé, un hameçon .... un hameçon amorcé
(4) azyme, du pain .... du pain azyme
(5) égaré, un pinson .... un pinson égaré
(6) ouvert, un balcon .... un balcon ouvert
(7) en éruption, un volcan .... un volcan en éruption
(8) engraissé, un cochon .... un cochon engraissé

Exercise 2
You will hear a noun-adjective sequence in the plural. Change them to the singular, making sure not to link.

(1) des garçons amusants .... un garçon amusant ....
(2) des flocons immaculés .... un flocon immaculé ....
(3) des enfants adoptés .... un enfant adopté ....
(4) des dindons endormis .... un dindon endormi ....
(5) des cochons engraissés .... un cochon engraissé ....
(6) des croutons émiettés .... un crouton émietté ....
(7) des fantassins embusqués ...... un fantassin embusqué ....
(8) des étudiants éveillés .... un étudiant éveillé ....

23.1.4.3.2 Odds and ends. Like *un*, the adjective *aucun* falls into the category of noun satellites. Consequently, it does not drop its final /n/, which provides phonetic reality for its syntactic closeness: /œ̃nami/ *un ami*, /okœ̃neko/ *aucun écho*. *Quelqu'un* and *chacun*, although they are called pronouns, behave more like nouns in that they do not allow liaison: */kɛlkœ̃nevəny/ *quelqu'un est venu*, */ʃakœ̃nãtãsõʃã/ *chacun entend son chant*. The so-called pronoun *aucun* would also behave identically, but the negative *ne* (which must occur in this syntactic context) is reduced to /n/ and occurs just before the verb, e.g. *aucun n'entendait ses appels*. The question is readily answered when *aucun* occurs before the adjective *autre*; there liaison does occur, i.e. *aucun autre* /okœ̃notʀ/.

23.2 Sound to letter relationship

214 / 23 Nasals and nasalized vowels

23.2.1 The spellings of /ã/. The segment /ã/ is spelled as follows:

23.2.1.1 an. *Pan, Antoine, nantir, dans, danse, panse, chant, plan,* and in borrowed words *covenant, fantasia, sandwich, handicap, gangster, Rembrandt* /ʀãbʀã/, but not in derivatives of English *man,* as *clubman, gentleman, policeman,* which rhyme with French *mane* /man/ 'manna (the heavenly food)'.

23.2.1.2 am. Before a consonant, *camp, jambe, Chambord, Samson* /sãsõ/, *ambiance, Cambridge* /kãbʀidʒ/, *ambassade*; but in final position, *macadam, islam, wigwam* rhyme with *madame.*

23.2.1.3 en. *en, s'ennorgueillir, s'enamourer, lent, vent, dépens, hareng*; but if not flanked by a word-final letter, the final *en* is pronounced /ɛ̃/, e.g. *Agen, examen, rien, bien.* The plural form of derivatives of *man* is always pronounced /-mɛn/; *policemen, gentlemen* rhyme with *Maine.*

23.2.1.4 em. *temps, embaucher, emmener, employeur, Rembrandt* but *emmenthal* /emɛ̃tal/ retains its original pronunciation.

23.2.1.5 aen, aon, ean. These are residual spellings of the same sound, as in *Caen, paon,* and *Jean. Caen* contrasts with *Caïn,* Abel's brother, which is pronounced /kaɛ̃/.

23.2.2 The spellings of /œ̃/. The segment /œ̃/ is spelled as follows:

23.2.2.1 un. *un, commun, chacun, tribun, embrun.*

23.2.2.2 um. *parfum.*

23.2.2.3 eun. *à jeun.*

23.2.3 The spellings of /õ/. The segment /õ/ is spelled as follows:

23.2.3.1 on. *mon, pont, onctueux, suction, honte*; but borrowed words ending with *on* retain the /n/ and are not nasalized; *Washington, Boston, Chatterton* rhyme with *tonne.*

23.2.3.2 om. *ombre, pompier, rompu, sombrero, dompteur* /dõtœʀ/; but *omnibus, omnipotent, somnambule* are pronounced with /ɔmn/.

23.2.3.3 un, um. These present a very special case, really an exception. The word *punch* is pronounced either /põʃ/ or /pœ̃ntʃ/. All words ending in *um,* e.g. *harmonium, uranium, speculum, minimum,* rhyme with *gentilhomme.*

23.2.4 The spellings of /ɛ̃/. The segment /ɛ̃/ is spelled as follows:

23.2.4.1 in. *lin, fin, insecte, succinct, insouciant, sanguin, Botin, Indes, Poitevin,* as long as the following segment is nonvocalic: but *inanité, inoxidable, inodore* begin with /in/; also words spelled with *nn,* e.g. *innocent, innombrable, inné, innovation* are also pronounced with /in/.

23.2.4.2 im. *timbre, impression, limbe.* Before a bilabial stop, *im* is always pronounced /ɛ̃/. Before a vowel, e.g. *image, immonde, immersion* and word-finally, e.g. *Olim,* where it occurs most infrequently, *im* is pronounced /im/.

23.2.4.3 ain. This segment is found only word-finally and preconsonantally, e.g. *nain, sainte, dizain, gain, pain, sainfoin, saindoux.*

23.2.4.4 aim. This segment is found only word-finally, e.g. *daim, faim, essaim, étaim.*

23.2.4.5 en. This segment is found generally word-finally, after the glide /j/, e.g. *Algérien, païen, rien, bohémien,* whether the glide is reduced from a vowel or added by Yod-Insertion, e.g. *Cambrien, Cyprien,* after /e/ as in *caldéen, galiléen, européen,* and exceptionally in *examen* and place names like *Agen.*

23.2.4.6 ein. *sein, feinte, rein, teinte, plein.*

23.2.4.7 eim. Rheims /ʀɛ̃s/.

23.2.4.8 yn and ym. *Thym, apocyn, Tirynthe.*

23.2.4.9 ing. *blanc-seing, coing, poing, shampooing.*

23.2.5 The spellings of /ɲ/. Generally, words with *gn* represent the segment /ɲ/, as shown in Section 23.2.5.1. But there are also some *gn* sequences which are pronounced /gn/, as illustrated in Section 23.2.5.2. Some words are pronounced either or both ways, as their 'nativeness' is still in question.

23.2.5.1 /ɲ/. *vigne, digne, signal, magnifique, oignon, Agnès, Guignol.*

23.2.5.2 /gn/. *gnome, stagnant, magnat, ignifuge* and its combustible relatives, *cognation, diagnostic, magnificat.*

23.2.5.3 Either /ɲ/ **or** /gn/. *magnolia, incognito, Agnus Dei.*

23.2.6 The spellings of /n/. The letter *n* is, of course, the orthographic sign which corresponds to /n/. There are a few instances where the influence of English can lead one to error, either by analogy with English or by hypercorrection.

23.2.6.1 pn for /pn/. *pneumonie, pneumatique.*

23.2.6.2 mn for /mn/. *mnémonique, amnésie;* but *damner, automne* drop the /m/.

23.2.6.3 Pronounced as /n/ **when Nasalization does not apply.** *abdomen, Eden, Carmen, specimen, Ibsen, Beethoven, pollen.*

23.2.7 The spelling of /m/.

23.2.7.1 See Section 23.2.6.2.

23.2.7.2 Pronounced as /m/ when Nasalization does not apply. *rhum, album, macadam, interim.*

Chapter 24
Schwa as 'mute *e*'

24.0 Introduction. This chapter discusses the problems consequent on assuming that some instances of schwa are instances of traditional 'mute *e*'. Discussion of these problems necessitates the introduction, addition, and use of another diacritic or symbol to the inventory of those symbols already employed up to this chapter to transcribe the sounds of French.

24.0.1 The diacritic (̩) for syllabic. Throughout this book, except in Chapter 15 and in this chapter, I have assumed in my transcription that schwa is a phonological entity. Consequently, this traditional view is the one represented by the transcription I have employed up to but exclusive of this chapter. However, in Chapter 15 I did say that I rejected this traditional view. Thus, in accord with that rejection, the phonological transcription in this chapter differs from that of the other chapters of this book solely in the way that schwa is transcribed. For here I have introduced and used the diacritic (̩), a short vertical bar under the segment to be modified, to indicate that the segment under which that diacritic occurs is syllabic.

24.0.2 Syllabicization. Chapter 15 explained that cluster simplification in French is accomplished in terms of syllabicization. In its effort to disallow certain clusters, the French sound system sets out to prevent their occurrence by insuring that one of the consonantal segments in that cluster is made syllabic. This generalized process, which can occur over several rules, explains why an extra syllable is added in *ours blanc, un yaourt cremeux, abrupt rocher, ballasts pleins,* by making the last consonant syllabic (note that the plural marker in this last word is not syllabicized but rather the /t/ is syllabicized). This generalized process also explains (1) why in *autrement, calmement,* etc., a syllabicized segment precedes /mã/ but does not occur in *maintenant, jugement,* or *clairement,* (2) why the final liquid in *probable, affable, susceptible,* is syllabic, whereas its equivalent in *possibilité, affabilité,* and *susceptibilité* is not syllabic, and (3) why /ilml̩ʁ dɔn/ is acceptable but not */ilml̩ʁdɔn/ for *il me le redonne.*

These 'tricks' are accomplished by creating syllabicized segments by means of different rules and then by selectively demoting these syllabicized segments to a nonsyllabic status. The exercises, therefore, suggested in this chapter are designed in accord with the theoretical framework discussed in the description given in Chapter 15.

24.0.3 A generative solution for traditional 'mute *e*'. Those who wish to use this book without relying heavily on the generative phonology developed in Chapters 8 to 15 may just keep in mind the fact that the term or rule of Demotion refers roughly to the deletion of the so-called 'mute *e*'. This rule of thumb will work in most, though not all, cases of Demotion. To illustrate this vague equivalency, consider *je comprends*, which at a point in our derivation is transcribed /ʒkɔ̃pʀã/. The syllabic /ʒ/ is demoted in fast speech and becomes a mere /ʒ/, whereupon Voicing Assimilation changes it to /ʃ/, yielding /ʃkɔ̃pʀã/. If Demotion does not apply, as would be the case in slow deliberate speech, /ʒ/ remains syllabic, just as it must remain in *je veux*. Essentially then, demoting is the same as deleting the schwa in the more traditional analysis. My reasons for this analysis are developed in Chapter 15 and will not be repeated here.

It should be understood that the concepts of 'syllabicized segments' and 'schwa deletion' are not incompatible. Schwa, as we now interpret it, is a phonological entity and is often referred to in alternations. Its phonetic reflex is the syllabicization of a preceding segment. This is accomplished by Syllabic Absorption (but see also Section 15.2.5).

24.0.4 Organization of the chapter. This chapter examines (1) those instances where syllables with schwa are not demoted, namely, in alternations (24.1) and before the so-called aspirated *h* (24.2), and (2) those instances where syllables with schwa are demoted (24.3). The chapter concludes with a discussion of schwa demotion in poetry (24.4).

24.1 Schwa in alternations

24.1.1 In verbs. In pretonic position there are vowel alternations involving schwa in the verb morphology. In the drill that follows, verbs of the first group are used in alternating forms and schwa is realized phonetically as /œ/ in some dialects, as /ø/ in others. The syllabicized segment can stand for both cases.

Exercise 1
Repeat after the speaker.
(1) porter .... portèrent .... porteront ....
(2) forcer .... forcèrent .... forceront ....
(3) capter .... captèrent .... capteront ....
(4) parler .... parlèrent .... parleront ....
(5) enfourner .... enfournèrent .... enfourneront ....
(6) récolter .... récoltèrent .... récolteront ....
(7) écarter .... écartèrent .... écarteront ....
(8) exister .... existèrent .... existeront ....

Exercise 2
Change to the future, then to the conditional, retaining the given person.
(1) gardent .... garderont .... garderaient ....

(2) masquent .... masqueront .... masqueraient ....
(3) confisquons ...... confisquerons .... confisquerions ....
(4) écartez .... écarterez .... écarteriez ....
(5) marquons .... marquerons .... marquerions ....
(6) sucres .... sucreras .... sucrerais ....
(7) dénombrent ...... dénombreront .... dénombreraient ....
(8) célébrez .... célébrerez .... célébreriez ....

There are alternations in verbs between schwa and /ɛ/, depending on word stress, but because of the ability of schwa to delete, only those cases where a cluster forces its retention can be used in the following drills.

Exercise 3
Change to the first person plural, retaining the same tense as given.
(1) Ils comprennent .... Nous comprenons ....
(2) Ils semaient .... Nous semions ....
(3) Ils apprennent .... Nous apprenons ....
(4) Ils égrennent .... Nous égrenons ....
(5) Elles dépeçaient .... Nous dépecions ....
(6) Elles menaient .... Nous menions ....
(7) Elles crèvent .... Nous crevons ....
(8) Elles surprennent .... Nous surprenons ....

Chapter 13 explained that /ɲ/ behaves like a cluster of consonants. A drill pitting /ɲ/ against the future and conditional markers is bound to create clusters where schwa cannot drop.

Exercise 4
Put the verb in the conditional. Repeat after the confirmation.
(1) Elle s'éloigne. .... Elle s'éloignerait. ....
(2) Nous nous résignons. .... Nous nous résignerions. ....
(3) Elle l'accompagne. .... Elle l'accompagnerait. ....
(4) Tu te soignes. .... Tu te soignerais. ....
(5) Elle gagne. .... Elle gagnerait. ....
(6) Ils vous dédaignent. .... Ils vous dédaigneraient. ....
(7) Elles égratignent. .... Elles égratigneraient. ....
(8) J'en répugne. .... J'en répugnerais. ....

Exercise 5
Put the verb in the future, retaining the same person as given. Repeat after the confirmation.
(1) Je signe. .... Je signerai. ....
(2) Tu te résignes. .... Tu te résigneras. ....
(3) Elle se renseigne. .... Elle se renseignera. ....
(4) Elles se peignent. .... Elles se peigneront. ....
(5) Tu nous accompagnes. .... Tu nous accompagneras. ....
(6) Je m'éloigne. .... Je m'éloignerai. ....

24.1.2 As an epenthetic segment / 219

(7) Nous nous soignons. .... Nous nous soignerons. ....
(8) Vous les dédaignez. .... Vous les dédaignerez. ....

In utterance-initial position, a syllabicized C is less likely to undergo demotion than if it were preceded by a vowel. This can be shown in a contrastive test pitting the second person plural of the present indicative against the imperative.

Exercise 6
Repeat after the speaker.
(1) Je tiens .... Vous tenez. .... Tenez! ....
(2) Je sème .... Vous semez. .... Semez! ....
(3) On vient .... Vous venez. .... Venez! ....
(4) On la lève. .... Vous la levez. .... Levez-la! ....
(5) Je jette ça .... Vous jetez ça. .... Jetez ça! ....
(6) Elle les mène ..... Vous les menez. .... Menez-les! ....
(7) Je gèle .... Vous gelez. .... Gelez! ....
(8) Elle chemine ..... Vous cheminez. .... Cheminez! ....

This next exercise on verbs anticipates Section 24.1.2 which deals with word-final schwa.

Exercise 7
Change the participle to the infinitive. Repeat after the speaker.
(1) pris .... prendre ....
(2) descendu .... descendre ....
(3) vendu .... vendre ....
(4) surpris .... surprendre ....
(5) déteint .... déteindre ....
(6) fondu .... fondre ....
(7) joint .... joindre ....
(8) cousu .... coudre ....

24.1.2 As an epenthetic segment.

Exercise 1
Repeat after the speaker.
(1) angulaire .... angle ....
(2) musculaire .... muscle ....
(3) populaire .... peuple ....
(4) séculaire .... siècle ....
(5) circulaire .... cercle ....

Following apocope, in alternations /-bilite/ ~ /-bļ/, drills of the following type may be employed.

Exercise 2
Repeat after the speaker.
(1) affabilité	affable ....
(2) navigabilité	navigable ....
(3) accessibilité	accessible ....
(4) compatibilité	compatible ....
(5) variabilité	variable ....
(6) culpabilité	coupable ....

With the suffix *-âtre*, drills such as Exercise 3 may be devised.

Exercise 3
Add the suffix *-âtre* to the following adjectives.
(1) fou	folâtre	(5) roux	roussâtre ....
(2) rouge	rougeâtre	(6) brun	brunâtre ....
(3) jaune	jaunâtre	(7) blanc	blanchâtre ....
(4) bleu	bleuâtre	(8) gris	grisâtre ....

The suffix *-mètre* can also be used as the basis of drills as in Exercise 4.

Exercise 4
Add the suffix *-mètre* to the following. Repeat after the confirmation.
(1) kilo	kilomètre	(4) tachy	tachymètre ......
(2) mono	monomètre	(5) milli	millimètre ....
(3) télé	télémètre	(6) péri	périmètre ....

A similar drill can be prepared by using the suffix *-forme*.

Exercise 5
Repeat after the speaker.
(1) fili	filiforme	(5) aéri	aériforme ....
(2) pisi	pisiforme	(6) cruci	cruciforme ......
(3) ongui	onguiforme	(7) uvi	uviforme ....
(4) lingui	linguiforme	(8) fusi	fusiforme ....

The suffix *-isme* can be used to prepare drills such as Exercise 6.

Exercise 6
Change to the *-isme* words, then repeat after the confirmation.
(1) alcool	alcoolisme ....
(2) dynamique	dynamisme ....
(3) urbain	urbanisme ....
(4) païen	paganisme ....
(5) cycle	cyclisme ....
(6) charlatan	charlatanisme ....
(7) idéal	idéalisme ....

Drills using the feminine marker *-e* after a cluster can be employed to prepare drills similar to Exercise 7.

Exercise 7
Repeat after the speaker.
(1) mort .... morte .... (5) lourd .... lourde ....
(2) vert .... verte .... (6) expert .... experte ....
(3) picard ..... picarde .... (7) bavard .... bavarde ....
(4) criard ...... criarde .... (8) fort .... forte ....

Some of these exercises can only be done as suggested by repeating after the speaker, but a few could be adapted to transformation drills.

24.1.3 Word-medially. When an adjective with a stop-liquid final sequence is changed into an adverb, the syllabicity of the liquid must remain to prevent a triconsonantal cluster.

Exercise 1
Repeat after the speaker.
(1) tendre .... tendrement ....
(2) pauvre .... pauvrement ....
(3) ample .... amplement ....
(4) aimable .... aimablement ....
(5) âpre .... âprement ....
(6) malingre .... malingrement ....
(7) moindre .... moindrement ....
(8) convenable .... convenablement ....

A variation of Exercise 1 would be the following.

Exercise 2
Repeat after the speaker.
(1) avec tendresse .... tendrement ....
(2) avec simplicité .... simplement ....
(3) avec amabilité .... aimablement ....
(4) avec charité .... charitablement ....
(5) avec confort .... confortablement ....
(6) par préférance .... préférablement ....
(7) avec peine .... péniblement ....
(8) avec gallardise .... gaillardement ....

Exercises 1 and 2 lend themselves to being used as transformation drills, particularly Exercise 2, which could be done with complete sentences to amplify the context, e.g. *Maman se penchait vers moi avec tendresse/tendrement*; *Elle répondait toujours à tout avec charité/charitablement*; *Ils se comportent tous avec simplicité/simplement.*

24.2 Before the so-called aspirated *h*.

Exercise 1
Put the object pronoun in the singular. Repeat after the confirmation.

(1) Il faut les hisser .... Il faut le hisser ....
(2) Il doit les hacher .... Il doit le hacher ....
(3) Il doit vous haïr .... Il doit te haïr ....
(4) Il faut les haler .... Il faut le haler ....
(5) Il veut nous hanter .... Il veut me hanter ....
(6) Il faut les herser .... Il faut le herser ....
(7) Il veut vous heurter .... Il veut te heurter ....
(8) Elle veut les houer .... Elle veut le houer ....

Exercise 2
Given the date in arabic numbers, make a sentence with *Nous sommes le
. . .* Repeat after the confirmation.

(1) 6-10 .... Nous sommes le six octobre ....
(2) 8-8 .... Nous sommes le huit août ....
(3) 11-11 .... Nous sommes le onze novembre ....
(4) 1-3 .... Nous sommes le premier mars ....
(5) 8-4 .... Nous sommes le huit avril ....

Exercise 3
Repeat after the speaker.

(1) ce héros .... (5) le hareng ....
(2) ce hameau .... (6) le homard ....
(3) le héron .... (7) ce harem ....
(4) ce hamac .... (8) le haschisch ....

Note: all derivations of *héros* have a mute *h*, e.g. *l'héroïne, l'héroïsme.*

24.3 Demotions. Syllabicized segments are all subject to Syllable Demotion except for those before 'aspirate *h*' and those in tonic position. The rule of Syllable Demotion applies selectively in such a way as not to create clusters with more than one desyllabicized segment in them. The only way that two desyllabicized segments can occur in a cluster is if the rightmost segment was desyllabicized by Elision. The selectivity exercised by the rule of Syllable Demotion is based on phonological factors: (1) whether neighboring segments are syllabic or not, (2) if not, whether they have been desyllabicized, and (3) whether postneighboring (next to the next) segments are consonantal or not.

These are obviously very abstract and complex conditions. Yet they seem to be shared quite generally by the vast majority of speakers. In this section they are taken up individually and, where appropriate, contrasted with the cases of non-Demotion discussed in Sections 24.1 and 24.2.

24.3.1 Word-final Demotion.

24.3.1 Word-final Demotion

Exercise 1
Change to the plural, retaining the same person in the pronoun and verb. Repeat after the confirmation.

(1) Nous mangeons	Je mange ....
(2) Nous parlons	Je parle ....
(3) Vous montez	Tu montes ....
(4) Nous réclamons	Je réclame ....
(5) Vous chantez	Je chante ....
(6) Nous l'otons	Je l'ote ....
(7) Vous cirez	Tu cires ....
(8) Vous signez	Tu signes ....
(9) Nous ouvrons	J'ouvre ....
(10) Vous doublez	Tu doubles ....

In the foregoing drill some demotions result in /VC/ and others in /VCC#/ sequences in word-final position. Drills that would yield /ɲ/ in word-final position are the reverse of Exercises 4 and 5 in Section 24.1.1. To work on /VCC#/ it is useful to use derivational morphology. In word-final position, after Apocope has created a cluster, Word-final Syllabicization makes the last segment syllabic. If the final C is a liquid, it may be deleted before a nonsyllabic segment in the next word, e.g. /katfwa/ for *quatre fois*. The syllabicized segment (i.e. /ʀ̩/) does occur in carefully enunciated speech (citation form, poetry), as was shown in all exercises in Section 24.1.2. Alternatively, in everyday speech Word-final Demotion demotes syllabic segments in final position to nonsyllabic status and, where appropriate, devoicing rules apply. To account for these facts a drill contrasting all derivationally related forms is most useful.

Exercise 2
Repeat after the speaker.

(1) angulaire	angle	angl¢ ....
(2) musculaire	muscle	muscl¢ ....
(3) navigabilité	navigable	navigabl¢ ....
(4) comptabilité	comptable	comptabl¢ ....
(5) circularité	cercle	cercl¢ ....
(6) vocabulaire	vocable	vocabl¢ ....
(7) séculaire	siècle	siècl¢ ....
(8) culpabilité	coupable	coupabl¢ ....

A contrasting drill is useful for drilling the deletion of the syllabic liquid.

Exercise 3
Repeat after the speaker.

(1) quatre amis	quatre camarades ....
(2) notre arrivée	notre départ ....
(3) un autre homme	un autre bonhomme ....

(4) notre entrée .... notre sortie ....
(5) quatre auteurs .... quatre poètes ....
(6) un angle aigu .... un angle fermé ....
(7) il faut être ici .... il faut être d'ici ....
(8) un mètre et demi .... un mètre cinquante ....

Alternatively, instead of the contrast between vowel and consonant one can utilize the formal versus colloquial contrast to serve as environment for a similar drill.

Exercise 4
Change to the colloquial style. Repeat after the confirmation.
(1) no*tre* frère .... notre /nɔt/ frère ....
(2) une au*tre* fois .... une autre /ot/ fois ....
(3) mes qua*tre* camarades .... mes quatre /kat/ camarades ....
(4) une tab*le* de nuit .... une table de nuit /tabdənɥi/ ....
(5) un pauv*re* bougre .... un pauvre bougre /povbugʀ/ ....
(6) un simp*le* soldat .... un simple soldat /sɛ̃psɔlda/ ....
(7) c'est vo*tre* tour .... c'est votre tour /vɔttuʀ/ ....
(8) un qua*tre*-pièces .... un quatre-pièces /katpjɛs/ ....

24.3.2 Postvocalic Demotion. A syllabicized segment after a vowel is a good candidate for Demotion. Compare, for example, *qui aime ce garçon?* and *qui est ce garçon?* In the first sentence, Word-final Demotion has changed /m̩/ to /m/ and the following /s/ cannot be demoted. In the second sentence /s̩/ may be demoted because it is preceded by a vowel (cf. Syllable Demotion for constraints on that rule). This demotion is not obligatory. It depends on speech speed and on the register which the speaker decided to use.

Exercise 1
In the following sentences you are to place *c'est* before the subject and the relative pronoun *qui* after it, demoting the syllabicized segment that constitutes the determiner.
(1) Le train entre en gare .... C'est le train qui entre en gare ....
(2) Ce garçon est insouciant .... C'est ce garçon qui est insouciant ....
(3) Ce pont est dangereux .... C'est ce pont qui est dangereux ....
(4) Le soleil fait ces ombres ..... C'est le soleil qui fait ces ombres .....
(5) Le quatorze est au troi- C'est le 14 qui est au troisième ....
    sième ....
(6) Le public se plaint .... C'est le public qui se plaint ....
(7) Ce produit me plaît .... C'est ce produit qui me plaît ....
(8) Ce pot est fleuri .... C'est ce pot qui est fleuri ....

The same type of drill can be devised with *voici* and *voilà*, both of which end with a vowel: *voici l*ę *bonhomme qui se plaint.*

Exercise 2
Change from the third person plural to the person indicated. Repeat after the confirmation.

(1) Ils lisent ce livre-là. Nous.
   Nous lisons ce livre-là.
(2) Ils écoutent ce disque en 45. Vous.
   Vous écoutez ce disque en 45.
(3) Ils connaissent ce langage. Nous.
   Nous connaissons ce langage.
(4) Ils admirent ce professeur. Vous.
   Vous admirez ce professeur.
(5) Ils prennent ce train-là. Nous.
   Nous prenons ce train-là.
(6) Ils chantent ce canon. Vous.
   Vous chantez ce canon.
(7) Ils coupent ce madrier. Nous.
   Nous coupons ce madrier.
(8) Ils aiment ce bistro. Vous.
   Vous aimez ce bistro.

An interesting fact should be conveyed to the students regarding the number of syllables after the demoted *ce* in the preceding drill. While 1, 2, 4, 5, and 8 are perfectly acceptable cases of demotion, they would be odd, somewhat unbalanced, if the noun in the direct object of these sentences were monosyllabic, e.g. *livre*, *disque*, *prof*, *train*, and *bar*, all occurring in sentence-final position. Consequently, it is possible to construct a drill that takes this contrast into account.

Exercise 3
Replace the noun in the direct object by the one in parentheses. Repeat after the confirmation.

(1) J'aimais ce livre. (bouquin)
   J'aimais ce bouquin.
(2) J'aime bien ce bar. (bistro)
   J'aime bien ce bistro.
(3) Achetez ce lit. (plumard)
   Achetez ce plumard.
(4) Goutez-moi ce vin. (bordeaux)
   Goutez-moi ce bordeaux.
(5) Donnez-moi ce verre. (gobelet)
   Donnez-moi ce gobelet.
(6) Appelons le frère. (frangin)
   Appelons le frangin.

To underscore the fact that the complexity of the cluster which follows the segment to be demoted is not a relevant factor in demotion, drills like the following may be used.

Exercise 4
Change the infinitive to the proper form of the future as per the pronoun given in parentheses. Repeat after the confirmation.

(1) se brosser (je) .... Je m¢ bross¢rai. ....
(2) se présenter (tu) .... Tu t¢ présent¢ra. ....
(3) vouloir le stopper (il) .... Il veut l¢ stopper. ....
(4) pouvoir le stériliser (on) .... On peut l¢ stériliser. ....
(5) devoir le transformer (tu) .... Tu doit l¢ transformer. ....
(6) falloir le gravir (il) .... Il faut l¢ gravir. ....

Exercise 5
Repeat after the speaker.

(1) sans l¢ sou .... (6) pas d¢ mal ....
(2) sans l¢ stylo .... (7) pas d¢ sculpteur ....
(3) pas d¢ splendeur .... (8) sans l¢ spectateur ....
(4) pas d¢ stratagème .... (9) sans l¢ stradivarius ....
(5) sans l¢ sculpteur .... (10) pas d¢ spectateur ....

24.3.3 Phrase-initial Demotion. In my own speech, strident obstruents that have been syllabicized are the only segments which I can demote at the beginning of an utterance. Furthermore, these are demoted if the next segment is not homorganic. For example, I do not accept as correct *L¢vez-vous!*, *T¢ rapelles-tu?*, or *C¢ zèle me dépasse*, which must begin with supported /l̩/, /t̩/, and /s̩/, respectively. To put this in simpler language, only *j¢*, *c¢*, and *s¢* can occur in my speech at the beginning of an utterance, and even then upon the following condition. The next word may not begin with /s,z,ʃ,ʒ/. The other words likely to occur in this environment (*que*, *de*, *le*, *me*, *ne*, *te*) are never demoted when they occur utterance-initially and before a word beginning with a consonantal segment.

Exercise 1
Repeat after the speaker.

(1) J¢ n'en sais rien. ....
(2) Je cherche sans trouver. ....
(3) C¢ garçon est sympathique. ....
(4) C¢ que tu dis m¢ plait. ....
(5) Ne sors pas sans moi. ....
(6) J¢ travaille tous les soirs. ....
(7) C¢ réveil sonne trop fort. ....
(8) S¢ taire ou ne pas s¢ taire. ....
(9) Ce journal se vend bien. ....
(10) Se gêner ou pas s¢ gêner. ....

24.3.4 Specific Demotion. Even in dialects where demotions are held to an almost absolute minimum (generally south of the Loire), the *ce* of *Est-ce que* is a mere /s/. Similarly, when demotion takes place in *ce que* as in *Voilà ce que je veux*, the resulting sequence is /sk̩/ not */s̩k/. *Ne*, the now weakened negative particle, tends to fall more easily than any other satellite. Furthermore, in those instances where it is not deleted completely, its syllabicity is often demoted. Consequently, *je ne lui ai rien donné* begins with /ʒn/ and never with */ʒn̩/. The demotion of *ne*, however, remains dependent on the environment specified for demotion, e.g. *Paul ne se tait pas* must be demoted to *Paul ne sé̸ tait pas*, not to *Paul né̸ se tait pas*, to avoid the /lns/ cluster.

Exercise 1
Repeat after the speaker.
(1) Est-c¢ que Paul sort?..............................
(2) Ça n¢ fait rien. ....
(3) On n¢ te répond pas. ....
(4) Je n¢ stoppe plus personne. ....
(5) Promettez de n¢ pas répondre. ....
(6) C'est encore c¢ que tu craignais. ....
(7) Paul ne s¢ tait pas. ....
(8) Marc ne m¢ donn¢ra rien. ....

24.3.5 Demotion of adjacent syllabicized segments. The rule of Syllable Demotion is stated in such a way that, in strings of syllabicized segments, every second segment may be demoted. It applies from right to left, mainly because these stringed segments occur in enclitic position (satellites preceding the nucleus) and the nucleus contains nondemotable syllabic segments (i.e. vowels).

Exercise 1
Repeat after the speaker.
(1a) Il *me le re*donn¢ ....
(1b) Il *me* l¢ *re*donn¢ ....
(1c) Il *me le r*¢donn¢ ....
(2a) *Je me le* pay¢ ....
(2b) J¢ *me* l¢ pay¢ ....
(2c) *Je* m¢ *le* pay¢ ....
(3a) plutôt *que de le* vendr¢ ....
(3b) plutôt *que* d¢ *le* vendr¢ ....
(3c) plutôt qu¢ *de* l¢ vendr¢ ....
(4a) il *me le re*demand¢ ....
(4b) il *me* l¢ *re*d¢mand¢ ....
(4c) il *me le r*¢demand¢ ....
(5a) *je ne te le re*donn¢ pas (?) ....
(5b) *je* n¢ *te le re*donn¢ pas ....

(5c) *je n¢ te l¢ r*edonn¢ pas ....
(5d) *je n¢ te le r¢donn¢* pas ....
(5e) *j¢ te l¢ r*edonn¢ pas ....
(6a) on *te le re*dira ....
(6b) on *te l¢ re*dira ....
(6c) on t¢ *le re*dira ....
(6d) on t¢ *le r¢*dira ....
(7) c¢ *que je n¢ te* dis pas ....

Note. Because of the demotion priority of *ce* and *ne*, no other demotion schema is possible in the foregoing. It is, of course, possible to retain all syllabicized segments in item (7), but their large number, as in (5a), makes the utterance very heavy: *ce que je ne te* dis pas (?).

24.4 Demotion in poetry. Essentially, the rules of Demotion are the same in poetry as for prose, with only minor modifications.

Unchanged is the rule of Elision which demotes a syllabicized segment at word-boundary. To illustrate, consider the last two words in the following line from *Phèdre*, where the syllabicized /R̩/ in /mœRtR̩/ is demoted to /R/ before a vowel, yielding /mœRtRɔnɔRe/.

Le ciel, le juste ciel, par le meurtre honoré

While Demotion occurs phrase- and word-finally in prose, it occurs only phrase-finally in poetry, where phrase is defined metrically. By and large, line ends and phrase ends coincide.

Si du crime d'Hélène / on punit sa famille /

Here the slanted line marks the end of each of the two halves of the alexandrine verse. The first of these cuts is called the *cesura* (*césure*). The rule is that syllabicized segments are demoted at the cesura and at the end of the line; but the other syllabicized segments are not demoted: *crime* is pronounced /kRim̩/, with two syllables. This may be further illustratd here by other lines from the same play.

Mais vous, quelles fureurs vous rendent sa victim¢
 1   2   1 2 3 4 / 1 2 1   2 3 4
Pourquoi vous imposer la peine de son crime
   1   2   1 2   3 4 /1 2 1 2 3   4

Note also Mallarmé's brilliant use of Syllabicization at word-boundary in the following, where *nul ptyx*, just like *ours blanc*, commands three syllables:

Sur la crédenc¢, au salon vide, nul ptyx
 1   2 3 4   1 2 3 4 1 2 3 4

Numerous poets and critics have wondered why the final mute *e* of words at the cesura and at the end of the line are not pronounced while others are retained. Martinon (1962) wonders: 'Mais pourquoi l'e muet non élidé est-il compté dans le corps d'un vers et ne l'ai pas à la fin, comme s'il était moins sensible ici que là?'

The scansion of these lines reveals the simple principle that obtains in this case, namely, given that verses are divided into syllable groups (the phrases of poetry) which end on a stressed vowel (the natural stress of French), then it follows that within these poetic phrases posttonic syllabicized segments are demoted while their pretonic equivalents are not.

Appendix 1
An IPA chart of English

	B	LD	I	A	AP		PV	G
Stops	p/b			t/d			k/g	
Nasals	m			n			ŋ	
Affricates					c/ɉ			
Fricatives		f/v	θ/ð	s/z	ʃ/ʒ			h
Liquids				l/ɫ	r/ɾ			
Glides					j		w	
Vowels: High					i/ɪ		u/ʊ	
Mid					e/ɛ	ʌ/ə	o/ɔ	
Low					æ	a	ɑ	

B:	Bilabial	AP:	Alveopalatal
LD:	Labiodental	V:	Velar
I:	Interdental	G:	Glottal
A:	Alveolar		

θ	*th*ick	ɉ	*j*u*dg*e	e	th*ey*
ð	*th*is	ɫ	peop*le*	ɛ	n*e*t
æ	th*a*t	l	*l*and	o	s*o*
ʌ	c*u*t	i	s*ea*t	ɔ	g*o*t
ə	sof*a*	ɪ	s*i*t	ɾ	thea*t*er
ɑ	f*a*ther	u	r*u*de	a	c*o*stume
c	*ch*ild	ʊ	g*oo*d		

Appendix 2
The RULES

This is a list of all rules discussed. They are ordered alphabetically by their names. After each name the abbreviated form is given in parentheses, followed by a reference to the section of the text where the rule is mentioned. For rules which were not specified in the text, the reference points to the allusion of their existence. The order of application of the rules is indicated in Appendix 3.

ALLO-COALESCENCE (ALLO) §12.3.
  In marked vocabulary, before a consonantal segment, /a/ and a following adjacent lateral segment coalesce to form /o/.
APOCOPE (Apoc.) Allusion in §6.2.1.
  Delete the last vowel of a word if it is posttonic and [nonlow].
BACK VOWEL RAISING (Back-V-Rais.) §10.3.4.
  All nonlow back vowels become [high].
CLOSED SYLLABLE ADJUSTMENT (Cl-Syl-Adjst.) §11.3.2
  In closed syllables, nonhigh segments are made [low].
DIPHTHONGIZATION (Diph.) §12.4.4.
  Strong nonhigh vowels are diphthongized; low front vowels become /jɛ/; nonlow vowels become /we/.
ELISION (Elision) §15.3.1.
  A syllabicized segment becomes [nonsyllabic] if it is followed by a vowel or a glide.
ELLO-COALESCENCE (ELLO) §11.3.2.3.
  In marked vocabulary, in phrase-final and preconsonantal position, /ɛl/ becomes /o/.
en-ADJUSTMENT (*en*-Adjst.) §14.2.4.
  In certain stems, the nasalized vowel /ɛ̃/ is made [nonfront].
EN-HAUT (En-Haut) §11.3.1.
  Stressed round vowels in open syllable position become [nonlow].
FINAL CONSONANT DELETION (Fin-C-Del.) Allusion throughout text.
  An obstruent is deleted obligatorily: (1) in phrase-final position, (2) in final position in singular polysyllabic nouns, or (3) in word-final position before a consonantal segment; or optionally: (1) in final position of plural nouns, or (2) in word-final position before a nonconsonantal segment.
GLIDING (Gliding) §12.2.3.
  A high vowel (HV) preceding an adjacent vowel (AV) becomes nonsyllabic under the following conditions: (1) if the HV is /i/ or /u/, then it cannot be preceded by two or more nonsyllabic segments as HV's onset; (2) if the HV is /y/, then the rule is applicable even if HV has a CC onset, provided that the AV is /i/.

232 / Appendix 2: The RULES

HIGH VOWEL ASSIMILATION (Hi-V-Assm.) §12.2.2.
   In native vocabulary, /o/ becomes /u/ before /i/.
HIGH VOWEL FRONTING (Hi-V-Frt.) §10.4.
   High vowels become [front].
HIGH VOWEL LOWERING (Hi-V-Low.) §10.3.2.
   In marked stems, high vowels become [nonhigh].
HOMORGANIC CONSONANT INSERTION (Homorg-C-Ins.) Allusion in §6.4.2.
   Insert a homorganic stop between a nasal and a following liquid.
/i/-FORMATION (/i/-Form.) §12.2.2.
   In native vocabulary, a velar stop followed by a dental stop becomes a high unrounded vowel.
/l/-DEVOICING (/l/-Devoicing) §15.3.4.
   In phrase-final position, in clusters with a voiceless obstruent, /l/ devoices.
/l/-/n/ PALATALIZATION (/l/-/n/-Palat.) §13.7.
   In stem-final position of native vocabulary, a segment which is [consonantal], [sonorant], [coronal], [anterior], [nonhigh], and [nonfront], and which is followed by a [nonconsonantal], [noncoronal], [nonanterior], [high], [front] segment becomes [noncoronal], [nonanterior], [high], and [front], and the conditioning segment deletes.
/la/-SYLLABE (/la/-Syll.) §15.3.1.
   The article or pronoun /la/ becomes /l̩/ if followed by a nonconsonantal segment.
LOW VOWEL FRONTING (Lo-V-Frt.) §10.4.
   Low vowels become [front] if they are marked strong.
LOW VOWEL REDUCTION (Lo-V-Red.) §15.1.2.
   In open syllable, in word-medial position, a weak low vowel becomes [central] and [lax].
NASAL DELETION (N-Del.) §14.2.2.
   A nonsyllabic nasal segment followed by a nonsyllabic segment (including a word boundary) is deleted if it is preceded by a nasalized vowel.
NASALIZATION (Nasltn.) §14.2.
   A vowel is nasalized if it is followed by a nasal and either a word boundary or a nonnasal consonantal segment.
NASALIZED VOWEL LOWERING (Nas-V-Low.) §9.4.3 and 14.2.3.
   All nasalized vowels become [low].
/ɔ̃/-ADJUSTMENT (/ɔ̃/-Adjst.) Allusion in Question 3, §14.5.
   The low back nasalized /ɔ̃/ becomes [nonlow].
/ɔs/-ADJUSTMENT (/ɔs/-Adjst.) §11.3.2.1.
   In native forms, before a consonantal segment, tonic /ɔs/ becomes /o:/ and atonic /ɔs/ drops the /s/.
PHRASE-FINAL SYLLABICIZATION (Phr-Fin-Sylbztn.) §15.2.2.
   In phrase-final position, a nonsyllabic segment preceded by one or more obstruents becomes [syllabic].

PHRASE-INITIAL DEMOTION (Phr-Inl-Dem.) §15.3.2.
  A phrase-initial syllabicized strident segment may become [nonsyllabic] if it is followed by a word boundary and a nonstrident segment.
POSTTONIC VOWEL REDUCTION (Posttonic-V-Red.) §15.1.1.
  A posttonic /a/ is reduced to schwa.
PRETONIC VOWEL ADJUSTMENT (Pretonic-V-Adjst.) §10.3.3.
  Pretonic vowels that are marked weak become [low] if they are [nonround] and [nonlow] if they are [round].
PRETONIC VOWEL RAISING (Pretonic-V-Rais.) §9.4.2.
  In open syllable, in learned vocabulary, pretonic low front segments become [nonlow].
/R/-DEVOICING (/R/-Devoicing) §7.2.1.
  /R/ is devoiced (1) in phrase-final position, or (2) by assimilating progressively and regressively to a voiceless obstruent, within words and at word boundaries.
SYLLABIC ABSORPTION (Syl-Abstn.) §15.2.2.
  In atonic position, schwa is absorbed into the immediately preceding segment which it makes [syllabic].
SYLLABIC DEMOTION (Syl-Dem.) §15.3.3.
A syllabicized segment may become [nonsyllabic] if it is preceded by a syllabic segment and followed by either (1) a syllabicized segment, (2) one and only one desyllabicized segment, if the next segment is [nonconsonantal], or (3) one or more never syllabicized segments. (This rule applies from right to left, iteratively.)
SYLLABIC LIQUID DELETION (Syl-Liq-Del.) §15.2.2.
  In fast speech, a syllabic liquid after an obstruent is deleted if it immediately precedes a word boundary followed by a consonantal segment.
SYNCOPE (Syncope) Allusion in §6.2.3.
  In native vocabulary, a posttonic vowel in a nonfinal syllable is deleted.
TONIC SCHWA (Tonic-Schwa) §15.2.5.
  In tonic position, schwa becomes /œ/.
VOICING ASSIMILATION (Voic-Assm.) Slightly amended from §7.1.2.
  In fast speech, a nonsyllabic obstruent agrees in voicing with an immediately following consonantal segment both at word boundary and word-internally.
VOWEL HARMONY (V-Harm.) §11.2.4.
  In open syllables, word-internally, a low vowel followed by a syllable whose peak is [nonlow] becomes [nonlow].
/wa/-ADJUSTMENT (/wa/-Adjst.) §9.4.3.
  The diphthong /we/ becomes low and nonfront (e.g. /we/ becomes /wa/).
WORD BOUNDARY SYLLABICIZATION (Word-Bndry-Sylbztn.) §15.2.2.
  A nonsyllabic segment preceded by a consonantal segment and followed by a word boundary and one or more consonantal segments becomes [syllabic].

WORD-FINAL DEMOTION (Word-Fin-Dem.) §15.3.4.
   In posttonic position, a syllabic segment is generally demoted if it is word-final or followed by inflectional markings.
YOD-CONVERSION (Yod-Conv.) §12.3.
   The lateral palatal /ʎ/ becomes [nonlateral].
YOD-INSERTION (Yod-Ins.) §12.2.4.
   Insert /j/ between /i/ and a following adjacent vowel.
ZAIZING (Zaizing) §11.3.1.
   Round vowels before /z/ becomes [nonlow] and [long].

Appendix 3
RULE-ordering chart

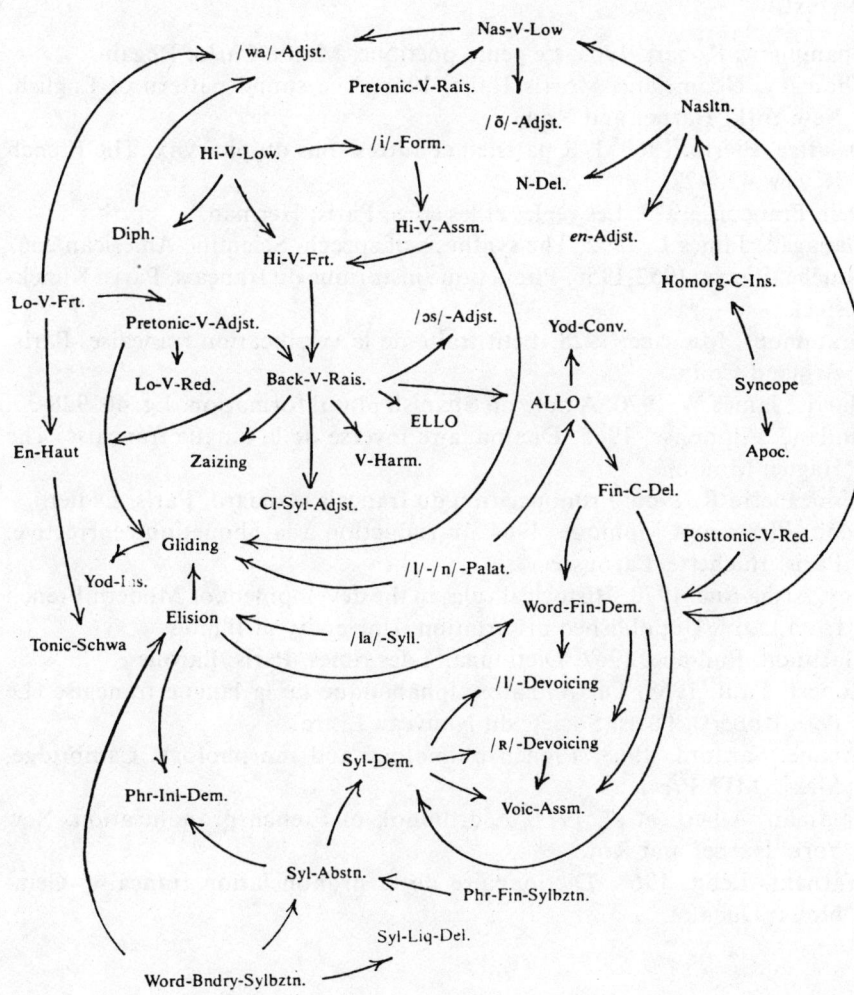

References

(This list is limited to those works which are specifically referred to in the text.)

Champigny, Robert. 1963. Le genre poétique. Monte Carlo: Regain.

Chomsky, Noam, and Morris Halle. 1968. The sound pattern of English. New York: Harper and Row.

Delattre, Pierre. 1969. L'R parisien et autres sons du pharynx. The French Review 43.5-22.

Dell, François. 1973. Les règles et les sons. Paris: Herman.

Flanagan, James L. 1972. The synthesis of speech. Scientific American 266.

Fouché, Pierre. 1952-1956. Phonétique historique du français. Paris: Klincksieck.

Grammont, Maurice. 1928. Petit traité de la versification française. Paris: Armand Colin.

Harris, James W. 1970. A note on Spanish plural formation. Lg. 46. 928-30.

Juilland, Alphonse. 1965. Dictionnaire inverse de la langue française. The Hague: Mouton.

Léon, Pierre R. 1966. Prononciation du français standard. Paris: Didier.

Léon, Pierre and Monique. 1964. Introduction à la phonétique corrective. Paris: Hachette/Larousse.

Loy, Artha Sue. 1970. Historical rules in the development of Modern French from Latin. Unpublished dissertation. University of Illinois.

Martinon, Philippe. 1962. Dictionnaire des rimes. Paris: Larousse.

Robert, Paul. 1968. Dictionnaire alphabétique de la langue française (Le Petit Robert). Paris: Société du Nouveau Littré.

Schane, Sanford. 1968. French phonology and morphology. Cambridge, Mass.: MIT Press.

Valdman, Albert, et al. 1971. A drillbook of French pronunciation. New York: Harper and Row.

Warnant, Léon. 1968. Dictionnaire de la prononciation française. Gembloux: Duculot.